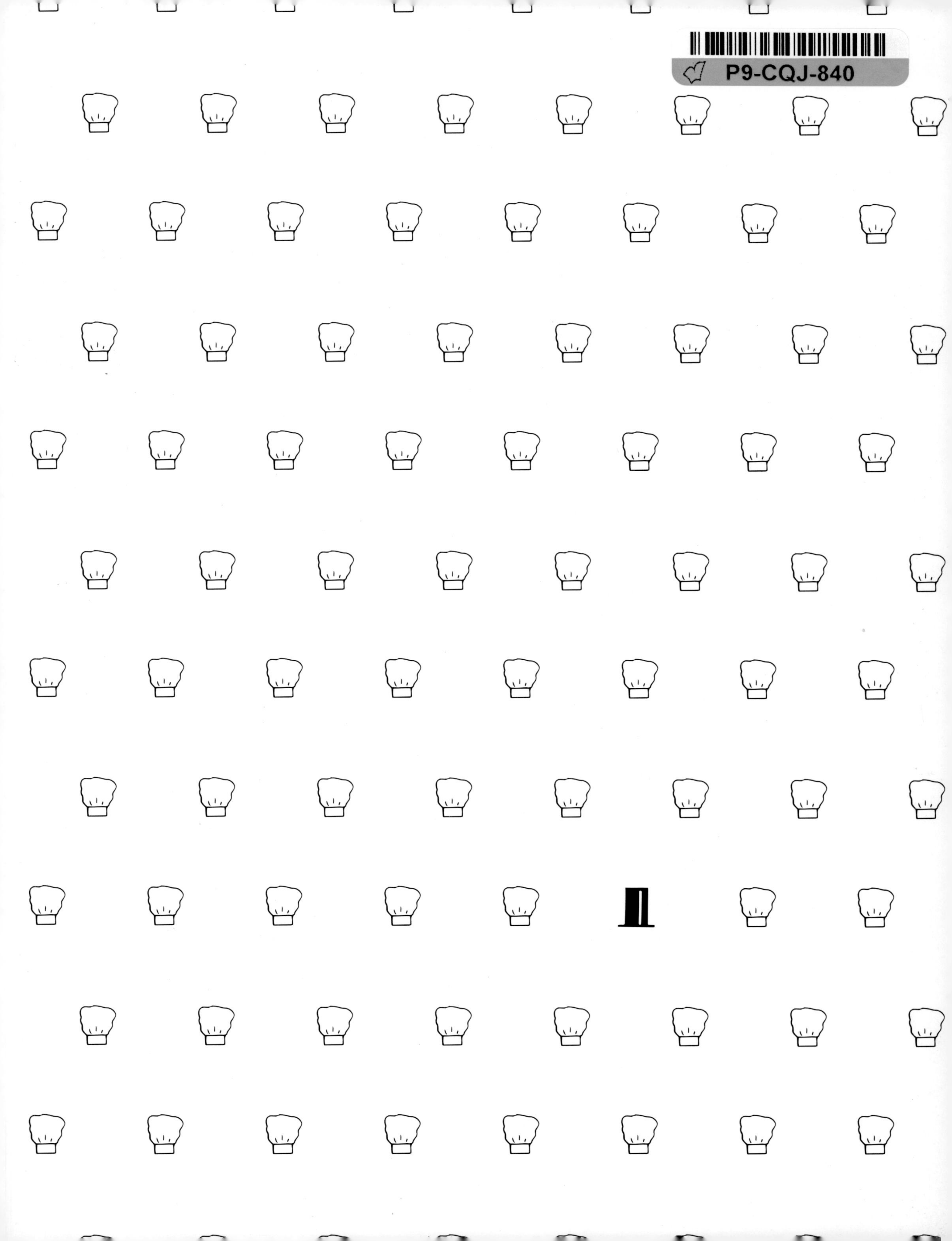

Honest to Goodness

My Friends: No one, not in my situation, can appreciate my feeling of sadness at this parting. To this place, and the kindness of these people, I owe everything.

Abraham Lincoln
February 11, 1861
Springfield, Illinois

It has been 129 years since Abraham Lincoln uttered these words as he boarded a train to leave Springfield, to return until another train, this one draped in black, brought him back to the people he had called neighbors.

Springfield, the only city the nation's 16th president ever called home.

Springfield, where honesty, fairness, and integrity are still an important part of our daily lives.

Those influences are felt in the foods we eat as well. Honestly good food — and plenty of it.

Native Illinois pork, beef, corn, garden crisp vegetables, fresh strawberries, apples and, yes, even horseradish are the staples of our culinary heritage, simply prepared with Midwestern flair and consumed with gusto.

Honest to Goodness is our celebration of that good food, a celebration of sweet ears of corn, fresh from the field, the aroma of oven-hot pies, the sweetness of dew-fresh strawberries and the rich ethnic dishes inspired by our forebearers.

We hope *Honest to Goodness* will inspire you. Enjoy the cooking of Springfield and savor the rich history that abounds in Illinois' capital city.

We have a tradition to be proud of.

Additional copies of *Honest to Goodness* may be obtained by writing the following address or by using the order blank in the back of this book:

Junior League of Springfield Publications
P.O. Box 1736
Springfield, Illinois 62705
(217) 787-7802

Please include your return address with a check payable to Junior League of Springfield Publications.

First Edition,
First printing: 10,000 copies
February 1990

Second Printing: 15,000 copies
March 1990

Third Printing: 7,500 copies
June 1994

Fourth Printing: 5,000 copies
June 2001

Fifth Printing: 5,000 copies
July 2004

ISBN 0-9624788-0-6
Library of Congress Catalog
Card Number 89-64324

Manufactured by
Favorite Recipes® Press
an imprint of

FRP™

P.O. Box 305142
Nashville, Tennessee 37230
1-800-358-0560

Printed in China

Honest to Goodness

Chairman and Editor
Susan Helm

Assistant Chairman and Recipe Editor
Sandy Bellatti

Special Editor
Trish Egler

Design/Art Direction
Baumgartner Graphic Design & Production

Chef Hat/Lincoln Hat Logo Design
Nancy Durbin

Photography
Robert Bullivant
cover
Doug Carr
section divider pages
Doug Bennington
introductory pages
Larry Kanfer
Lincoln Home

Food Styling
Joy Bullivant
cover

The Junior League of Springfield, Incorporated, is an organization of women committed to promoting voluntarism and to improving the community through the effective action and leadership of trained volunteers. Its purpose is exclusively educational and charitable.

The proceeds realized from the sale of *Honest to Goodness* will be returned to the community through programs of The Junior League of Springfield, Incorporated.

There was a Springfield before Abraham Lincoln moved to town as a young attorney and politician. But since Mr. Lincoln, as a member of the Illinois House of Representatives, and his "Long Nine" coalition convinced the state legislature to move the Illinois capital to Springfield in 1837, the name Abraham Lincoln has been synonymous with Springfield. He is the reason that hundreds of thousands of tourists from across the world visit our city every year. From the Old State Capitol where he delivered his revered "House Divided" speech, to the law office where he developed his renowned reputation as a railroad lawyer, to his stately home on Eighth Street, Mr. Lincoln pervades our historic city.

The Junior League of Springfield and Mr. Lincoln in fact became neighbors. Since 1985, the Junior League of Springfield has been headquartered at the Corneau House, a cottage once owned by Lincoln's druggist, Charles Corneau, and now located next door to the only house that Mr. Lincoln and his wife, Mary Todd, ever owned.

The sun sets on Lincoln's home.

So it was only natural that the Junior League of Springfield pay tribute to the city's most famous resident. A creative team, consisting of a food stylist, two art directors and a photographer, created the exciting food mosaic used for the cover of *Honest to Goodness.*

Creating all the subtle shading in Mr. Lincoln's famous hat begins by using black popcorn and coffee beans.

What could be more honest and good than a portrait of Mr. Lincoln tastefully designed from all natural food ingredients?

Layered, dried apple slices were considered for the skin, but rejected as not giving the right feel for one of the nation's most famous faces. Brown rice was substituted for the base of the skin tone and, in one of the most exciting discoveries of the two-day styling session, was enhanced with red lentils — without which Mr. Lincoln looked quite anemic. Oriental black string beans gave Mr. Lincoln's face his recognizable character and depth.

The most critical area in maintaining the dignity of Abraham Lincoln, the eye and mouth, were also the two areas most difficult to portray in the food mosaic. Skinned plum slices were carved and sprinkled with paprika for the mouth. For the eye, an apple slice was positioned for the eyelid, black olive and paella rice for the eye, black string beans for an outline, and black sesame seeds for critical shading. The "perfect" coffee bean was carefully sought out for Mr. Lincoln's familiar mole.

With the string beans in place for character lines, added shading is created with black sesame seeds.

Chinese cabbage leaves became a delicate lace collar, and the ascot was fashioned from leek leaves. Mr. Lincoln's trademark hat and coat were created from popcorn, black beans and coffee beans.

The final image was close to four feet long, three feet wide and extremely fragile.

Lincoln's heritage also is found on the section divider pages throughout the book.

Surrounded by a rich copper background, the photographs capture the essence of artifacts used by President and Mrs. Lincoln and their contemporaries. From the rustic bowls, crockery

The food stylist adds an ascot tie of leek leaves as the portrait nears completion.

and copperware from New Salem where Mr. Lincoln studied by candlelight, to his personal gloves and Mrs. Lincoln's handwritten invitation, the images convey a feeling of history and tradition.

Many of the artifacts that

Last minute coloring, shading and brushing away of excess material is carefully completed in preparation for the actual photo shoot.

were photographed are stored at the Illinois State Historical Library and have never been seen by the public.

Honest to Goodness, a collection of recipes from the Illinois heartland by the Junior League of Springfield, is the result of literally thousands of hours of work by one of Springfield's most valued assets — its volunteers.

More than 2,000 recipes were submitted by League members, community organizations, local restaurants and interested area cooks. The selection process took almost 18 months, from gathering the recipes and testing them at least 3 times, to final editing.

We hope *Honest to Goodness* will inspire you. We appreciate your contribution to our community efforts. We want you to experience all the fine recipes presented in this cookbook and hope you will enjoy the efforts of all the people who helped make *Honest to Goodness* possible. And we hope you will also savor the rich history that abounds in the Springfield area. We have a tradition to be proud of, as we learned in producing this book.

Partake.

No Springfield celebration is complete without fragrant bowls of "chilli" with all the trimmings, seen here nestled among a shiny copper kettle and two antique dippers from the Rutledge Tavern at New Salem State Park.

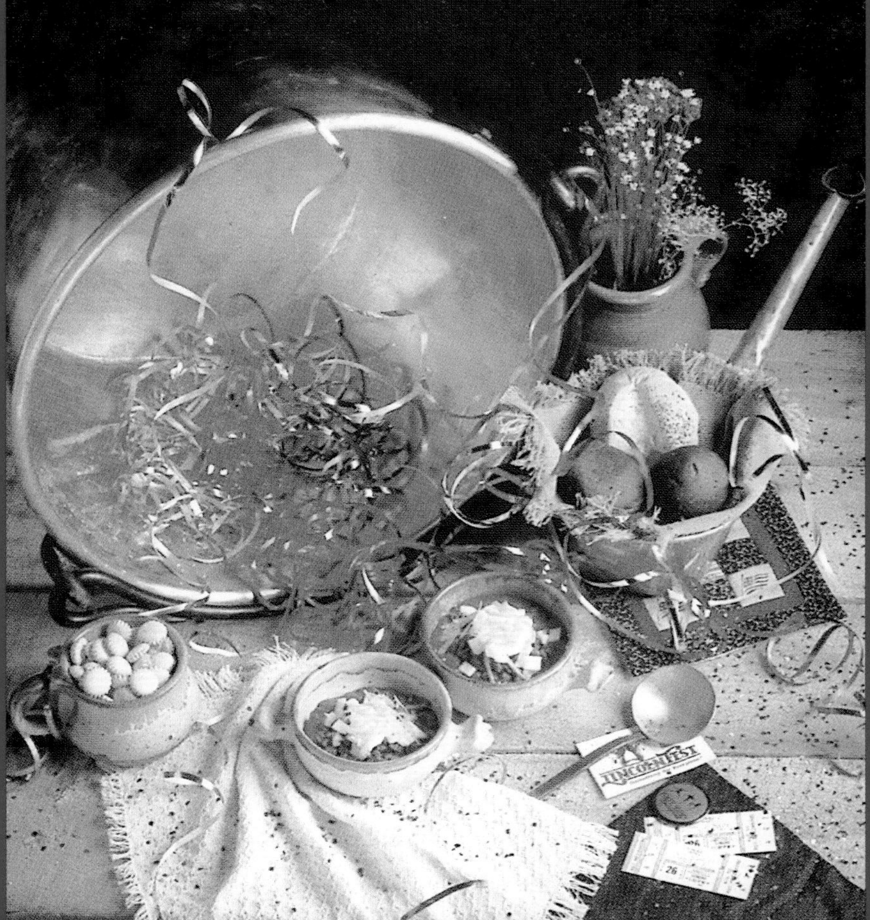

Hometown Favorites

Butterfly Pork Chop Sandwiches

Cabbage Slaw

Clayville Sugars

Elephant Ears

Fried Catfish

Fried Pumpkin & Zucchini Blossoms

Gooey Butter Cake

Grandma's Tea Cake

Grilled Corn on the Cob with Herb Butter

Grove Park Corn Soup

Horseshoes

Lemon Shake-Ups

Mrs. Lincoln's White Cake

Rod's Chilli

Horseshoes

4 servings

The head chef at the old Leland Hotel is generally credited with inventing Springfield's famous horseshoe sandwich in 1928. The recipe has had endless variations over the years - everything from shrimp to turkey has been added and beer is a hotly contested ingredient. But the original recipe called for ham and a fried egg. The shape of the ham prompted the "horseshoe" name, with the fries representing the nails and the heated steak platter an anvil.

- *½ cup butter or margarine*
- *¼ cup flour*
- *1 teaspoon salt*
- *½ teaspoon freshly ground black pepper*
- *2 cups light cream or half and half*
- *½ teaspoon cayenne pepper*
- *2 cups shredded Cheddar cheese, sharp or mild*

Melt butter in saucepan. Blend in flour and cook over low heat until mixture is smooth and bubbly. Remove from heat; stir in salt, pepper, cream, cayenne, and cheese. Return to heat, stirring constantly to make a smooth thick sauce. Keep warm until sandwiches are assembled.

- *8 slices bread, toasted*
- *Sliced or shaved ham, chicken, or turkey or cooked ground beef patty*
- *Cooked French Fries*

Place 2 slices of toast on serving plate; top with meat of your choice and cover with cheese sauce. Mound french fries on top. Serve immediately.
A smaller sandwich, using only 1 slice of toast, is a Ponyshoe.

Grove Park Corn Soup

4 servings

- *6 ears yellow sweet corn, old enough to be starchy - not fresh*
- *3 tablespoons butter*
- *1½ to 2 cups chopped onion*
- *3 cups whole milk*
- *½ cup finely crushed saltine crackers*
- *½ to 1 teaspoon sugar*
- *Salt*
- *Freshly ground black pepper*
- *¾ cup chopped green pepper (optional)*
- *1 cup diced ham (optional)*

Garnish

- *Butter*
- *Crumbled crisp bacon*

Grate corn off cob using coarse grater or cut off with sharp knife, close to cob. Be sure to remove all the starchy pulp. In large pot, sauté onion in butter untill tender but not brown. Add corn and cook a few minutes, stirring constantly to keep corn from sticking.

Mash crackers in a small amount of milk; add to pot. Add remaining milk and sugar. Season with salt and pepper to taste. If desired, add green pepper and ham. Heat carefully 10 to 15 minutes, stirring often to avoid scorching soup. Serve topped with crumbled, crisp bacon or a pat of butter.

Butterfly Pork Chop Sandwiches

8 servings

1 cup ketchup
2 tablespoons cider vinegar
2 tablespoons brown sugar
½ teaspoon dry mustard
2 drops hot pepper sauce
1 tablespoon minced onion
1 teaspoon hickory barbecue smoke seasoning
¼ cup water
8 4-ounce butterfly pork chops
Seasoned salt
8 sandwich buns

Garnish

Dill pickle slices
Prepared mustard

Combine ketchup, vinegar, brown sugar, mustard, hot pepper sauce, onion, seasoning, and water in a saucepan. Simmer uncovered for 10 to 15 minutes, stirring often. Cool.

Place pork chops in a non-metallic pan; liberally coat both sides of chops with barbecue sauce. Cover and let marinate overnight in refrigerator.

Sprinkle pork chops with seasoned salt. Grill. Place cooked chops on buns and serve. Garnish with pickles and mustard if desired.

Your favorite barbecue sauce may be used to marinate pork chops.

No central Illinois fest or fair is complete without at least one smoky grill where row after row of butterflied pork chops sends up an appetizing sizzle. Basted with a little sauce, the "Original State Fair Butterfly Pork Chop Sandwich" has become one of the most popular items at the fair, often requested by visiting entertainers.

Fried Catfish

4 to 6 servings

4 cups seasoned croutons
2 pounds catfish fillets
3 cups buttermilk
Salt
Freshly ground black pepper
Cayenne pepper
Oil for frying
Lemon wedges

Process croutons in food processor or blender to make fine crumbs. Place fillets in a non-metallic pan. Pour buttermilk over the fillets; let set for 30 minutes.

Remove fillets; season with salt, pepper, and cayenne to taste. Coat fillets with crouton crumbs. Let set for 30 minutes. Fry fillets in 375 degree oil, turning once, until coating is dark golden brown. Serve immediately with lemon wedges.

Area fishermen take pride in reeling in catfish — the size of which gets bigger with every telling. Catfish can be dressed up with elegant sauces and delicate coatings, but the down-home version calls for a dusting of cornmeal, an ironstone plate, a slice of lemon, and a sprig of parsley.

ELEPHANT EARS

4 large servings

Elephant ears, a perennial fair favorite, take two hands and a lot of nerve to eat. Don't worry if it crumbles as you bite into it - the experts say the sign of a properly crisped elephant ear is that you end up wearing a great deal of it.

½ cup sugar
1 teaspoon cinnamon
⅓ batch Prize-Winning Potato Bread dough, punched down and ready to shape
Oil for deep frying

Combine sugar and cinnamon; set aside. Divide dough into 4 balls; let rest on floured surface for 10 minutes. Roll our dough into large oval about ¼ - to ½ - inch thick. Let rest 5 to 10 minutes.

Heat oil in deep fryer, electric wok or skillet to 375 degrees. Carefully place oval of dough in hot oil. Fry until side becomes dark golden brown; using tongs turn elephant ear and cook other side. Remove and drain on paper towel. Sprinkle with cinnamon-sugar mixture. Fry remaining dough. Serve immediately.

One pound of frozen bread dough, thawed and at room temperature, may be substituted for potato bread dough.

LEMON SHAKE-UPS

1 serving

The drink of choice between Memorial Day and Labor Day in Springfield is the lemon shake-up. No powdery mix or imitation flavors are permitted, and every shake-up is a made-to-order original. An authentic shake-up uses a glass and a shaker, lots of ice, sugar, and one or more cut lemons. After that, it's all in the wrist.

½ large lemon or 1 small lemon, cut in half
2 tablespoons plus 2 teaspoons sugar
Ice
Water

Squeeze juice from lemon into 16-ounce glass; drop in lemon. Add sugar. Fill glass with ice; fill glass with water. Place a large-mouth glass over filled glass. Shake for 30 seconds to dissolve sugar and mix together lemon and water. Uncover and serve.

For orange shake-up, substitute ½ medium orange for lemon. Or substitute ¼ medium orange and ¼ large lemon for lemon-orange shake-up.

Rod's Chilli

4 servings

1 pound finely ground beef	*1 small onion*
3 tablespoons chili powder	*4 ounces ground beef suet*
2 tablespoons ground cumin	*1 garlic clove*
2 teaspoons oregano	*2 15 ¾-ounce cans chili beans, hot or mild*
1 ½ cups water	*1 tablespoon vinegar*
1 celery stalk	*Salt*

Garnish

Oyster crackers	*Shredded Cheddar cheese*
Chopped onions	*Sour cream*

Slowly brown beef in oven-proof skillet, stirring constantly. Add chili powder, cumin, and oregano. Let simmer for about 5 minutes. Add water.

Meanwhile, cut celery and onion into small pieces; puree in food processor or electric blender. Melt suet in skillet; add garlic clove and pureed vegetables. Cook over low heat about 30 minutes. Strain. Add strained mixture (flavored suet) to meat mixture. Discard vegetables and garlic remaining in strainer.

Cover and bake in 250 degree oven for 2 to 3 hours or longer so seasonings will slowly permeate the meat, stirring occasionally.

Heat beans and their liquid and vinegar together in saucepan for 30 minutes just before serving. Salt to taste. Ladle beans into soup bowl; add meat mixture into center of beans. There should be twice the amount of beans as meat. Serve with oyster crackers, chopped onions, shredded Cheddar cheese, and sour cream.

Meat sauce may be cooked longer in the oven but add more water if necessary to keep it moist.

In 1909, J.A. Bockelman ordered a sign for his new restaurant, the Dew Chilli Parlor, which he was inspired to name after the sparkling morning dew. The sign painter quibbled over the spelling of "chilli", but Bockelman protested that the dictionary spelled it both ways. The local variation - with 2 "l"s, just like "Illinois" - has stuck to this day.

Grilled Corn On The Cob With Herb Butter

8 servings

There are 10,000 acres of sweet corn planted in Illinois each year. Popular varieties include Sun Dance, Gold Cup, Jubilee, Kandy Korn, Platinum Lady, Illini Supersweet, and Peaches and Cream. Many of the newer varieties boast superior "keeping" qualities, but old-time Illinois cooks still insist that the best sweet corn recipes have "start water boiling" as the first step and "go pick the corn" as the second.

8 ears fresh corn, husks and silk intact
3 gallons salted water

Soak corn in salted water for 10 to 20 minutes. Remove from water. Grill ears of corn over medium coals, turning often to cook evenly. Grill for approximately 20 minutes or until the kernels emit water when pierced with a sharp knife. The husks will be slightly charred and hot. Carefully husk corn and serve with Herb Butter.

Herb Butter

½ cup butter, softened
½ teaspoon basil
½ teaspoon oregano
½ teaspoon parsley flakes
1 garlic clove, minced

Mix together butter, basil, oregano, parsley and garlic. Cover and refrigerate until ready to serve.

Cabbage Slaw

8 to 10 servings

2 heads cabbage, cut coarsely
1 large red onion, thinly sliced
¾ cup plus 2 tablespoons sugar
¾ cup oil
½ cup white wine vinegar
½ teaspoon salt
½ teaspoon celery salt
½ teaspoon dry mustard

In a bowl, layer cabbage and onion; sprinkle sugar between vegetables. Bring to a boil oil, vinegar, salt, celery salt, and mustard. Pour over cabbage and onion. Cover and refrigerate at least 8 hours or overnight, stirring occasionally.

Fried Pumpkin & Zucchini Blossoms

4 to 6 servings

20 pumpkin or zucchini blossoms
3 eggs, beaten
1 cup milk
1 teaspoon baking powder
¼ teaspoon salt
1 teaspoon vanilla
1 cup flour
½ cup oil or shortening for frying
Sugar (optional)

It is said that fried zucchini blossoms were created by a gardener desperately trying to keep the zucchini harvest down to manageable proportions — but too thrifty to throw the plucked blossoms away.

Wash blossoms and drain on paper towels. Cut off green ends of flowers. Mix together eggs, milk, baking powder, salt, and vanilla to make a batter. Dip blossoms in batter and then roll in flour until completely coated.

Heat oil to 375 degrees. Fry blossoms, turning to brown on all sides, until golden brown. Drain on paper towels. Sprinkle with sugar if desired. Serve immediately.

For a simpler batter, beat together 2 eggs, and 2 tablespoons ice water. Dip blossoms in batter and roll in 1 cup finely crushed cracker crumbs.

Clayville Sugars

6 dozen

4 cups flour
1 teaspoon cream of tartar
1 teaspoon baking soda
½ teaspoon salt
1 cup butter
1/3 cup oil
1 cup granulated sugar
1 cup powdered sugar
2 eggs
1 teaspoon vanilla
Granulated sugar

A similar cookie is sold at the Clayville Rural Life Center, a restored 19th century inn and farmhouse west of Springfield.

Sift together flour, cream of tartar, baking soda, and salt; set aside. Cream together butter, oil, and sugars. Add eggs and vanilla. Stir in dry ingredients.

Drop rounded tablespoonful of dough onto ungreased baking sheets. Moisten bottom of glass in water, dip bottom in granulated sugar and press on top cookies. Bake at 375 degrees for 8 to 10 minutes or until edges of cookies are slightly browned.

If dough is too soft to handle, chill until ready to bake.

Some people say Gooey Butter Cake was the result of an accident in a Springfield bakery. Others say it was created in St. Louis. Whatever the source, buttery, rich Gooey Butter Cakes are a Springfield tradition.

Gooey Butter Cake

16x 11 inch cake

3 cups cake flour
1 3/4 cups sugar
1/3 cup dry milk powder
2 1/2 teaspoons baking powder
1 teaspoon salt
1 cup plus 2 tablespoons butter, melted
2 eggs
1 1/2 teaspoons vanilla

Topping

8 ounces cream cheese, softened
2 eggs
1 teaspoon vanilla
1 pound powdered sugar

Sift together cake flour, sugar, dry milk, baking powder, and salt in large bowl. Add melted butter, eggs, and vanilla. Beat together to make a thick batter. Spread into greased 16x11 inch jelly roll pan.

Prepare topping by beating cream cheese until creamy; add eggs and vanilla. Blend in powdered sugar. Spread topping on cake batter. Bake at 350 degrees for 25 to 30 minutes until top is golden brown. Cool and cut into 2-inch squares.

An 18 1/4-ounce yellow cake mix, without pudding added, may be substituted for dry cake ingredients. Reduce melted butter to 1/2 cup and omit vanilla. Prepare cake batter by combining cake mix, melted butter, and eggs.

From Mary Todd Lincoln's letters to close friend Hannah Shearer, Springfield, June 26, 1859: "For the last two weeks, we have had a continual round of strawberry parties, this last week I have spent five evenings out... After raspberry time, we will resume, doubtless our usual quiet."

Grandma's Tea Cake

12 servings

1/2 cup butter
1/2 cup sugar
1 egg, well-beaten
Dash of salt
1/2 cup milk
2 cups flour, sifted
2 teaspoons baking powder
Fresh strawberries, sliced and sweetened to taste

Cream together butter and sugar; add egg, salt, milk, flower, and baking powder. Mix well. Pour batter into greased 8-inch round baking pan. Bake at 350 degrees for 30 minutes or until done. Cool to room temperature. Cut into wedges and top with strawberries. Serve.

Other fresh fruit may be substituted for strawberries.

Mrs. Lincoln's White Cake

8- or 9-inch layer cake

1 cup butter	*1 teaspoon vanilla*
2 cups sugar	*1 teaspoon almond extract*
3 cups cake flour	*1 cup chopped blanched almonds*
2 teaspoons baking powder	*6 egg whites*
1 cup milk	*¼ teaspoon salt*

Cream butter and sugar until light and fluffy. Sift together flour and baking powder; remove 2 tablespoons and set aside. Add sifted ingredients, alternating with milk, to creamed mixture. Stir in vanilla and almond extract. Combine almonds with reserved flour and add to batter.

Beat egg whites until stiff; add in salt. Fold into batter. Pour into 3 greased and floured 8- or 9-inch cake pans. Bake at 350 degrees until cake tester comes out clean, 20 to 25 minutes. Cool 5 to 10 minutes; remove from pans and cool on racks. Frost.

Frosting

2 cups sugar	*½ cup chopped candied cherries*
1 cup water	*½ cup chopped candied pineapple*
2 egg whites	*Few drops vanilla or almond extract*

Combine sugar and water in a saucepan, stirring until sugar is dissolved. Bring to a boil; cover and cook about 3 minutes until the steam has washed down any sugar crystals that may have formed on side of pan. Uncover and cook until syrup reaches 238 to 240 degrees.

Whip egg whites until frothy; pour in syrup in thin stream, whipping egg whites constantly until frosting is spreading consistency. Add cherries, pineapple and flavoring.

Mary Todd Lincoln's White Cake recipe was actually created by M. Giron, a famous Lexington, Kentucky, confectioner on the occasion of Lafayette's visit to that city in 1825. The Todd family received the recipe from M. Giron and treasured it thereafter. It was served on special occasions in Springfield and at the White House. Legend has it that Mary Todd Lincoln often made this cake for the president, and he always commented, "Mary's White Cake is the best I have ever eaten." However, according to many Lincoln historians it was never served with frosting.

The stage is set for an evening of old Springfield elegance, pictured here with Mary Todd's tortoise-shell fan, a reproduction of an invitation to dinner in her handwriting, and her sealing-wax stamp, used on all her correspondence thoughtout the Springfield years. A plateful of Savory Stuffed Mushrooms, Crab Puffs, and Baked Brie in Puff Pastry completes the scene.

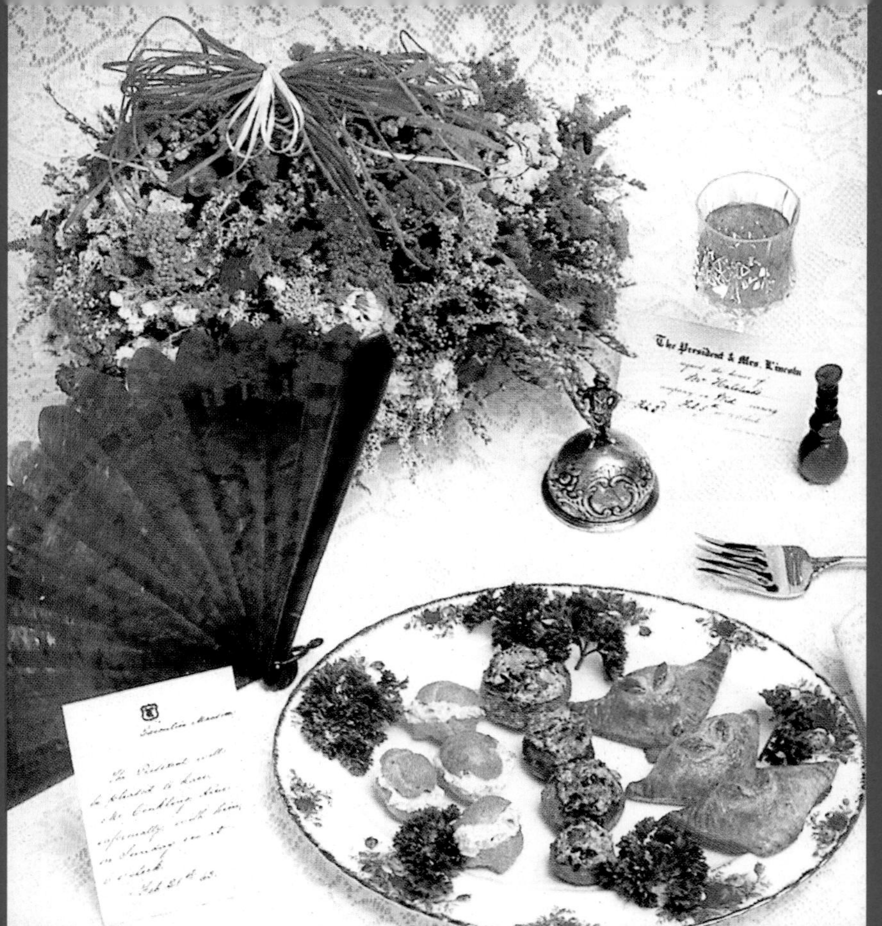

Appetizers

From Mary Todd Lincoln's letter to close friend Hannah Shearer, Springfield, January 1, 1860:

"Gov. and Mrs. Matteson, give a large entertainment on Wednesday evening, Mr L- gives me permission to go, but declines the honor himself."

Baked Brie in Puff Pastry with Orange Blackberry Sauce

8 servings

➤ An elegant, festive delight.

1 sheet frozen puff pastry, approximately 9 ounces, thawed

6 ounces Brie cheese

1 egg, slightly beaten

1 tablespoon milk

Cut puff pastry into 16 squares. Press down edges to make more pliable. Cut Brie into 16 triangles, approximately 1 ½ x 1 ½ x 2 inches. Place Brie triangles on pastry squares. Beat together egg and milk. Brush pastry edges with egg wash. Fold pastry over Brie forming a triangular turnover and press to seal all the edges. To completely seal and make a decorative edge, press edge with tines of fork. Brush top and sides lightly with wash. Bake at 400 degrees for 10 to 13 minutes or until golden brown. Remove from oven and let cool 2 to 3 minutes. Spoon 1 to 2 tablespoons Orange-Blackberry Sauce on individual plates; place 2 pastries on top of sauce. Serve.

Orange Blackberry Sauce

1 10-ounce package frozen blackberries, thawed

¼ cup sugar

1 tablespoon orange-flavored liqueur

Purée blackberries in food processor. Add sugar and liqueur and process again. Refrigerate until ready to use.

Substitute raspberries for blackberries for a different treat. Cut scraps of puff pastry into leaf shapes and use to decorate tops of pastries.

Curried Onion Canapes

24 servings

➤ When Vidalia onions are in season, try this.

¼ cup mayonnaise or salad dressing

1 egg yolk

1 teaspoon salt

1 teaspoon curry powder

½ teaspoon sugar

1 large onion, finely chopped

1 package party rye bread

Butter or margarine

Parmesan cheese

Paprika

Mix first 6 ingredients in a bowl. Butter party rye slices. Spread about 1 tablespoon curry mixture on each slice of bread. Sprinkle with Parmesan cheese. Accent with paprika. Place on baking sheet. Bake at 350 degrees for 15 to 20 minutes or until hot and bubbly. Serve immediately.

Honey Garlic Chicken Wings

24 wings

24 chicken wings
½ cup freshly squeezed lemon juice
2 tablespoons soy sauce
4 tablespoons honey
Salt
Freshly ground black pepper
1 ½ to 2 tablespoons garlic powder

Wash chicken wings and pat dry. Spread on baking sheet. Bake at 250 degrees for 30 minutes. Combine lemon juice, soy sauce, and honey to make sauce; heat in microwave oven on high for 1 to 1 ½ minutes. Remove wings from oven, sprinkle with salt, pepper, and garlic powder. Pour sauce over wings. Return to oven and bake at 350 degrees for 60 minutes. Baste every 15 minutes with sauce. Turn wings over after 30 minutes. Serve immediately.

Savory Stuffed Mushrooms

15 mushrooms

15 medium to large mushrooms
½ pound bacon
½ cup chopped onion
8 ounces of cream cheese
1 6-ounce can pitted ripe olives, chopped
Dash of garlic powder
Seasoned bread crumbs

Wash mushrooms; remove stems and chop very finely. Fry bacon until crisp; remove from grease and crumble. Sauté onion and stems in remaining grease. In mixing bowl, blend cream cheese, bacon, olives, garlic powder, onions, and mushroom stems; set aside. Press bottoms of mushrooms in seasoned bread crumbs and place on greased baking sheet. Fill each with cream cheese mixture. Bake at 325 degrees for 15 to 20 minutes.

For a little different flavor, substitute 2 tablespoons fresh chives for onions.

Peppy Almonds

1 cup

2 tablespoons butter
1 ½ teaspoons chili powder
1 teaspoon celery salt
1 teaspoon Worcestershire sauce
½ teaspoon salt
⅛ teaspoon cayenne pepper
8 ounces whole almonds

➤ Top a taco salad with these almonds for a unique touch.

Mix all ingredients together in a microwave-safe dish. Cook on high in microwave oven for 7 minutes, stirring after 3 minutes and 6 minutes.

Stuffed Artichokes

2 servings

- *2 artichokes, trimmed and steamed*
- *1 cup Italian bread crumbs*
- *¼ cup Parmesan cheese*
- *1 teaspoon oregano*
- *1 teaspoon basil*
- *½ teaspoon salt*
- *1 to 2 garlic cloves, minced*
- *⅓ cup olive oil*
- *4 tablespoons butter (divided use)*
- *¼ cup water*
- *8 medium mushrooms, chopped*

Cool artichokes and spread leaves; remove a few of the center leaves and scrape out choke with a spoon. Place in individual microwave-safe serving bowls. Mix together bread crumbs, Parmesan cheese, oregano, basil, salt, garlic, and olive oil. Combine 2 tablespoons butter, water, and mushrooms. Cook in microwave oven 2 to 4 minutes or until tender; add to dry mixture. Blend together and spoon into center of artichoke and fill leaves; drizzle one tablespoon melted butter over each artichoke and heat in microwave oven for 1 to 2 minutes until hot.

Turkey Pecan Tea Sandwiches

12 sandwiches

- *4 tablespoons butter, softened*
- *½ cup finely chopped pecans*
- *1 ½ teaspoons grated orange peel*
- *8 thin slices whole grain wheat bread, crusts removed*
- *4 ounces thinly sliced cooked turkey breast*
- *Salt*
- *Freshly ground black pepper*
- *4 large lettuce leaves*

Blend together butter, pecans, and orange peel. Spread on one side of each bread slice. Top half the bread with turkey, and salt and pepper to taste. Add lettuce and other bread slices to each sandwich. Cut each into 3 finger sandwiches. If prepared ahead, cover with barely damp paper towels and plastic wrap and chill.

For milder flavor, use less orange peel.

Coconut Chicken Fingers

8 servings

1 pound boneless chicken breasts
Salt
Freshly ground black pepper
Garlic powder
1 cup cornstarch
3 eggs, beaten
2 cups flaked coconut
Oil for deep frying

Garnish

Orange slices
Pineapple chunks
Grapes
Fresh mint leaves

Cut chicken breasts into strips. Sprinkle with salt, pepper, and garlic powder to taste. Coat breast strips in cornstarch. Dip in beaten eggs and roll in coconut. Refrigerate at least 1 hour. Heat oil in deep fryer or electric skillet to 350 degrees; fry chicken strips until golden on both sides. Drain on paper towels. Place on serving dish. Garnish with fruit and fresh mint. Serve immediately with Orange Mint Sauce.

Orange Mint Sauce

Grated peel of 1 orange
8 ounces orange marmalade
4 tablespoons chopped fresh mint
4 ounces freshly squeezed orange juice
2 tablespoons cornstarch
2 ounces orange-flavored liqueur

Place orange peel in saucepan. Add orange marmalade, mint, and orange juice. Bring to full boil over medium heat. Add cornstarch and orange liqueur and continue to boil until thickened. Refrigerate. Serve with Coconut Chicken Fingers or other poultry.

Rummy Sausage Links

8 servings

1 pound cocktail sausages
1 cup brown sugar
¾ cup soy sauce
¾ cup golden rum

Sauté sausages until browned. Add sugar and soy sauce; simmer until mixture thickens. Place in a chafing dish. Add rum, ignite and serve.

Layered Brie

30 servings

➤ One 4-inch wheel of Brie serves 8.

1 8-inch wheel Brie cheese (about 2 ¼ pounds)
⅔ pound bleu cheese, rind removed
⅔ cup Peach Chutney or apricot preserves
¼ cup chopped pecans
¼ cup sliced almonds
Fresh fruit
Crackers

Freeze Brie 30 minutes on a serving platter. With a long sharp knife, cut Brie in half horizontally. Place bleu cheese on a microwave-safe plate. Heat in microwave oven on low (10% power) 1 to 2 minutes until spreadable. Spread bleu cheese onto one cut surface of Brie; top with second piece of Brie. Return layered Brie to freezer for 30 minutes. With sharp knife, cut off and discard top rind.

In small bowl heat chutney or preserves in microwave oven on high 1 minute. Spread evenly on Brie. Top with almonds and pecans. Cover loosely and chill.

To serve, heat in microwave on low for 2 to 3 minutes until Brie is softened, rotating dish twice. Serve with fruit or crackers.

Curry Chutney Dip

6 to 8 servings

➤ Attractive when served in pineapple boat

8 ounces cream cheese, softened
¼ cup chutney
¼ teaspoon dry mustard
1 teaspoon curry powder
¼ cup finely chopped fresh pineapple
¼ cup sliced almonds, toasted
Crackers
Fresh fruit

Combine cream cheese, chutney, mustard, and curry powder; mix well. Stir in pineapple. Chill at least 3 hours. Sprinkle with almonds and serve with crackers or fresh fruit.

Frosted Party Nuts

3 cups

➤ Pack these nuts in pretty tins for great holiday gifts.

1 cup sugar
1 teaspoon cinnamon
½ cup water
3 cups raw peanuts with skins

Bring sugar, cinnamon, and water to a boil in iron skillet. Add raw peanuts. Cook over medium heat, stirring constantly with wooden spoon until liquid is evaporated and peanuts are coated, about 20 minutes. Spread on baking sheet. Bake at 300 degrees for 30 minutes, stirring every 10 minutes. Cool.

South of the Border Shrimp

25 to 30 servings

1 cup oil (divided use)
5 garlic cloves
3 medium onions, chopped
3 pounds large shrimp, peeled and deveined
3 onions, thinly sliced
⅔ cup white wine vinegar
1 ½ teaspoons salt
½ teaspoon coarsely ground black pepper
2 pickled jalapeno peppers, cut into strips

Heat ⅓ cup oil in large frying pan. Add garlic and chopped onions and sauté for 10 minutes. Add shrimp and sauté 5 minutes. Combine the sliced onions, remaining oil, vinegar, salt, pepper, and jalapeño peppers in a bowl. Add shrimp and stir. Marinate for at least 12 hours or longer, if possible. Serve cold.

Jalapeños are a must.

Shrimp Boats

20 shrimp boats

1 envelope dry Italian dressing mix
¼ cup vinegar
¼ cup water
¼ cup vegetable oil
¼ cup olive oil
¼ cup Parmesan cheese
1 pound cooked, shelled and deveined shrimp
Fresh spinach leaves
3 eggs, hard boiled and sliced

➤ A beautiful appetizer submitted by professional chef Jim Hampton.

Garnish
Purple kale

Pour dressing mix into cruêt or jar. Add vinegar, water, vegetable oil, olive oil, and Parmesan cheese. Shake. Chill well. Shake again and pour over cooked shrimp. Allow shrimp to marinate in dressing for 24 hours.

Using half of the shrimp, wrap each in a spinach leaf. Place a slice of boiled egg and another shrimp on top of wrapped shrimp. Put a fancy toothpick through the center to secure. Serve. Garnish serving platter with purple kale.

Crusty Crab Points

3 dozen points

6 ounces crabmeat
½ cup butter, softened
1 5-ounce jar sharp Cheddar cheese spread
½ teaspoon mayonnaise
½ teaspoon seasoned salt
½ teaspoon garlic powder
3 English muffins, sliced in half

When using canned crabmeat, drain. Combine all ingredients except English muffins with electric mixer. Spread on English muffin halves. Freeze for 1 to 1 ½ hours. Cut each muffin half into 6 wedges. Refreeze in plastic bags until ready to serve. Broil until golden brown and bubbly, about 5 minutes. Serve immediately.

Filling is also good on party rye or leave the English muffin halves uncut and serve as an open face sandwich.

Spinach Wedges

12 servings

➤ For a Sunday supper, cut in larger servings and add a salad and fresh crusty bread.

4 frozen puff pastry shells, thawed for 2 hours
6 eggs
3 ounces cream cheese, softened
¼ cup sharp Cheddar cheese, shredded
1 10-ounce package frozen spinach, cooked and drained
2 tablespoons chopped green onion
1 tablespoon parsley
½ teaspoon salt
Freshly ground black pepper
Freshly grated Parmesan cheese

Roll 4 pastry shells together to make a 10-inch pie crust. Allow pastry to rest 5 minutes before putting into pie pan. Flute edges. Combine eggs, cream cheese, and shredded cheese. Fold in spinach, onion, parsley, and salt. Add pepper to taste. Place in pie crust and top with Parmesan cheese.

Bake at 425 degrees for 15 minutes, or until edges are set. Allow to stand for 10 minutes before cutting into small wedges and serving.

Lobster Rolls

60 1-inch rolls

20 slices white bread, crusts removed	*6 to 7 ounces fresh lobster, broiled and shredded*
8 ounces cream cheese	*2 teaspoons snipped parsley*
¼ cup plus 2 tablespoons butter (divided use)	*Sesame seed*

Flatten bread slices with a rolling pin. In saucepan, heat cream cheese with 2 tablespoons butter until cream cheese is melted and mixture is smooth. Add shredded lobster and parsley to mixture. Spread about 1 tablespoon of lobster mixture on bread and roll up. Melt remaining butter and brush over rolls. Sprinkle with sesame seed. Cut rolls crosswise into thirds. Place on baking sheet and broil 3 to 4 minutes. Serve immediately.

Try substituting crabmeat or chopped mushrooms for lobster.

Crab Puffs

Approximately 36 puffs

½ cup water	*1 ½ cups finely chopped crabmeat*
¼ cup butter or margarine	*½ cup mayonnaise or salad dressing*
½ cup flour	*½ cup shredded Swish cheese*
Dash of salt	*¼ cup chopped green onion*
2 eggs	*1 teaspoon prepared mustard*

Bring water and butter to a boil. Add flour and salt; stir vigorously over low heat until mixture forms a ball. Remove from heat. Beat eggs in a food processor or blender; add spoonfuls of the dough while processing to a smooth paste. Drop small rounded teaspoonfuls of dough onto greased baking sheet. Bake at 400 degrees for 20 to 25 minutes or until golden brown. Remove immediately and cool on rack.

When using canned crabmeat, drain. Combine crabmeat, mayonnaise, cheese, onion, and mustard; mix well. Cut tops from puffs and remove any doughy center. Fill with crabmeat mixture and replace tops.

Make puffs ahead and freeze. Thaw and fill just before serving.

Salmon Pâté with Cucumber Sauce

24 servings

➤ Shrimp is an excellent alternative for this appetizer, which can also double as a salad.

1 10 ½ -ounce can tomato soup
1 8-ounce package cream cheese
2 tablespoons unflavored gelatin, dissolved in ¼ cup water
1 7 ¾ -ounce can salmon, drained and flaked
1 cup mayonnaise
1 green pepper, finely chopped
1 cup chopped celery
1 small onion, grated
1 tablespoon Worcestershire sauce
½ teaspoon salt
¼ teaspoon freshly ground black pepper

Heat soup and cheese, stirring until thoroughly mixed. Add softened gelatin; stir well. Add remaining ingredients. Mix well. Place in well greased 9x5 inch loaf pan or 4-cup mold; chill several hours or overnight. Slice and serve with Cucumber Sauce.

Cucumber Sauce

¾ cup chopped cucumber, well drained
1 tablespoon chopped fresh dill or 1 ½ teaspoons dried
2 tablespoons fresh chives or chopped green onion
½ teaspoon salt
2 cups sour cream

Combine ingredients; mix thoroughly. Chill several hours. Serve separately with pâté.

Spicy Herring

2 cups

➤ Even those who don't think they like herring will like this appetizer.

8 ounces diced herring in wine
½ cup finely chopped green pepper
½ cup finely chopped red onion
½ cup diced celery
4 tablespoons diced ripe olives
½ cup ketchup
1 teaspoon prepared horseradish
Crackers
Rye bread rounds

Mix herring, green pepper, onion, celery, olives, ketchup, and horseradish. Refrigerate 2 hours or more. Serve with crackers or rye rounds.

Herbed Feta Wedges

12 servings

1 ½ cups fresh rye bread crumbs
2 tablespoons sesame seed
1 ½ tablespoons margarine, melted
8 ounces cream cheese, softened
5 ounces feta cheese, room temperature
1 egg, beaten
1 teaspoon basil
½ teaspoon rosemary
¼ teaspoon freshly ground black pepper
1 teaspoon finely chopped onion
½ cup sour cream

Mix bread crumbs, sesame seed and margarine; press into 8-inch pan. Chill. Cream cheeses in food processor; add egg, seasonings, and onion. Mix in sour cream until completely blended. Pour into crust. Bake at 325 degrees for 40 minutes, or until center is set. Cool. Cut into wedges or squares and serve.

Tortilla Temptations

24 pieces

8 ounces cream cheese, softened
1 2 ¼-ounce can ripe olives, drained and sliced or chopped
4 green onions, including tops, chopped
4 small flour tortillas
Picante or salsa sauce

Combine cream cheese, olives, and green onions with an electric mixer until mixed well. Evenly spread thin layer of filling on tortillas. Roll up tortillas jellyroll fashion. Cover and refrigerate at least 2 hours until the cream cheese mixture sets. Cut each tortilla into 1-inch slices. Serve with picante or salsa sauce for dipping.

Fruit with Lemon Cream Dip

8 to 12 servings

8 ounces cream cheese, softened
⅓ cup powdered sugar
1 teaspoon grated lemon peel
1 tablespoon fresh lemon juice
Assorted fresh fruits for dipping

Beat cream cheese, sugar, lemon peel, and lemon juice until smooth. Refrigerate 2 to 4 hours. Serve chilled dip with fresh fruit.

Nacho Shrimp Spread

6 to 8 servings

8 ounces cream cheese
1/4 cup whipping cream
3/4 cup chili sauce
4 ounces medium or large cooked shrimp, chopped
6 scallions, chopped
3/4 green pepper, chopped
3 to 4 ounces pitted ripe olives, chopped
8 ounces grated mozzarella cheese
Plain round tortilla chips

Mix cream cheese and whipping cream. Mound on a platter or large plate. Spread remaining ingredients over cream cheese in order listed. Be sure all moisture has been removed from the olives and shrimp. Chill at least 1 hour. Just before serving, broil or microwave on high until cheese on top bubbles. Serve with tortilla chips.

Super Bowl Popcorn

6 to 8 servings

1 teaspoon paprika
1/2 teaspoon crushed red pepper
1/2 teaspoon ground cumin
5 tablespoons margarine, melted
1/2 cup popcorn, popped
6 tablespoons freshly grated Parmesan cheese

Stir paprika, red pepper, and cumin into melted margarine. Allow to cool about 5 minutes. Place popcorn in large bowl. Pour spice mixture over top. Sprinkle with cheese. Toss popcorn with forks to coat evenly. Serve hot or cold.

Savory Edam Cheese

16 servings

➤ Perfect to serve when neighbors drop by.

2 7-ounce packages Edam cheese, room temperature
1/2 cup beer
2 tablespoons butter, softened
1/2 teaspoon caraway seed
1/2 teaspoon dry mustard
1/4 teaspoon celery salt
Crackers

Carefully remove small circle-shaped slice of red wax covering on cheese. Scoop out cheese, keeping shell intact. Mix cheese with remaining ingredients in food processor. Fill cheese shell with mixture, mounding high. To retain moisture prior to serving, replace circle-shaped slice on top. Serve with crackers.

Will keep covered in refrigerator up to 2 weeks.

Oyster Caps

2 dozen caps

24 large mushroom caps	*Melted butter*
⅔ cup butter, softened	*Salt*
2 tablespoons finely chopped green onion	*Freshly ground black pepper*
24 oysters	*Parsley, finely chopped*

Place mushroom caps in baking dish. Blend butter and onion; put ¼ teaspoon of mixture into mushrooms. Dip oysters in melted butter and place one in each cap. Sprinkle with salt and pepper to taste. Bake at 375 degrees until edges of oysters curl. Sprinkle with parsley and serve immediately.

Try this with snails instead of oysters!

In 1828, a jobless Lincoln signed on with James Gentry to take a boat of grain and meat to New Orleans. It's said that while there, Lincoln developed a taste for oysters.

Tangy Shrimp

6 servings

1 quart water	*⅓ cup cottonseed or safflower oil*
1 tablespoon salt	*1 teaspoon tarragon leaves*
10 ounces yellow onion, thinly sliced	*1 ¼ pounds large or jumbo shrimp, cooked, peeled, and deveined*
⅓ cup fresh lemon juice	
4 bay leaves	

Garnish

1 ½ lemons, very thinly sliced	*Fresh parsley sprigs*

Combine water, salt, onion, lemon juice, bay leaves, oil, and tarragon in a bowl; add shrimp. Cover and refrigerate for 2 to 12 hours. Remove bay leaves. Serve in chilled seafood cocktail servers. Garnish with lemon slices and parsley sprigs.

Pineapple Shrimp Crown

12 servings

8 ounces sour cream

1 tablespoon curry powder

1 fresh pineapple

1 pound cooked shrimp

1 20-ounce can pineapple chunks or 1 fresh pineapple, cut up into chunks

1 8-ounce jar maraschino cherries

Mix together sour cream and curry powder; set aside while preparing pineapple. Cut off top of pineapple; remove enough pineapple from shell to accommodate the curry-sour cream dip.

Skewer shrimp and pineapple chunks on decorative toothpicks. Alternate shrimp and pineapple and insert in sides of pineapple. At top of pineapple, insert a row of skewered maraschino cherries. Place pineapple on serving platter and fill center with curry dip.

Pita Triangles

20 servings

➤ These appetizers will disappear before your eyes. Graciously submitted for use in *Honest To Goodness* by professional cook Gloria Schwartz.

1 14-ounce package pita bread

1 cup butter

Mixed dried herbs (paprika, dill, oregano, or garlic)

½ cup freshly grated Parmesan cheese

Split pita and cut each half into 6 triangles. Melt butter and add any combination of two herbs. Brush pita triangles with butter mixture. Sprinkle with cheese. Arrange buttered side up on baking sheet and place in 250 degree oven for 20 minutes or until crisp and lightly browned. Can be kept in an airtight container for months.

For a dessert variation, brush pita with butter and sprinkle with mixture of sugar and cinnamon. Great with ice cream.

Quick and Easy Appetizers

➤ These quick and easy appetizers were developed especially for those who love to entertain but don't have the time to make elaborate appetizers.

Pineapple and Strawberry Kebabs

Create fresh fruit kebabs using pineapple, strawberries, or other fresh fruits in season. Sprinkle with cherry-flavored liqueur and refrigerate for 1 hour before serving.

Salami on Rye

Top party rye bread with shredded sharp Cheddar cheese and top with bite-sized pieces of hard salami. Broil until bubbly.

Caper Lovers Spread

Combine 3 ounces cream cheese, 1 tablespoon milk, 1 tablespoon capers, 1 tablespoon liquid from capers container, and a dash of white pepper. Fill celery or spread on crackers.

Onion on Rye

Combine ¾ cup diced green onion, ½ cup mayonnaise, and ½ cup freshly grated Parmesan cheese. Spread on party rye bread or thin white bread squares. Sprinkle with paprika. Broil until bubbly.

Gingersnaps with a Snap

Mix bleu cheese or cream cheese with a touch of chutney or chopped pistachio nuts. Spread on gingersnaps.

It's a Date

Insert almonds into pitted dates and roll in sugar.

Stuffed Cherry Tomatoes

Using a pastry tube, stuff cherry tomatoes with egg pâté combined with cream cheese and chives, or cream cheese and horseradish mixed with a touch of lemon juice.

Orange Apricots

With pastry tube, fill dried whole apricots with a combination of 1 tablespoon cream cheese and a dash of orange-flavored liqueur. Add fresh mint leaf as a garnish.

Bourbon Slush

About 1 gallon

➤ Keep this in the freezer for coolers all summer long.

4 tea bags
2 cups boiling water
2 cups sugar
1 cup bourbon
2 6-ounce cans frozen orange juice concentrate, thawed
1 6-ounce can frozen lemonade concentrate, thawed
7 cups water

Steep tea bags in boiling water for 2 to 3 minutes. Remove tea bags and stir in sugar. Add remaining ingredients and mix until sugar is totally dissolved. Freeze until firm. Remove from freezer at least 20 minutes before serving. Spoon into cocktail glasses.

For a different summer treat, substitute apricot brandy for bourbon.

Peachy Keen Slush

22 servings

¼ cup sugar
5 cups water (divided use)
1 12-ounce can frozen orange juice concentrate, thawed
1 12-ounce can frozen lemonade concentrate, thawed
2 ½ cups peach schnapps
⅓ cup lemon juice
2 28-ounce bottles ginger ale, chilled

Boil sugar and 2 cups of water for 3 minutes in medium saucepan. Allow to cool. Combine sugar mixture, orange juice, lemonade, 3 cups water, peach schnapps, and lemon juice in a large freezer container. Cover and freeze at least 24 hours.

To serve, spoon ½ cup slush into each serving glass and stir in ¼ cup ginger ale.

Margarita Slush

1 gallon or 20 servings

- *9 cups water*
- *2 cups tequila*
- *1 ½ cups orange-flavored liqueur*
- *1 12-ounce can frozen limeade concentrate, thawed*
- *1 12-ounce can frozen lemonade concentrate, thawed*

➤ Easy to make and delicious with Mexican food.

Mix all ingredients together in freezer container and freeze for at least 1 day before serving. Remove from freezer about 1 ½ hours before serving.

May serve in salt-rimmed glasses with lime or lemon wedges.

Spiced Wine Cup

10 to 12 servings

- *1 pint cranberry juice*
- *½ cup sugar*
- *3 strips lemon peel*
- *2 cinnamon sticks*
- *10 whole cloves*
- *1 3-liter bottle Burgundy wine*

➤ Just the thing to warm your guests on a cold, snowy evening.

Place cranberry juice, sugar, lemon peel, cinnamon, and cloves in saucepan. Bring to a boil, then simmer 10 minutes; strain. Add Burgundy and heat just to simmering; do not let mixture boil. Keep warm in carafe. Serve hot in punch glasses or mugs.

Tomato Bouillon

15 servings

➤ A wonderful aroma on a cold winter day.

- *1 46-ounce can tomato juice*
- *46 ounces water*
- *5 bouillon cubes, chicken or beef*
- *1 stick cinnamon*
- *1 ½ teaspoons whole cloves*

Garnish

- *Twists of lemon*
- *Celery*

Mix together tomato juice, water, bouillon cubes, and cinnamon in a large pan. Place cloves in tea ball or cheesecloth bag and secure tightly; add to tomato mixture. Heat thoroughly. Garnish with lemon for soup or with celery stalks for a drink.

Fresh salad ingredients create a beautiful cornucopia with the wooden mush ladle and solid brass candlestick from the Rutledge Tavern at New Salem.

Salads

Lincoln's friends and associates knew well that the man ate for sustenance, not usually for the sheer enjoyment of fine cuisine. William H. Herndon, Lincoln's law partner, said that Lincoln *"filled up and that is all."*

Oriental Spinach Salad

10 servings

10 to 12 ounces fresh spinach, torn
½ pound bacon, cooked and crumbled
4 eggs, hard boiled and sliced
½ cup bean sprouts
1 8-ounce can sliced water chestnuts, drained
1 6-ounce can Chinese noodles

Dressing (Enough for 2 salads)

1 teaspoon salt
⅓ cup vinegar
1 cup oil
¾ cup sugar
1 tablespoon Worcestershire sauce
1 tablespoon diced onion

Toss salad ingredients in large bowl. Mix all ingredients for dressing in blender. Pour half of dressing on salad and toss again. Serve immediately.

Napa Cabbage Salad

10 to 12 servings

1 medium head napa cabbage
1 bunch green onions, chopped
3 to 5 tablespoons margarine
2 3-ounce packages Oriental noodles
2 ½ ounces sliced almonds
4 tablespoons sesame seed
¼ cup white wine vinegar
¾ cup vegetable oil
2 tablespoons soy sauce
½ cup sugar

Thinly slice cabbage. Add onions. Melt margarine and brown noodles. Be sure to break noodles into small pieces and do not use packaged noodle seasoning. When noodles are golden brown, add almonds and sesame seed; finish browning, watching carefully. Remove and set aside. Combine remaining ingredients and boil for 1 minute. Let cool. Stir dressing well. Toss with salad greens and noodle mixture 15 to 30 minutes before serving.

Simply Caesar Salad

4 to 6 servings

1 large head romaine lettuce	*3 tablespoons lemon juice*
2 large garlic cloves, minced	*4 tablespoons olive oil*
½ teaspoon salt	*2 tablespoons corn oil*
¼ teaspoon freshly ground black pepper	*1 egg yolk*
¼ teaspoon Dijon mustard	*½ cup freshly grated Parmesan cheese*
⅓ teaspoon Worcestershire sauce	*Croutons*

Wash, dry, and break romaine into bite-sized pieces; refrigerate until ready to use. Combine remaining ingredients, except croutons, in the order given. Mix thoroughly in large bowl. Add the salad greens and toss to coat leaves well. Add croutons and toss again. Serve immediately.

Dressing may be prepared in advance. However, do not add the egg yolk or Parmesan cheese until you are ready to toss and serve the salad.

Wilted Lettuce Salad

4 to 6 servings

6 cups torn lettuce	*2 tablespoons sugar*
5 slices bacon, diced	*½ teaspoon salt*
1 egg, beaten	*⅓ cup vinegar*
¼ cup minced onion	*2 tablespoons water*

Place torn lettuce in serving bowl. Cook bacon in a heavy skillet; remove bacon and drain off grease. Combine egg, onion, sugar, salt, vinegar, and water; add to skillet. Heat to boiling and pour over lettuce. Sprinkle on bacon and serve immediately.

Spinach may be substituted for lettuce.

Easy Summer Tomato Special

6 servings

3 medium tomatoes, sliced ½-inch thick	*⅔ cup olive oil*
5 fresh basil leaves, snipped in half	*1 clove garlic, minced or crushed*
1 green pepper, julienned	*1 teaspoon salt*
¼ to ½ sweet yellow onion, sliced ¼-inch thick	*1 teaspoon freshly ground black pepper*
⅓ cup red wine vinegar	*2 teaspoons fresh chopped oregano or ½ teaspoon dried*

Overlap tomatoes in a circle in shallow dish. Tuck basil leaf between each tomato. Sprinkle onion and green pepper over all.

Combine remaining ingredients in a jar and shake well. Pour over vegetables and let marinate at least 8 hours.

Sugar Creek Salad

➤ This unusual salad is delicious. Even those who dislike sauerkraut will love this!

8 to 10 servings

¾ cup sugar	*½ cup chopped celery*
½ cup vinegar	*½ cup chopped green pepper*
⅓ cup oil	*½ cup chopped onion*
32 ounces canned sauerkraut, rinsed and drained	*½ cup chopped carrots*

Mix sugar, vinegar, and oil together until sugar dissolves. Set aside. Combine sauerkraut and vegetables in large non-metallic container; pour dressing over vegetables. Cover and refrigerate. Serve well chilled.

This salad will keep for up to 2 weeks

Cauliflower En Salade

6 to 8 servings

1 medium head cauliflower
3 ripe avocados, peeled and mashed
1 tablespoon lemon juice
1 teaspoon garlic salt
2 tablespoons sour cream
2 green onions, chopped
2 tablespoons salsa

➤ A unique combination!

Place cauliflower in a microwave-safe dish; cook on high for 4 minutes. Chill. Mash avocados and add remaining ingredients. Top chilled cauliflower with avocado mixture.

Serve cauliflower whole for buffet or chopped for individual servings.

Fourth of July Salad

8 to 10 servings

1 head cauliflower, separated into small florets
1 medium bunch fresh broccoli, chopped
1 small red onion, sliced and separated into rings
¼ pound bacon, cooked and crumbled
⅓ cup freshly graded Parmesan cheese
⅓ cup sugar
1 cup mayonnaise
Salt
Freshly ground black pepper

Combine cauliflower, broccoli, onion, bacon, and cheese. Mix sugar and mayonnaise. Add to vegetables. Add salt and pepper to taste. Mix well. Refrigerate at least 8 hours to blend flavors.

Icy Crab Vinaigrette

3 to 4 servings

1 medium onion, finely chopped (divided use)
1 pound fresh lump crabmeat
Salt
Freshly ground black pepper
½ cup oil
¼ cup plus 2 tablespoons cider vinegar
½ cup ice water

➤ Fresh and light, either as a salad or as an appetizer.

Spread half of the chopped onion over the bottom of large glass bowl. Separate crabmeat and place on top of onion. Top with remaining onion. Salt and pepper to taste. Pour oil, vinegar, and ice water over all. Cover and chill 2 to 12 hours. Toss lightly before serving. Serve in chilled seafood cocktail servers or salad bowls.

Sweet and Sour Cucumbers

8 to 10 servings

1 tablespoon salt

1 teaspoon celery seed

2 cups sugar

1 cup vinegar

6 medium cucumbers, peeled and thinly sliced

1 large onion, thinly sliced

3 tablespoons chopped parsley

1 green pepper, diced

1 carrot, finely chopped

In a large bowl, mix salt, celery seed, sugar, and vinegar until sugar dissolves. Add cucumbers, onion, chopped parsley, green pepper and carrot to vinegar mixture. Refrigerate 2 to 3 days and serve.

Try zucchini instead of cucumbers.

Mushroom Salad

6 to 8 servings

1 pound fresh mushrooms, thinly sliced

6 tablespoons lemon juice

1 tablespoon freshly snipped chives

1 tablespoon chopped parsley

1 teaspoon tarragon

½ cup Italian salad dressing

¼ cup pimientos, chopped

½ teaspoon salt

⅛ teaspoon freshly ground black pepper

1 ½ teaspoons sugar

2 teaspoons Dijon mustard

Place mushrooms in large glass bowl and sprinkle with lemon juice, chives, parsley, and tarragon. Stir gently. Cover and refrigerate for at least 1 and no more than 24 hours, stirring occasionally if marinating more than 2 hours.

Combine Italian salad dressing, pimentos, salt, pepper, sugar, and mustard; stir well. Refrigerate for at least 1 hour. Toss mushrooms with dressing and serve.

Easy Gourmet Chicken Salad

10 servings

1 10-ounce package long grain and wild rice
6 green onions, sliced
½ cup chopped green pepper
½ cup chopped celery
¼ cup sliced green olives
½ cup slivered almonds
2 6-ounce jars marinated artichokes
¼ teaspoon curry powder
⅓ cup mayonnaise
2 to 3 cups cubed cooked chicken

Prepare rice according to package directions for less moist rice. Combine rice, onions, pepper, celery, olives, and almonds. Drain and slice artichokes, saving the juice. Mix artichoke juice with curry powder and mayonnaise; stir into rice mixture. Add artichokes and chicken. Toss lightly. Serve warm or cold.

For a vegetarian rice salad, omit chicken and add ½ cup chopped red pepper.

Zesty Green Beans

8 servings

➤ A fresh, crisp green bean salad.

2 pounds fresh green beans
1 small onion, minced
1 small garlic clove, minced
½ cup freshly grated Parmesan cheese
6 tablespoons oil
2 tablespoons white wine vinegar
1 teaspoon salt
¼ teaspoon freshly ground black pepper

Garnish

Lettuce
Tomato wedges
Ripe olives

Wash and trim green beans. Leave whole and cook in boiling salted water just until tender. Drain and cool. Combine cooked green beans with onion and garlic. Sprinkle with cheese. Set aside. Combine the oil, vinegar, salt, and pepper and pour over green bean mixture. Toss. Cover and refrigerate at least 8 hours. Serve at room temperature on lettuce bed with tomato wedges and ripe olives.

Country Corn Salad

6 to 8 servings

1 16-ounce can yellow corn, drained (reserve liquid)	*1 to 2 tablespoons chopped red pepper*
1 cup shredded cabbage	*1 teaspoon flour*
½ large onion, chopped	*¼ teaspoon turmeric*
1 to 2 tablespoons c hopped green pepper	*¼ cup sugar*
	½ teaspoon salt

Combine vegetables in a bowl and set aside. In a small saucepan, mix remaining ingredients and reserved liquid. Bring to a boil; remove from heat and pour over vegetables. Chill and serve.

Creamy Asparagus Salad

4 servings

1 ½ pounds fresh asparagus	*¼ cup grated Cheddar cheese*
Salt	*2 eggs, hard boiled and sliced*
Freshly ground black pepper	*Buttermilk salad dressing*
Parsley	*Croutons*
Chives	

Steam asparagus 3 minutes or until tender. Drain and place in serving dish. Season to taste with salt, pepper, parsley, and chives. Top with grated cheese and sliced eggs; cover and refrigerate until cold. Pour buttermilk dressing over and top with croutons just before serving.

Robust Pasta Salad

10 to 12 servings

1 12-ounce package tomato, spinach, and macaroni twirls, cooked and drained	*2 cups sliced fresh mushrooms*
3 plum tomatoes, chopped	*1 cup sliced ripe olives*
1 green pepper, chopped	*1 cup robust Italian salad dressing*
1 bunch green onions, chopped	*2 cups shredded Mozzarella cheese*

Mix pasta, chopped vegetables, and dressing. Chill thoroughly. Add cheese before serving.

May be served hot or cold. Add your choice of meat, chicken, or seafood for a one-dish meal.

Asparagus Vinaigrette

4 servings

1 to 1 ½ pounds fresh asparagus, steamed
⅓ cup olive oil
1 teaspoon Dijon mustard
1 to 2 garlic cloves, minced
1 tablespoon finely chopped fresh herbs (basil, oregano, parsley, or dill)
⅓ cup white wine vinegar
Freshly ground black pepper
Salt (optional)

Garnish

Other chilled marinated vegetables
Fresh herbs

Place steamed asparagus in a shallow container. Combine olive oil, mustard, garlic, and herbs in a cruet or jar with a tight seal. Stir to blend. Add vinegar, pepper, and salt, if desired. Shake well.

Pour vinaigrette over asparagus. Cover and refrigerate for at least 2 hours. If desired, marinate green, yellow, or sweet red pepper strips, red or Vidalia onion rings, 2-inch zucchini strips, or lightly steamed carrot strips or rounds in separate containers. Serve on platter, garnished with other chilled, marinated vegetables and fresh herbs.

Double the vinaigrette recipe if you use other marinated vegetables as a garnish. Asparagus spears may be prepared in the microwave oven, but be careful not to overcook them.

Tomato Aspic

12 to 15 servings

1 3-ounce package lemon-flavored gelatin
2 cups tomato-vegetable juice (divided use)
1 tablespoon vinegar
Pinch of salt
¾ cup chopped cucumber
1 small green pepper, chopped
2 stalks celery, finely chopped
1 teaspoon finely chopped onion
4 to 5 pimento-stuffed olives, thinly sliced
Lettuce

Dissolve gelatin in 1 cup boiling tomato-vegetable juice. Add remaining juice, vinegar and salt. Set aside to cool. Chill until partially set. Add remaining ingredients except lettuce. Mix and pour into oiled 4-cup ring mold. Chill. Unmold and serve on a bed of lettuce.

Shrimp Mousse

20 servings

1 10 ¾-ounce can tomato soup	*1 tablespoon Worcestershire sauce*
8 ounces cream cheese	*2 garlic cloves, pressed*
1 envelope (¼ounce) unflavored gelatin	*2 to 4 drops hot pepper sauce*
¼ cup cold water	*1 tablespoon fresh lemon juice*
1 cup mayonnaise	*Salt*
¼ cup chopped green onion	*Freshly ground black pepper*
½ cup chopped green pepper	*2 pounds fresh shrimp, boiled, peeled, and chopped*
½ cup chopped celery	*Lettuce leaves*

In small microwave-safe bowl, combine soup and cream cheese and heat in microwave oven until warm. Beat until smooth and mixed. Dissolve gelatin in water and add to cheese-tomato mixture. Stir. Add mayonnaise and remaining ingredients except lettuce; mix. Place in well-oiled 4-cup mold; chill overnight until firm. Unmold, slice, and serve on a bed of lettuce.

May use 14 ounces of crabmeat instead of shrimp. For an appetizer, unmold on lettuce leaves and serve with crackers.

Holiday Cranberry Ring

8 to 10 servings

1 6-ounce package strawberry-flavored gelatin	*Peel from ½ orange*
16 ounces fresh cranberries	*1 ½ cups sugar*
2 medium tart apples, cored	*1 cup pecans, finely chopped*
1 orange, peeled	

Garnish

Lettuce	*Sugar-glazed green grapes*

Prepare gelatin according to package directions and set aside to cool. Grind cranberries, apples, orange, and peel. Add sugar and nuts to fruit mixture and mix well. Pour into gelatin and refrigerate in 9x13 pan or large ring mold until firm. Unmold on a bed of lettuce and serve with sugar-glazed green grapes in center.

Lincoln proclaimed the first official celebration of Thanksgiving in 1863, setting a side the last Thursday of November. This tradition was broken in 1865, the year of his death, and for several years following.

Fresh Pear Salad

6 to 8 servings

3 pears (divided use)	*1 teaspoon salt*
3 tablespoons lemon juice (divided use)	*¼ teaspoon freshly ground black pepper*
1 ½ quarts mixed salad greens, torn	*2 tablespoons red wine vinegar*
2 tablespoons minced green onion	*3 tablespoons orange juice*
½ cup chopped walnuts	*¼ cup oil*
2 tablespoons sugar	*3 tablespoons mayonnaise*

Garnish

Endive	*Fresh raspberries or blueberries*
Orange slices	

Peel, core and coarsely chop 2 pears. Place in salad bowl and toss with 2 tablespoons lemon juice. Add salad greens, onions, and walnuts. Toss gently to blend. In small bowl, combine sugar, salt, pepper, vinegar, and orange juice. Add oil and mayonnaise. Blend until smooth.

Core and slice remaining pear. Toss with remaining tablespoon lemon juice. Arrange pear slices on salad. Garnish with endive and orange slices or fresh raspberries or blueberries, if desired. Pass dressing separately.

Brandied Oranges

8 servings

8 to 10 oranges, peeled and sliced	*¼ cup brandy*
⅓ cup honey	*¼ teaspoon cinnamon*
½ cup fresh orange juice	

Garnish

Lettuce leaves	*Whipped cream flavored with rose water*

Arrange orange slices in large shallow dish. Heat honey in small pan; stir in juice and brandy. Pour over oranges and sprinkle with cinnamon. Cover and refrigerate at least 3 hours. Serve on lettuce leaf, and garnish with whipped cream flavored with rose water.

Rose water may be found at your neighborhood pharmacy.

Just Like Home Potato Salad

10 servings

6 to 7 medium red potatoes
2 to 3 eggs, hard boiled and chopped
½ cup chopped green pepper
½ cup chopped onion
½ cup chopped celery
1 cup mayonnaise
2 tablespoons sugar
½ teaspoon salt
1 ½ teaspoons prepared mustard
2 tablespoons milk

Garnish

Green or red pepper

Boil potatoes until split and soft. Run under cold water. Peal and cube in large salad bowl. Add all other ingredients and mix well. Refrigerate at least 2 hours. Garnish with thin rings or strips of pepper.

Chicken Pecan Salad

6 to 8 servings

½ cup broken pecans
5 cups diced, cooked chicken
1 ½ cups diced celery
2 green onions, diced
5 slices bacon, cooked and crumbled
1 cup mayonnaise
1 cup sour cream
½ teaspoon seasoned salt
1 tablespoon lemon juice

Garnish

Lettuce leaves
Tomato wedges
Asparagus spears
Hard-boiled eggs

Toast pecans in 350 degree oven for 8 to 10 minutes. In large bowl, combine pecans, chicken, celery, onions, and bacon. Add mayonnaise, sour cream, salt, and lemon juice, tossing well after each addition.

Arrange salad on individual beds of lettuce, and garnish with tomato wedges, cold asparagus spears, or hard-boiled egg halves.

Ginger Beef Salad

6 servings

1 pound fresh asparagus, sliced diagonally into 2-inch pieces

1 bunch broccoli, cut into bite-sized florets

1 pound top sirloin, all fat removed and sliced thinly

2 teaspoons sesame oil

2 tablespoons vegetable oil

1 garlic clove, crushed

Lettuce leaves

2 ounces slivered almonds, toasted

➤ A hearty salad. Add a hard roll and you'll have a lunch with flair.

Dressing

⅓ cup soy sauce

¼ cup rice vinegar

2 teaspoons sesame oil

1 1-inch piece fresh ginger root, peeled and grated

1 ½ teaspoons sugar

Freshly ground black pepper

Blanch asparagus and broccoli in salted water for 30 seconds. Rinse in cold water and drain. Sauté beef strips in oils with garlic in wok or large frying pan to desired doneness. Remove from pan to cool.

Combine all ingredients for dressing. When ready to serve, toss beef slices with dressing; add vegetables; toss again.

Serve on lettuce leaves and sprinkle with toasted almonds.

To toast almonds, spread on baking sheet. Toast in 350-degree oven about 30 minutes, stirring every 10 minutes.

Crunchy Broccoli Salad

6 servings

4 cups chopped broccoli

1 ½ cups seedless red grapes, halved

1 cup mayonnaise

⅓ cup sugar

2 tablespoons cider vinegar

12 slices bacon, cooked and crumbled

¼ cup sunflower nuts

Combine broccoli and grapes. Mix mayonnaise, sugar, and vinegar. Add to broccoli and toss. Chill. Before serving, add bacon and sunflower nuts. Toss well.

May substitute chopped pecans for sunflower nuts or raisins for grapes.

Mexican Chicken Salad

8 servings

- *4 whole chicken breasts, split, cooked and boned*
- *2 cups chunky salsa*
- *¼ cup coarsely chopped green onion*
- *1 avocado, peeled, seeded and coarsely chopped*
- *1 tomato, coarsely chopped*
- *1 3-ounce can ripe olives, sliced*
- *1 15-ounce can garbanzo beans, drained*
- *Garlic powder*
- *Freshly ground black pepper*
- *1 cup shredded Monterey Jack cheese*
- *Tortilla chips (optional)*

Cut chicken into 1-inch pieces and combine with salsa. Refrigerate overnight. When ready to serve, place in large bowl and layer other ingredients, except cheese, one at a time over the chicken. Season to taste with garlic powder and pepper and toss lightly. Top with cheese and serve with tortilla chips.

Soak avocado briefly in lemon juice and water to retain color. Salad is pretty served in individual edible tortilla baskets.

German Potato Salad

8 to 10 servings

- *2 pounds red potatoes, cooked, skinned, and sliced*
- *½ pound bacon*
- *2 tablespoons flour*
- *2 tablespoons sugar*
- *1 teaspoon salt*
- *¼ cup vinegar*
- *1 cup water or beef bouillon*
- *1 medium onion, grated*
- *Freshly ground black pepper*
- *2 eggs, hard boiled and sliced*

Place potatoes in a serving dish. Fry bacon in skillet; drain, reserving 1 tablespoon of grease in skillet. Crumble bacon and set aside. Mix flour, sugar, and salt in a small bowl; add to grease in skillet. Gradually add vinegar and water, stirring until mixture has thickened. Add onion and black pepper as desired. Pour sauce over potatoes. Top with crumbled bacon and sliced eggs.

Spoon River Dressing

3 ½ cups

2 cups red wine vinegar	*1 cup oil*
1 ½ cups sugar	*Juice of 1 lemon*
1 cup water	*1 teaspoon salt*
½ cup prepared mustard	*1 to 2 cloves garlic minced*

Blend all ingredients well. Put in 1-quart jar and refrigerate at least 24 hours. Serve on your favorite salad greens.

Feta Cheese Dressing

3 cups

2 cups crumbled feta cheese	*2 garlic cloves, minced*
2 cups mayonnaise	*2 tablespoons green onion tops*
½ cup red wine vinegar	*1 teaspoon salad herbs*
1 tablespoon Worcestershire sauce	*1 teaspoon oregano*
2 tablespoons olive oil	*Freshly ground black pepper*

In a bowl, blend all ingredients until smooth. Refrigerate in covered container. Serve over salad greens. Keeps up to 2 weeks.

White French Dressing

2 cups

2 teaspoons dry mustard	*2 teaspoons salt*
2 teaspoons water	*1 cup white wine vinegar (divided use)*
2 teaspoons onion juice	*2 cups oil*
¾ cup sugar	*2 teaspoons celery seed*
4 garlic cloves, minced	

Combine dry mustard and water; mix well and set aside. Blend together onion juice, sugar, garlic, salt, and ½ cup of vinegar. Slowly add oil while beating constantly with electric mixer. Continue beating and add remaining ½ cup of vinegar, celery seed, and mustard mixture. Chill to thicken. Keeps several weeks.

You can almost smell the fresh bread and taste the spicy Italian Sausage Soup. Someone has been busy making bread, using the 19th century rolling pin and buttermold, both original pieces seen at New Salem.

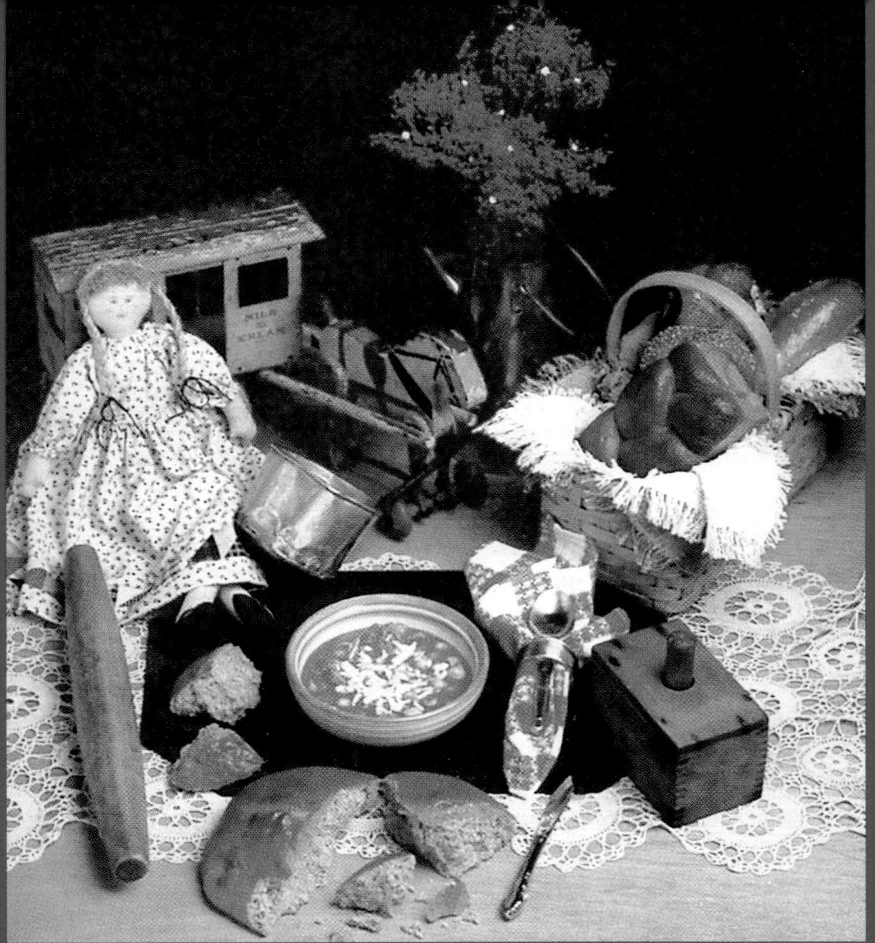

Soups and Breads

In 1876 Mary Todd Lincoln traveled abroad and settled in Pau, France, for four years. She found the privacy she desired in Europe, but missed the hearty American food she had enjoyed in Kentucky, Illinois, and Washington, D.C. She wrote to her grandnephew, Edward Lewis Baker, Jr., from Pau on October 4, 1876:

". . . How much I long to see you all — to have a taste of your dear Grandma's good food — waffles, batter cakes, egg corn bread — are all unknown here — as to biscuits, light rolls & (sic) they have never been dreamed of — not to speak of buckwheat cakes . . ."

Pumpkin Grand Marnier Soup

6 to 8 servings

➤ Different and delicious!

4 tablespoons butter	*1 ½ cups chicken broth*
½ cup chopped white onion	*½ cup orange juice*
1 16-ounce can pumpkin	*¼ cup brown sugar*
½ to ⅔ cup Grand Marnier	*1 to 2 cups half and half*

Garnish

Sour cream	*Freshly grated orange peel*

Melt butter in large saucepan and sauté onion over medium heat until onion is soft, about 5 minutes. Stir in pumpkin, liqueur, chicken broth, orange juice, and brown sugar. Bring to a simmer, while stirring. Reduce heat and continue simmering, uncovered for 15 minutes. Remove from heat and cool slightly. Purée soup in batches in blender or food processor until smooth. Return to saucepan and stir in half and half to desired consistency. Simmer for 5 to 10 minutes, stirring to avoid scorching. Ladle into warm bowls. Garnish with dollop of sour cream and a sprinkle of orange peel.

If made a day ahead, do not add half and half until ready to heat and serve.

Zucchini Soup

6 servings

➤ Quick and colorful!

2 cups sliced zucchini, ½-inch thick	*4 chicken bouillon cubes dissolved in 2 cups hot water*
⅔ cup sliced onion	*Oregano*
2 tablespoons butter	*Freshly ground black pepper*
1 ½ cups coarsely chopped tomato	*Salt (optional)*
½ cup sliced mushrooms	

Garnish

Grated mozzarella cheese

Cook zucchini and onion in melted butter over medium heat, covered, for 7 to 10 minutes. Add tomato, mushrooms and bouillon. Season to taste with oregano, pepper, and salt. Cook 20 minutes. Garnish with grated mozzarella cheese.

If prepared ahead, do not freeze. Variation: Omit chicken bouillon and water and serve as a vegetable.

Creamy Vegetable Chowder

12 servings

3 cups diced, peeled potatoes
2 ½ cups water
¾ cup chopped onion
¾ cup chopped green pepper
½ cup chopped celery
12 ounces fresh mushrooms, sliced
1 garlic clove, minced
¾ cup butter (divided use)
¼ cup flour
1 ¼ teaspoons salt
½ teaspoon dry mustard
¼ teaspoon freshly ground black pepper
2 cups milk
1 ½ teaspoons Worcestershire sauce
¾ cup cubed processed cheese
1 16-ounce can stewed tomatoes, chopped (reserve juice)
1 tablespoon chopped parsley
5 drops hot pepper sauce

Garnish

Dill
Chives
Paprika

Place potatoes in a bowl and add water. Sauté onions, green pepper, celery, mushrooms, and garlic in ½ cup butter in 5-quart Dutch oven over medium heat for 10 minutes. Increase heat to high, adding potatoes and water to vegetables. Bring to boil. Reduce heat; cover and simmer for 20 minutes or until potatoes are fork-tender.

In medium saucepan, melt ¼ cup butter. Stir in flour, salt, mustard, and pepper. Cook 3 minutes, stirring constantly until smooth and bubbly. Gradually stir in milk and Worcestershire sauce; cook until thickened, stirring constantly. Add cheese, stir until melted.

Add sauce to potato mixture. Add stewed tomatoes and juice, parsley, and hot pepper sauce. Heat through, stirring frequently. Do not boil. Serve immediately. Garnish with dill, snippets of chives, or a sprinkle of paprika.

Sunday Night Soup

12 servings

➤ This thick spicy soup really hits the spot on a crisp, fall evening.

2 teaspoons oil
1 pound lean ground beef
1 cup chopped onion
1 11-ounce can chopped tomatoes
3 cups water
2 beef bouillon cubes
1 teaspoon salt
1 teaspoon freshly ground black pepper
1 large bay leaf
¾ cup chopped celery
1 teaspoon Worcestershire sauce
1 package dry onion soup mix
2 ½ cups tomato-vegetable juice
1 8-ounce can mushroom stems and pieces, drained
1 16-ounce package frozen vegetables for soup
6 to 8 ounces vermicelli, broken into 2-inch pieces
½ teaspoon thyme
¼ teaspoon garlic powder

Garnish

Sprigs of parsley
Toasted garlic croutons

In large saucepan, cook ground beef and onion in oil over medium heat until lightly browned. Drain thoroughly. Add tomatoes, water, bouillon cubes, salt, pepper, bay leaf, celery, Worcestershire sauce, onion soup mix, tomato-vegetable juice, and mushrooms to saucepan and bring to a boil. Reduce heat to simmer, cover, and cook for 30 minutes.

Add frozen vegetables, uncooked vermicelli, thyme, and garlic powder. Bring to a second boil. Reduce heat and simmer soup for an additional 20 to 30 minutes. Remove bay leaf. Serve in bowls topped with toasted garlic croutons or sprigs of parsley for color.

Hearty Tortellini Soup with Pesto Sauce

8 servings

½ package 15-bean soup mix	*1 16-ounce bag frozen Italian vegetables (zucchini, cauliflower, carrots, Italian green beans and lima beans)*
2 quarts water	*Salt*
1 large onion, coarsely chopped	*Freshly ground black pepper*
1 28-ounce can stewed tomatoes	
1 large garlic clove, minced	
1 7-ounce box cheese-filled tortellini	

➤ Serve with hard, crusty rolls for a complete meal!

Rinse beans thoroughly, cover with water, and soak overnight. Drain and place beans in 5-quart stockpot with 2 quarts of water, onion, tomatoes, and garlic. Bring to boil and simmer, covered, for 2 ½ to 3 hours, or until beans are tender. Thirty minutes before serving, add tortellini and cook 15 minutes. Add frozen Italian vegetables and cook 15 minutes more. Season to taste with salt and pepper. Serve hot with a tablespoon of Pesto Sauce on each serving.

Pesto Sauce

1 cup butter or margarine, softened	*¼ cup chopped fresh basil*
1 garlic clove, minced	*¼ cup chopped walnuts or pinenuts*
1 cup freshly grated Parmesan cheese	

Process all sauce ingredients in a blender or food processor until smooth.

Pasta "swells" and absorbs soup if added much before serving.

Mansion Chilli

6 to 8 servings

➤ This is Illinois Executive Mansion Chef Gary Piper's recipe. One famous country singer's contract calls for this "chilli" to be served before his Illinois State Fair performance.

1 ½ pounds lean ground beef
3 tablespoons suet
1 medium onion, chopped
1 ½ tablespoons minced garlic
1 green pepper, chopped
Brown sugar
1 ½ teaspoons freshly ground black pepper
1 ½ teaspoons salt
2 tablespoons chili powder
½ teaspoon cumin
1 16-ounce can stewed tomatoes
1 8-ounce can tomato sauce
¼ cup water
¼ cup ketchup
1 15-ounce can dark red kidney beans, undrained

Garnish

Grated cheese
Oyster crackers
Chopped onion

Brown ground beef and suet. Add onion, garlic, green pepper, brown sugar to taste, seasonings, tomatoes, tomato sauce, water, and ketchup. Let simmer for several hours. Ten minutes before serving, add beans. Serve with "help yourself" bowls of grated cheese, oyster crackers, and chopped onions.

Cheesy Vegetable Soup

12 to 14 servings

4 cups chicken broth
2 ½ cups diced potatoes
1 cup chopped celery
½ cup chopped onion
2 10 ¾-ounce cans cream of chicken soup
1 cup chopped fresh mushrooms
1 pound processed cheese
1 package frozen mixed carrots, broccoli, and cauliflower

Combine chicken broth, potatoes, celery, and onion in a large saucepan or kettle; simmer for 20 minutes or until vegetables are fork-tender. Add the cream of chicken soup and stir well until blended. Add the mushrooms, cheese, and frozen vegetables. Cook over low heat for an additional 30 minutes, stirring occasionally.

Wild Rice Soup

6 to 8 servings

1 3/4 cups water
1/2 cup wild rice
1/4 pound bacon, diced
1/2 cup diced onion
1/3 cup diced celery
12 ounces fresh mushrooms, sliced
14 ounces chicken broth
2 10 3/4-ounce cans cream of mushroom soup
2 1/4 cups milk
1 teaspoon Beau Monde seasoning
Freshly ground black pepper
1 1/2 to 2 cups shredded chicken (optional)

Garnish

Dry sherry

Bring water to boil. Add rice; cover and cook over low heat for 35 to 40 minutes. While rice is cooking, fry bacon; drain and reserve 2 tablespoons of drippings. Sauté onions, celery and mushrooms in the bacon drippings; drain. Add bacon, sautéed vegetables, chicken broth, mushroom soup, milk and seasonings to the cooked rice. Simmer at least 20 minutes or longer. For a heartier soup, shredded cooked chicken may be added. A few drops of sherry may be added to each bowl when served or place a small pitcher of sherry on the side.

Simmering improves the flavor of this tasty soup. It is especially good reheated.

Pumpkin Spice Soup

8 to 10 servings

3 cups chicken broth
1 cup applesauce
1 16-ounce can pumpkin
1/2 cup sugar
1 teaspoon cinnamon
1/4 teaspoon ground cloves
1/4 teaspoon ground ginger
2 tablespoons bourbon
1 cup half and half

Garnish

Animal crackers

➤ If you like pumpkin pie, you'll like this. No need to wait for the holidays!

Heat chicken broth in saucepan. Stir in the applesauce, pumpkin, sugar, spices, and bourbon; simmer uncovered on low heat for 15 to 20 minutes. Remove from heat and cool slightly. Purée soup in batches in blender or food processor. Return to pan and stir in half and half. Return to stove top just enough to heat through, 5 to 10 minutes.

Ladle into heated bowls. Float 2 to 3 animal crackers on top.

Chicken Lime Soup

8 to 10 servings

➤ The cilantro makes this soup! Very pretty served in clear glass bowls.

1 3- to 3 ½-pound chicken
6 cups water
1 medium onion, quartered
1 stalk celery
Small bunch fresh cilantro (divided use)
6 whole peppercorns
1 teaspoon salt
½ teaspoon thyme
1 medium green pepper, diced
½ medium onion, diced
2 tablespoons oil
1 16-ounce can whole tomatoes, drained, seeded, and diced
1 ½ teaspoons freshly grated lime peel
Juice of 2 limes
¼ teaspoon freshly ground black pepper
¼ teaspoon salt (optional)
8 small corn tortillas
Oil for frying

Garnish

Lime slices
Cilantro

Place chicken, water, quartered onion, celery, 3 cilantro sprigs, peppercorns, 1 teaspoon salt, and thyme in Dutch oven. Bring to boil; cover and simmer for 1 hour. Remove chicken and cool. Skin and bone chicken; cut into ½-inch cubes. Strain broth and discard vegetables.

In same Dutch oven, sauté green pepper and chopped onion in oil. Add tomato pieces and cook a few more minutes. Add broth, grated lime peel, lime juice, and 3 tablespoons chopped cilantro. Bring to a boil; reduce heat and simmer uncovered for 30 minutes. Stir in chicken and pepper. Add salt to taste. Simmer 10 minutes longer.

Cut each tortilla in 8 wedges and fry in hot oil, stirring gently until crisp and lightly browned. Drain on paper towel. Place 8 wedges in each bowl and ladle soup over wedges. Garnish with thin lime slice and small sprigs of cilantro or serve from large glass bowl with tortilla wedges on the side.

Cream of Broccoli Soup

8 servings

1 cup thinly sliced onion	*¼ cup flour*
6 cups chopped broccoli	*2 cups half and half*
4 cups chicken broth	*Dash of paprika*
⅛ teaspoon Beau Monde seasoning	*¼ teaspoon Worcestershire sauce*
¼ cup butter	*Dash of salt*

Garnish

Whole wheat croutons	*Sour cream*

Combine sliced onion, broccoli, chicken broth, and Beau Monde seasoning in large saucepan; simmer, covered, for 20 to 25 minutes or until vegetables are very tender. Cool. Blend in batches in blender or food processor until very smooth. Return broccoli purée to large saucepan.

Melt butter in top of double boiler and add flour; whisk while cooking until flour is bubbly. Add the half and half slowly, while whisking, and stir until thickened. Add paprika, Worcestershire sauce, and salt.

Add cream sauce slowly to the broccoli mixture and whisk until blended. Keep soup warm over low heat. Do not boil. Serve in heated bowls. Serve with whole wheat croutons and a dollop of sour cream.

Prepare the broccoli purée and refrigerate up to several days ahead or freeze. Make the cream sauce when ready to serve. Blend the two and heat. Easy and delicious!

Shrimp Chowder

8 servings

2 tablespoons butter or margarine	*1 cup grated American cheese*
3 medium onions, chopped	*1 quart milk, heated*
1 cup boiling water	*1 pound large fresh shrimp, cooked and cut in pieces or 20 ounces frozen salad-size shrimp*
5 medium potatoes, peeled and cubed	
2 teaspoons salt	
¼ teaspoon freshly ground black pepper	*2 tablespoons fresh minced parsley*

Melt butter or margarine in a large pan; add chopped onions and sauté until tender. Add water, potatoes, salt, and pepper. Simmer, covered, for at least 15 minutes, until potatoes are fork-tender. In separate pan, melt grated cheese in hot milk. Combine with potato mixture. Just before serving, add shrimp and parsley.

Mushroom Bisque

4 to 6 servings

¼ pound butter
2 leeks, sliced (white part only)
½ pound mushrooms, sliced
1 teaspoon basil
4 teaspoons Spice Island Chicken Stock base
2 tablespoons cornstarch
1 ¾ cups milk
½ cup half and half
¼ cup cream sherry

Lightly sauté leeks, mushrooms, and basil in butter. Whisk in chicken stock base and cornstarch to make a roux, stirring constantly over medium heat. Blend in milk and half and half until smooth. Do not boil. If bisque is kept on stove and cooks down, add more milk or half and half. Stir in sherry just before serving.

Cauliflower Soup

8 to 10 servings

1 medium head cauliflower
2 to 3 carrots, cut in ¼-inch slices
1 to 2 celery stalks, cut in ¼-inch slices
¼ lemon
¼ cup butter
1 medium onion, chopped
4 to 6 fresh mushrooms, sliced
3 to 4 tablespoons flour
4 cups chicken broth
¾ teaspoon salt
¼ teaspoon white pepper
¼ pound American or processed cheese, cut in chunks
1 cup cream or half and half

Garnish

Parsley
Freshly grated nutmeg

Add cauliflower head, carrots, celery, and lemon to large pot of boiling water; simmer for about 10 minutes or until cauliflower is tender. Discard lemon. Drain vegetables, reserving 1 cup of liquid. Break cauliflower into florets. Set aside.

In the same pot, melt butter; sauté onions and mushrooms until onions are translucent, about 5 minutes. Stir in flour and cook 1 to 2 minutes over low heat, stirring constantly to avoid browning flour. Slowly add reserved cooking liquid; cook, stirring until mixture is thick and smooth. Add chicken broth, cauliflower, celery, carrots, salt, and pepper. Reduce amount of salt to ¼ teaspoon, if canned chicken broth is used. Simmer 15 to 20 minutes. Add cheese and stir until smooth. Add cream just before serving and heat through. Top with a sprig of parsley or freshly grated nutmeg.

Elegant Carrot Soup

6 servings

3 cups sliced carrots
¾ cup sliced onion
4 cups chicken broth
2 teaspoons tomato paste
2 tablespoons butter
2 tablespoons brown rice, uncooked
1 teaspoon ground cardamom
½ teaspoon salt
⅛ teaspoon white pepper

Garnish

Fresh parsley
Paprika
Carrot curls

Combine all ingredients in large saucepan, cover, and bring to a boil. Reduce heat and simmer until carrots are very tender and rice is soft, about 45 minutes. Cool slightly. Purée in small batches in blender or food processor. To serve hot, return to pan and heat through. Serve in warm bowls and garnish with chopped parsley or a dash of paprika.

If serving cold, ladle into chilled bowls and top with carrot curls or chopped parsley.

➤ Serve with buttered English muffins topped with freshly grated Parmesan cheese and lightly browned.

Country Potato Soup

8 servings

3 tablespoons butter or margarine
2 cups chopped onion
4 cups chicken broth
3 pounds potatoes, peeled, cut in quarters
1 cup half and half
1 ½ cups grated Cheddar cheese
1 to 2 teaspoons fresh dill
Freshly ground black pepper

Garnish

Paprika
Sprigs of fresh dill
Sprigs of fresh parsley
Curls of Cheddar cheese

Melt butter in large saucepan. Add onion, cover and cook until onion is soft. Add broth and potatoes. Simmer, covered, about 30 minutes, or until potatoes are very tender. Put ⅓ of mixture into blender or food processor and blend until soup is chunky, but not perfectly smooth. Process remaining thirds. Return to pan; stir in half and half, cheese, dill, and pepper to taste. Heat gently until cheese is melted. Sprinkle each serving lightly with paprika, add a sprig of fresh dill or parsley, or curls of Cheddar cheese.

May be prepared up to 3 days in advance, but do not freeze. Great reheated in a double boiler.

Family Chilli

8 servings

Because of the number of "chilli" parlors in Springfield, the city for many years laid claim to the title "chilli capital of the world."

2 slices smoked bacon, diced
1 ½ pounds ground beef
⅔ cup diced onion
2 teaspoons minced garlic
3 tablespoons chili powder diluted in 3 tablespoons hot water
1 16-ounce can tomatoes
2 8-ounce cans tomato sauce
3 16-ounce cans dark red kidney beans, partially drained
8 ounces beer
Salt

Garnish

Cheddar cheese
Oyster crackers

Brown bacon, ground beef, onion, and garlic together in Dutch oven. Pour off any excess drippings. Add all other ingredients. Cover and simmer for at least 1 hour to blend well. Serve with grated Cheddar cheese and oyster crackers.

This chilli is best when prepared a day ahead and served the next day. Flavor will be better developed if chilli is simmered longer than 1 hour.

Seafood Gumbo

8 servings

¼ cup plus 1 tablespoon oil (divided use)	*2 16-ounce cans tomatoes*
¼ cup flour	*2 chicken bouillon cubes*
1 large onion, diced	*1 pound shrimp, shelled and deveined*
1 large green pepper, cut in ½-inch pieces	*½ pound crabmeat*
1 garlic clove, mashed	*12 oysters, drained with liquid reserved (optional)*
2 teaspoons salt	*¼ to ½ teaspoon hot pepper sauce*
¾ teaspoon thyme	*Filé powder*
10 to 12 ounces fresh okra, caps removed, and sliced in ½-inch pieces	*4 to 6 cups cooked rice*
6 cups water (divided use)	*Dry sherry (optional)*

➤ For quick and easy gumbo, prepare soup base a day ahead and add seafood just before serving.

In a large saucepan, cook flour in ¼ cup oil until dark brown, stirring constantly. Add onion, green pepper, garlic, salt, and thyme. Cook until tender, stirring occasionally.

Put okra in skillet with additional tablespoon hot oil and cook a few minutes, stirring to keep from sticking. Add some water to loosen browned bits and add to soup pot with tomatoes and their liquid, oyster liquid (if used), remaining water, and chicken bouillon cubes. Bring to boil and simmer about 30 minutes or until soup thickens slightly. Add shrimp, crabmeat, oysters, and hot pepper sauce. Simmer 10 minutes, stirring occasionally.

Ladle into shallow bowls or onto plates. Sprinkle with filé and place a scoop of rice in center. May serve with a small pitcher of sherry on the side.

Ten ounces frozen okra may be substituted.

Hungarian Bean Soup

8 servings

➤ This soup is a meal in itself! Serve with corn bread or corn muffins.

8 ounces dried Great Northern beans	*3 tablespoons oil*
1 teaspoon salt	*3 to 4 tablespoons flour*
2 to 3 carrots, chopped	*3 garlic cloves, minced*
2 parsnips, chopped	*¼ cup fresh minced parsley*
2 to 3 stalks celery, chopped	*1 tablespoon mild Hungarian paprika*
1 leek, chopped (white part only)	*4 Debrecen sausages or 1 Kielbasa, cut into slices*
1 ½ to 2 green peppers, chopped	*1 to 2 tablespoons white wine vinegar*
2 to 3 tomatoes, fresh or canned, coarsely chopped	*½ cup tomato juice*

Soak beans overnight in cold water. Drain and rinse well. Place in stockpot and add enough cold water to cover by 3 inches. Add salt and bring to a boil. Simmer 30 minutes. Add carrots, parsnips, celery, leek, green pepper, and tomatoes. Cover pot; continue simmering until vegetables are tender and beans are completely cooked, but not mushy. Add a little water if needed.

In skillet, heat oil and stir in flour. Stir and cook roux until it begins to turn golden. Stir in garlic and parsley. Remove from heat and stir in paprika. Return skillet to heat; add 1 to 2 cups liquid from the soup and stir until mixture is thick and smooth.

Add contents of skillet to soup pot and stir well to combine. Add tomato juice and stir. Stir in sausage pieces and simmer soup for an additional 10 minutes. Stir in vinegar just prior to serving.

Ladle into heated bowls.

Avocado Salsa Surprise

6 servings

4 very ripe avocados, peeled and chopped	*½ teaspoon salt*
3 cups cold chicken broth	*⅛ teaspoon garlic powder*
3 ⅓ tablespoons lime juice	*2 cups whipping cream*
4 drops hot pepper sauce	*Salsa*

➤ Smooth and delicious.

Garnish

Sour cream	*Crisp bacon, crumbled*
Thin slices of lime	*Chopped fresh chives and tomatoes*

Blend avocados, chicken broth, lime juice, hot pepper sauce, salt, and garlic powder in blender or food processor until smooth. Divide ingredients into batches if necessary. Whisk in whipping cream. Chill in covered container for 4 to 6 hours to develop flavor.

Place 1 teaspoon salsa in bottom of individual soup bowl; add ¾ to 1 cup soup. Garnish with a teaspoon of sour cream and thin lime slices, crumbled bacon, or chopped chives and tomatoes. Serve immediately.

Must be prepared 4 to 6 hours ahead. May not be frozen.

Italian Sausage Soup

6 servings

1 pound link Italian sausage, cut in ½-inch pieces
½ cup chopped green pepper
½ cup chopped onion
½ cup sliced mushrooms
½ cup butter
1 28-ounce can chopped tomatoes, undrained
2 8-ounce cans tomato sauce
2 cups water
1 tablespoon chicken bouillon granules
½ teaspoon garlic powder
¾ cup small shell macaroni, cooked al dente and drained

Garnish

Shredded mozzarella cheese

Brown sausage in large pot; pour off grease. In separate skillet, sauté green pepper, onion, and mushrooms in butter; add to sausage. Stir in all remaining ingredients except macaroni. Cover and simmer 30 minutes or longer. Add cooked macaroni; simmer 5 minutes. Ladle into warm soup bowls and garnish with cheese.

If prepared ahead or frozen do not add cooked macaroni until ready to serve.

Crab Bisque

8 servings

➤ An elegant way to start a meal.

¾ cup butter (divided use)
⅔ cup finely chopped onion
2 scallions, chopped
¼ cup chopped parsley
11 ounces fresh mushrooms, sliced
¼ cup flour
2 cups milk
½ teaspoon salt
¼ teaspoon white pepper
Dash of hot pepper sauce
3 cups half and half
3 cups cooked crabmeat
6 tablespoons dry sherry

Heat ½ cup butter in skillet; add onion, scallions, parsley, and mushrooms and sauté until soft, about 5 minutes. In a saucepan, heat remaining ¼ cup butter. Stir in flour; add milk. Cook, stirring, until thickened and smooth. Stir in salt, pepper, and hot pepper sauce. Add sautéed vegetables and half and half. Bring just to a boil, stirring; reduce heat. Add crabmeat and simmer, uncovered, for 5 minutes. Do not boil. Just before serving, add the sherry and stir.

Cooked shrimp or crab sticks may be substituted for the crabmeat.

French Onion Soup

8 servings

1 tablespoon oil
3 tablespoons butter or margarine
5 to 6 cups yellow onions, thinly sliced
1 teaspoon salt
Pinch of sugar
2 tablespoons flour
48 ounces homemade beef stock, canned bouillon or combination of stock and water
1 cup dry white wine or dry white vermouth
Salt
Freshly ground black pepper
1 ½ tablespoons cognac (optional)
Toasted French bread slices
Freshly grated Parmesan cheese or grated Swiss cheese

➤ This superb onion soup is a specialty of local professional chef Gloria Schwartz.

Melt butter and oil in a large saucepan. Add onions and cook slowly, covered, for 15 minutes. Uncover, raise heat to moderate and stir in 1 teaspoon salt and sugar. Cook for 30 to 40 minutes, stirring often, until onions are a dark, golden brown. Do not let the onions burn. Sprinkle in flour and stir for 3 minutes. Remove pan from heat. Bring beef stock to a boil; whisk in beef stock slowly until blended into onions. Add wine; add salt and pepper to taste. Bring soup to a boil; lower heat and simmer partially covered for 30 to 40 minutes. If desired, stir in cognac just before serving.

Pour into heated soup bowls over toasted slices of french bread. Pass bowls of freshly grated Parmesan or Swill cheese.

Summer Strawberry Soup

6 servings

➤ Delicious frozen and served as a sorbet!

3 pints strawberries	*1 ½ cups sugar*
1 ½ cups Chablis	*6 tablespoons fresh lemon juice*
3 teaspoons grated lemon peel	*6 tablespoons sour cream*

Garnish

Whipped cream	*Slivered almonds*
Sprigs of fresh mint	

Remove stems from strawberries and slice. Place in bowl with rest of ingredients. Purée in batches in blender at medium speed. Chill.

When serving this beautiful and elegant soup, garnish with a dollop of whipped cream, a small sprig of mint, or a sprinkle of slivered almonds.

Peach Soup

6 servings

1 cup water	*1 ½ tablespoons arrowroot*
⅓ cup sugar	*2 cups white wine*
1 teaspoon whole cloves	*2 16-ounce packages frozen sliced peaches, defrosted, and undrained*
1 cinnamon stick	

Garnish

Mint sprigs	*Violets*
Whipped cream	*Sweetened whipped cream*
Nasturtiums	*Almond extract*

Combine water, sugar, whole cloves, and cinnamon stick in medium saucepan and bring to a boil over medium high heat. Reduce heat, cover, and simmer 30 minutes. Strain syrup and return to pan. Dissolve arrowroot in wine; add to syrup and blend thoroughly. Bring to a boil, stirring occasionally. Cool.

Purée thawed peaches in blender in batches. Add cooled syrup for ease in blending. Combine puréed peaches with rest of syrup. Chill. Serve in chilled bowls garnished with mint sprigs, nasturtiums, or violets. Delicious topped with a dollop of sweetened whipped cream lightly flavored with almond extract.

If prepared 1 or 2 days ahead or frozen, whirl in blender again before serving. If arrowroot is not available, substitute 1⅓ tablespoons cornstarch.

Chilled Senegalese Soup

8 servings

½ cup butter	*¼ teaspoon chili powder*
2⅓ cups diced onion	*1 ½ teaspoons salt*
1 large apple, cored, peeled, and chopped	*2 4 ½-ounce jars strained peas (baby food)*
4 teaspoons curry powder	*4 cups chicken broth*
3 tablespoons flour	*3 cups whipping cream*

➤ Unique flavor!

Garnish

Slivered almonds	*Shredded chicken*
Chives	*Chopped fresh parsley*

Sauté onion and apple in butter until soft but not brown. Add curry and simmer about 7 minutes. Blend in flour, chili powder, salt, and strained peas. Add chicken broth. Bring to a boil. Remove from heat. Put mixture through a fine sieve; chill several hours. Before serving, stir in cream. Garnish with slivered almonds, chives, shredded chicken, or chopped parsley.

Gazpacho Slimmer

4 to 6 servings

1 cup peeled, seeded, and diced tomato	*1 small garlic clove, minced*
½ cup finely chopped celery	*2 tablespoons olive oil*
½ cup peeled, seeded, and finely chopped cucumber	*1 teaspoon salt*
	¼ teaspoon freshly ground black pepper
½ cup minced green pepper	*½ teaspoon Worcestershire sauce*
⅓ cup snipped parsley	*3 cups tomato-vegetable juice*

➤ An easy, refreshing summer soup!

Garnish

Chopped hard boiled eggs	*Cucumber slices*
Yogurt or sour cream	

Combine all ingredients in a stainless steel or glass bowl. Cover and chill thoroughly for 4 hours or overnight. Serve in chilled bowls. Garnish with chopped hard boiled eggs, a dollop of yogurt or sour cream or float a cucumber slice on top.

Bran Muffins

6 dozen

1 15-ounce box raisin bran cereal	*2 teaspoons salt*
2 ¾ cups sugar	*4 eggs, beaten*
5 cups flour	*1 cup shortening*
5 teaspoons baking soda	*1 quart buttermilk*

Mix dry ingredients. Mix eggs, shortening and buttermilk. Combine mixtures. Store in a covered container in the refrigerator. When ready to use, fill greased muffin tins ⅔ full. Bake at 400 degrees for 15 minutes.

Batter can be stored in the refrigerator for up to two months.

Chunky Applesauce Muffins

3 dozen

➤ Great for brown bag lunches.

4 cups flour	*1 teaspoon vanilla*
½ teaspoon cloves	*12 ounces applesauce*
½ teaspoon allspice	*2 teaspoons baking soda*
2 teaspoons cinnamon	*1 cup chopped apples*
1 cup margarine	*1 cup chopped pecans*
2 cups sugar	*1 cup raisins*
2 eggs	

Sift together flour, cloves, allspice, and cinnamon; set aside. Cream together margarine and sugar; add eggs and vanilla. Mix applesauce and baking soda together; add to creamed mixture. Stir in dry ingredients. Fold in apples, pecans, and raisins. Pour batter into greased muffin tins. Bake at 400 degrees for 15 to 20 minutes.

Batter can be refrigerated up to 2 weeks.

Buttermilk Herb Biscuits

32 biscuits

5 cups flour
⅓ cup sugar
1 tablespoon baking powder
1 teaspoon baking soda
2 teaspoons salt
1 cup shortening
1 teaspoon oregano
1 teaspoon dried celery leaves, crumbled, hard stalks removed
1 teaspoon chopped freeze-dried chives
2 teaspoons chervil
2 teaspoons herbs de Provence
2 teaspoons crushed thyme leaves
2 teaspoons parsley leaves
2 packages dry yeast
¼ cup warm water
2 cups buttermilk

➤ A welcome complement to any dinner.

Stir together flour, sugar, baking powder, baking soda, and salt. Cut in shortening until mixture resembles coarse meal. Add herbs; mixing well to distribute evenly. Dissolve yeast in warm water; stir into buttermilk. Add liquid to dry ingredients, stirring well until blended. On floured surface knead just enough to hold dough together. Roll out ½-inch thick. Cut with biscuit cutter. Place on greased baking sheet; cover and let rise 1 hour. Bake at 450 degrees for 10 minutes.

For freezing, bake only 5 minutes; cool and freeze. When ready to serve, place on greased baking sheet and bake at 450 degrees for about 8 minutes.

For plain biscuits, simply omit the 7 herbs and follow the basic recipe.

Soft Pretzels

1 dozen

1 package dry yeast
¾ cup warm water
¼ teaspoon salt
2 ½ cups flour
¼ cup water
1 teaspoon baking soda
Pretzel salt
¼ cup butter, melted

➤ Kids of all ages love to make these.

Dissolve yeast in warm water. Blend salt and flour in food processor with a steel blade. Add yeast mixture and process until dough forms ball. Process for 1 minute to knead dough. Place dough in greased bowl; cover and let rise 15 minutes. Punch down and divide into 12 balls. Roll each ball into a long strip on a floured surface; shape into pretzels.

Combine water and baking soda to make solution. Dip pretzels in soda solution; sprinkle with salt. Place on a greased baking sheet. Bake at 400 degrees for 20 minutes. Remove from oven; brush with melted butter.

Prairie Popovers

6 popovers

➤ Delicious with a salad lunch.

2 eggs, room temperature	*1 cup milk*
1 cup flour	*Sugar*

Beat eggs, flour, and milk until smooth. Grease popover pans and sprinkle with sugar. Fill pans ¾ full. Place in cold oven. Bake at 450 degrees for 30 minutes. Do not open oven door until done. Serve with Bing Cherry Butter, Honey Butter, or Strawberry Butter.

Bing Cherry Butter

½ cup

2 tablespoons Bing cherry preserves	*½ cup butter, softened*

Combine both ingredients in a mixing bowl. Mix until blended and smooth. Store in refrigerator.

Honey Butter

1 ¼ cups

➤ Particularly good with waffles or pancakes.

½ cup butter	*¼ cup honey*
½ cup margarine	*¼ cup half and half*

Mix butter and margarine with electric mixer; add honey, one tablespoon at a time. Slowly blend in half and half until smooth and fluffy. Store in refrigerator.

Strawberry Butter

1 ½ cups

➤ A touch of red for your Valentine table.

10 ounces frozen strawberries, thawed	*½ cup powdered sugar*
1 cup unsalted butter, softened	

Combine all ingredients in a mixing bowl. Mix until well blended and smooth. Store in refrigerator.

Harvest Pumpkin Bread

2 loaves

3 cups sugar	*1 tablespoon cinnamon*
1 cup oil	*1 tablespoon nutmeg*
4 eggs	*1 teaspoon baking powder*
2 cups canned pumpkin	*½ teaspoon ground cloves (optional)*
3 ½ cups flour	*⅔ cup water*
2 teaspoons baking soda	*2 cups chopped walnuts (optional)*
1 teaspoon salt	*2 cups raisins (optional)*

➤ Great for brunch, lunch or a kid's snack!

Cream together sugar and oil. Add eggs and pumpkin; mix well. Add all dry ingredients and water; beat well. Stir in walnuts and raisins. Pour batter into 2 greased and floured 9x5 inch loaf pans. Bake at 350 degrees for 1 hour or until done.

Cranberry Bread

1 loaf

➤ Makes decorative tea sandwiches when thinly sliced and spread with cream cheese or orange butter.

2 cups sifted flour	*2 tablespoons butter, melted*
½ teaspoon baking soda	*2 tablespoons hot water*
½ teaspoon baking powder	*½ cup orange juice*
½ teaspoon salt	*½ cup chopped nuts*
1 egg	*½ cup halved cranberries*
1 cup sugar	

Topping

2 tablespoons butter, melted	*1 tablespoon sugar*

Sift together flour, baking soda, baking powder, and salt; reserve ¼ cup of mixture. Beat egg, sugar, and liquids in a large bowl. Stir in dry ingredients. Coat nuts and cranberries with reserved flour mixture; fold into batter. Pour into greased and floured 9x5 inch loaf pan. Bake at 350 degrees for 1 hour and 10 minutes.

Remove from pan; brush top with butter and sprinkle with sugar. Wrap in double thickness of waxed paper. Refrigerate 2 hours. Rewrap and refrigerate for additional 24 hours before slicing. Store in refrigerator.

Poppy Seed Bread

2 loaves

3 cups flour
1 ½ teaspoons salt
1 ½ teaspoons baking powder
3 eggs
1 ½ cups milk
1 cup plus 2 tablespoons oil
2 ½ cups sugar
2 tablespoons poppy seed
1 ½ teaspoons vanilla
1 ½ teaspoons almond extract
1 ½ teaspoons butter flavoring

Glaze

½ teaspoon butter flavoring
½ teaspoon almond extract
½ teaspoon vanilla
¾ cup sugar
¼ cup orange juice

Sift together flour, salt, and baking powder; set aside. Cream together eggs, milk, oil, and sugar in a large bowl. Add poppy seed, vanilla, almond extract, and butter flavoring. Mix in dry ingredients until batter is smooth.

Pour batter into 2 greased and floured 9x5 inch loaf pans. Bake at 350 degrees for 1 to 1 ¼ hours. Remove loaves from pans and place on rack to cool.

Mix together the glaze ingredients in a small bowl. Spoon glaze over warm loaves.

Very Very Banana Bread

2 loaves

1 cup butter or shortening
2 cups sugar
4 eggs, well beaten
6 ripe bananas, mashed
2 ½ cups flour
1 teaspoon salt
1 ½ teaspoons baking soda
1 cup chopped walnuts (optional)

Grease two 9x5 inch loaf pans. Cream together butter and sugar. Mix together eggs and bananas. Combine these two mixtures. Add remaining ingredients and blend.

Bake at 350 degrees for 50 to 60 minutes or until done. Wrap in foil while still warm to keep moist.

Zucchini Bread

2 loaves

4 eggs
3 cups sugar
1 ½ cups oil
1 ½ teaspoons vanilla
3 cups zucchini, peeled, grated, and loosely packed
3 cups flour
1 tablespoon baking soda
1 teaspoon baking powder
1 ½ teaspoons salt
3 teaspoons cinnamon
1 teaspoon grated orange peel
1 ½ cups chopped nuts

➤ A delicious use of your abundant zucchini crop.

Beat eggs until frothy. Add sugar, oil, and vanilla; beat well until thick and lemony color. Stir in zucchini. Sift together flour, baking soda, baking powder, salt, and cinnamon; add to zucchini mixture. Fold in orange peel and nuts. Pour into 2 greased and floured 9 x 5 inch loaf pans. Bake at 350 degrees for 1 hour or until done. Let cool in pans for 10 minutes before removing.

Cream Cheese Cinnamon Swirls

30 servings

16 ounces cream cheese, softened
1 egg yolk
1 teaspoon vanilla
1 loaf sliced white bread, crusts removed
½ cup butter, melted
½ cup sugar
2 tablespoons cinnamon

➤ Serve at brunch with fresh fruit salad.

Beat cream cheese, egg yolk, and vanilla until smooth. Flatten each slice of bread and spread with cream cheese mixture. Roll up and brush with melted butter. Roll in cinnamon and sugar mixture and cut into fourths. Place on greased baking sheet. Bake at 350 degrees for 10 to 15 minutes.

May be frozen before baking, thawed and then baked.

Coconut Crumb Cake

24 to 30 servings

3 cups light brown sugar	*1 ½ cups buttermilk*
¾ cup oil	*3 eggs, beaten*
3 cups flour	*1 teaspoon salt*
1 teaspoon cinnamon	*1 ½ teaspoons baking soda*
2 cups flaked coconut	*1 tablespoon hot water*
1 cup chopped pecans	*1 teaspoon vanilla*

Glaze

2 cups powdered sugar	*Hot water*
1 teaspoon rum or vanilla extract	

Mix together brown sugar, oil, flour, and cinnamon in large bowl. Reserve 1 ½ cups of crumbs in another bowl and stir in coconut and pecans. Add buttermilk, eggs, salt, baking soda, water, and vanilla to large bowl of crumbs. Mix at low speed with electric mixer until blended. Pour batter into greased and floured 13 ½ x 17 ½ inch baking pan. Cover with reserved crumb mixture. Bake at 350 degrees for 20 minutes. Combine glaze ingredients, using enough hot water to make a very thin icing. Drizzle over cooled coffee cake.

Berry Blue Tea Cake

9 servings

2 cups sifted flour	*¾ cup sugar*
2 teaspoons baking powder	*1 egg, beaten*
½ teaspoon salt	*½ cup milk*
¼ cup butter or margarine	*2 cups blueberries*

Topping

¼ cup sugar	*¼ teaspoon cinnamon*
2 tablespoons flour	*2 tablespoons butter or margarine*

Sift together dry ingredients. Cream butter; gradually beat in sugar. Add egg and milk; beat until smooth. Add dry ingredients; fold in blueberries. Pour into greased and floured 9-inch square pan.

For topping, mix sugar, flour, and cinnamon. Cut in butter until crumbly. Sprinkle topping over dough. Bake at 375 degrees for 40 to 45 minutes.

Gooey Pecan Rolls

12 rolls

Filling and Topping

1 cup brown sugar (divided use)
1 cup plus 2 tablespoons butter, melted and cooled (divided use)
1 tablespoon water
¾ cup chopped pecans
1 teaspoon cinnamon

➤ So finger-lickin' good, you may need to serve them with a fork.

Dough

1 package dry yeast
¼ cup warm water
3 tablespoons butter, softened
2 ½ cups sifted flour
¾ cup lukewarm buttermilk
1 teaspoon sugar
1 teaspoon salt
½ teaspoon baking soda

Mix ½ cup brown sugar and 1 cup melted butter with 1 tablespoon water. Spread in bottom of 12 extra large muffin cups or 9-inch square baking pan and sprinkle with pecans.

Dissolve yeast in warm water in large mixing bowl. Add softened butter and 1 ¼ cups flour, buttermilk, sugar, salt, and baking soda. Beat thoroughly. Add remaining flour gradually.

Turn out on lightly floured surface. Knead until smooth and elastic. Roll dough into 16 x 8 inch rectangle. Spread remaining melted butter and sprinkle with cinnamon and remaining ½ cup brown sugar. Roll up from long side and cut into 12 pieces. Arrange in cups or pan and let rise until double.

Bake at 375 degrees for 25 minutes. While still warm, turn out onto serving plate.

May substitute frozen bread dough.

Almond Streusel Coffee Cake

8 servings

1 cup sugar
2 cups flour (divided use)
½ cup margarine
2 eggs, well beaten
2 teaspoons baking powder
½ teaspoon salt
⅔ cup milk
1 teaspoon almond extract
½ cup sliced almonds

Combine sugar, 1 cup flour, and margarine to make a crumbly mixture. Set aside. Mix eggs, 1 cup flour, baking powder, salt, milk, and almond extract. Spread in greased 9 x 13 inch baking pan. Top with crumb mixture, and sprinkle with almonds. Bake at 350 degrees for 25 to 30 minutes.

Coffee Lovers' Coffee Cake

12 servings

During Lincoln's White House years, he was known to become so preoccupied with his work that at times he would forget to eat. One morning, while artist Francis B. Carpenter was in the White House painting "The First Reading of the Emancipation Proclamation," Lincoln heard the clock strike noon and interrupted the artist's work saying, "I believe, by the by, that I have not yet had my breakfast, -- this business has been so absorbing that it has crowded everything else out of my mind."

2 cups sifted flour
2 teaspoons instant coffee granules or 2 tablespoons Turkish coffee
½ cup butter
2 cups brown sugar
½ teaspoon salt
1 teaspoon cinnamon
¼ teaspoon nutmeg
1 teaspoon baking soda
1 cup sour cream
1 egg
½ cup chopped nuts

Sift together flour and coffee into a large bowl. Add butter, brown sugar, salt, cinnamon, and nutmeg; combine until mixture is crumbly. Lightly pat one half of crumb mixture into greased 9-inch square or round baking pan.

Mix together baking soda and sour cream; add to remaining crumb mixture. Add egg and blend. Pour over crumb mixture in pan. Top with nuts. Bake at 350 degrees for approximately 45 minutes.

Substitute 2 teaspoons of cocoa for coffee for a milder flavor.

Sour Cream Walnut Streusel Cake

1 large bundt cake

3 cups flour
1 ½ teaspoons baking powder
1 ½ teaspoons baking soda
½ teaspoon salt
¾ cup butter
1 ½ cups sugar
3 eggs
2 teaspoons vanilla
2 cups sour cream
¾ cup light brown sugar
2 teaspoons cinnamon
1 cup chopped walnuts
Powdered sugar

Mix together flour, baking powder, baking soda, and salt; set aside. Cream butter, gradually add sugar, and beat well until fluffy. Add eggs one at a time, mixing well after each. Add vanilla and mix. Add flour mixture alternately with sour cream, blending well.

Mix brown sugar, cinnamon, and walnuts together. Spoon small amount of batter into greased and floured bundt pan. Layer on ⅓ of nut mixture. Spoon on half of the remaining batter, then another ⅓ of nut mixture. Repeat with remaining batter and nut mixture.

Bake at 350 degrees for 1 hour. Cool cake in pan on wire rack for 5 minutes. Turn out and cool completely. Dust with powdered sugar.

Cinnamon Swirl Orange Bread

2 loaves

1 package dry yeast	*1 tablespoon grated orange peel*
¼ cup warm water	*¾ cup orange juice*
1 cup warm milk	*6 ½ to 7 cups flour (divided use)*
1 cup sugar (divided use)	*1 egg, slightly beaten*
¼ cup margarine	*1 tablespoon cinnamon*
1 ½ teaspoons salt	*2 tablespoons water*

➤ Best cinnamon bread ever!

Glaze

1 cup sifted powdered sugar	*4 teaspoons orange juice*
1 teaspoon orange peel	

Dissolve yeast in warm water. Combine milk, ½ cup sugar, margarine, salt, orange peel, and juice. Cool to lukewarm; stir in 2 cups of flour and beat until smooth. Stir in yeast and egg; beat well. Add enough flour to make a soft dough. Turn onto a floured surface and knead until smooth and elastic, 8 to 10 minutes. Place dough in greased bowl and turn over so the top is greased. Cover and let rise until double in size, about 1 hour.

Punch down, and divide into 2 balls. Cover and let rest 10 minutes. Roll dough into a 15x7 inch rectangle. Sprinkle with ¼ cup of sugar, 1 ½ teaspoons cinnamon, and 1 tablespoon water. Roll up rectangle along the 7-inch side. Pinch edges together to seal the loaf. Place seam side down in greased 9x5 inch loaf pan. Repeat to form the second loaf. Cover and place in warm place to rise until double, about 50 to 60 minutes.

Bake at 350 degrees for 30 to 40 minutes or until golden brown. Remove from pans and cool. Combine powdered sugar, orange peel, and orange juice. Frost with glaze.

➤ Cardamom gives this bread a unique flavor.

CARDOMOM BRAIDED BREAD

2 loaves

1 package dry yeast
¼ cup warm water
1 cup warm milk
½ cup sugar
¼ teaspoon salt
1 teaspoon ground cardamom
½ cup melted butter
1 egg, well beaten
3 to 4 cups flour
1 egg yolk, beaten with 1 tablespoon water
Granulated sugar

Dissolve yeast in water. Mix milk, sugar, salt, cardamom, butter, and egg. Cool to lukewarm. Add yeast to mixture. Work in enough flour to make stiff but not sticky dough. Knead well for several minutes. Cut dough in half and let rise until double. Divide each half into 3 parts. Shape each part into a 12-inch long rope. Braid 3 ropes together, pressing ends together and tucking them under. Place on greased baking sheet; repeat with other 3 ropes. Cover and let rise until double again. Brush top with egg yolk and sprinkle with sugar. Bake at 375 degrees for 20 minutes.

➤ Toast this hearty bread for a treat on a wintery morning.

HEARTLAND WHOLE WHEAT BREAD

4 large loaves

4 cups milk
¼ cup shortening
½ cup molasses or honey
2 teaspoons salt
2 packages dry yeast
½ cup lukewarm water
9 ⅓ cups whole wheat flour
1 ½ cups finely chopped walnuts (optional)
1 ½ cups finely chopped dates (optional)
Melted butter

Combine milk, shortening, molasses or honey, and salt in saucepan and heat until lukewarm. Dissolve yeast in lukewarm water and add to liquid mixture. Stir in flour, one cup at a time. Add more if needed. May add walnuts and dates for a unique, flavorful taste. Knead on floured surface for 8 to 10 minutes. Place in greased bowl; cover and let rise until double, about 1 hour.

Punch down dough; turn onto floured surface. Shape into 4 loaves and place in greased 9 x 5 inch loaf pans. Cover and let rise until nearly double, about 50 minutes.

Bake at 350 degrees for 50 minutes. Remove from pans and brush tops with melted butter.

To save time buttering hot loaves, simply rub the tops with a stick of butter.

Fruit-Filled Coffee Bread

2 large coffee cakes

2 packages dry yeast	*½ cup butter*
½ cup plus 1 teaspoon sugar (divided use)	*2 teaspoons salt*
¼ cup lukewarm water	*2 eggs, beaten*
1 cup boiling water	*5 cups sifted flour*
	Sliced fresh peaches or strawberries

Topping

¼ cup sugar	*¼ cup shortening*
1 cup flour	*Cinnamon*

➤ A Russian immigrant brought this coffee cake to Springfield in the early 1900s.

Add yeast and 1 teaspoon sugar to lukewarm water. Set aside for 15 minutes. Combine boiling water, butter, ½ cup sugar, and salt in large bowl; cool to lukewarm. Add yeast mixture and beaten eggs. Add flour and knead until dough is smooth. Add more flour if needed. Cover and let rise until double in size.

Punch down. Divide dough in half and roll out ½-inch thick on floured surface. Put on greased 14-inch round or 10x15 inch baking pan. Layer half of fruit on top of dough. Repeat with remaining dough and fruit.

Mix topping ingredients, except cinnamon, until crumbly and spoon over fruit. Lightly sprinkle with cinnamon and extra sugar. Bake at 400 degrees for 20 minutes or until golden brown.

No Knead Butter Rolls

4 dozen

2 packages dry yeast	*1 egg*
¼ cup warm water	*1 teaspoon salt*
2 cups warm milk	*6 ¼ cups flour (divided use)*
¾ cup sugar	*1 cup butter (divided use)*

Dissolve yeast in warm water and let stand 10 minutes. Combine yeast mixture with milk, sugar, egg, salt, and 3 cups flour. Beat until smooth. Add ½ cup melted butter gradually and continue beating. Stir in remaining flour. Cover and refrigerate overnight.

Divide dough into 4 balls on floured surface. Roll each ball into 10-inch rounds. Brush rounds with ½ cup melted butter. Cut each into 12 wedges. Roll up to shape into crescents. Place on lightly greased baking sheet. Let rise for 2 hours. Bake at 350 degrees for 15 minutes or until golden brown.

Easy Italian Bread

1 large loaf

➤ A delicious bread that is prepared in the food processor and refrigerated until ready to bake.

3 cups flour (divided use)
1 tablespoon sugar
1 tablespoon butter or margarine
1 package dry yeast
1 cup plus 2 tablespoons very warm water

Cornmeal
Oil
1 egg white
1 tablespoon cold water

Using metal blade in food processor, combine 2 cups flour, salt, sugar, butter, and yeast until butter is thoroughly cut into dry ingredients. Add half the warm water and turn processor on and off 4 times. Add remaining flour and warm water. Again turn processor on and off 4 times; let run until a ball of dough forms on the blade. If dough is too sticky, add more flour 1 tablespoon at a time. When dough is desired consistency, let processor run 60 seconds to knead dough.

Turn out dough onto lightly floured surface. Cover and let rest for 20 minutes. Roll dough into a 15x10 inch rectangle. Beginning with longest side, roll tightly. Pinch seam to seal and taper ends by rolling gently back and forth. Place on a greased baking sheet that has been sprinkled with cornmeal. Brush dough with oil and loosely cover. Refrigerate for 2 to 24 hours.

Remove from refrigerator when ready to bake. Uncover carefully and let stand at room temperature for 10 minutes. Lightly cut 3 or 4 diagonal slits in the top of the loaf with a sharp knife. Beat together egg white and cold water.

Bake at 425 degrees for 20 minutes. Remove loaf from oven; brush top with egg white mixture; return to oven for 5 to 10 more minutes or until loaf is golden brown.

Oatmeal Bran Bread

3 loaves

1 ¼ cups warm water	*⅓ cup dry milk powder*
1 package dry yeast	*1 cup boiling water*
¼ cup butter or margarine	*½ cup quick oatmeal*
3 tablespoons brown sugar	*½ cup bran cereal flakes*
3 tablespoons molasses	*1 ½ cups whole wheat flour*
1 teaspoon salt	*3 cups white flour (divided use)*

➤ *Delicious sandwich bread.*

Combine warm water and yeast; set aside. Combine butter, brown sugar, molasses, salt, and dry milk in a large bowl. Add boiling water and stir. Add dissolved yeast and mix together with electric mixer on low speed. Mix in oatmeal, bran cereal, and whole wheat flour. Stir in 2 cups of white flour, 1 cup at a time.

On a floured surface, knead in the remaining cup of white flour. Continue kneading until smooth and elastic, about 8 to 10 minutes. Place dough in greased bowl. Cover and let rise until double in size, about 1 ½ hours. Punch down dough and let rise again until double. Punch down, turn out on a floured surface, and shape into 3 loaves. Place in greased 9 x 5 inch loaf pans. Cover and let rise until loaves are nearly double. Bake at 350 degrees for 30 to 40 minutes.

Italian Sausage Bread

2 loaves

16 ounces Italian sausage	*1 cup freshly grated Parmesan cheese*
1 onion, chopped	*2 16-ounce loaves frozen bread dough, thawed*
3 eggs	

➤ *A hearty lunch that everyone loves.*

Sauté sausage with chopped onion; drain and pat mixture with paper towel to remove excess grease. Beat eggs thoroughly with Parmesan cheese.

Roll out half of dough into a 15x10 inch rectangle. Spread half of cheese mixture on dough, leaving a 1-inch rim uncovered. Sprinkle half of sausage mixture on top. Roll up along the longer side. Pinch edges to seal. Place on a greased baking sheet. Repeat with remaining dough and mixtures. Bake at 350 degrees for 45 minutes. Slice and serve warm.

Prize-Winning Potato Bread

2 loaves

➤ Blue ribbon winner at the Illinois State Fair.

Instant mashed potato buds
2 packages dry yeast
2 cups warm water
¼ cup sugar
1 tablespoon salt
½ cup butter or margarine, softened
7 ½ to 7 ¾ cups flour (divided use)
2 tablespoons butter or margarine, melted

Prepare 2 servings of mashed potatoes as package label directs, omitting butter and seasonings. Measure 1 cup.

Sprinkle yeast over warm water in a large bowl and stir until dissolved. Stir in sugar and salt until dissolved. Add mashed potatoes, softened butter, and 3 ½ cups flour. Using electric mixer at medium speed, beat until smooth, about 2 minutes. Gradually add 4 cups more flour, mixing by hand until dough is stiff enough to leave sides of bowl. Mix in remaining ¼ cup flour, if needed.

Turn out dough onto a lightly floured surface. Knead dough 8 to 10 minutes until it is smooth and elastic and small blisters appear on surface. Place in greased bowl; turn dough to bring up greased side. Cover and let rise in a warm place until double in bulk, about one hour.

Punch down. Divide in half. Roll out one half into a 16x8 inch rectangle; roll up along narrow side; pinch edge to seal. Place seam side down in greased 9x5 inch loaf pan. Brush surface lightly with butter. Repeat with remaining dough.

Let rise until nearly double. Bake at 350 degrees for 30 to 40 minutes until crust is deep golden brown. Remove from pans and brush tops with remaining melted butter.

German Dark Rye Bread

2 loaves

3 cups unbleached or bread flour	*1 tablespoon salt*
2 packages dry yeast	*1 tablespoon cinnamon (optional)*
¼ cup sweetened cocoa powder	*3 to 3 ½ cups rye flour*
1 tablespoon caraway seed, crushed	*2 tablespoons, cornmeal*
2 cups warm water	*1 egg white, beaten*
⅓ cup molasses	*1 teaspoon water*
¼ cup butter or oil (divided use)	*Caraway seed*
1 tablespoon sugar	

In large mixing bowl, combine the unbleached or bread flour, yeast, cocoa powder, and caraway seed until well blended. Combine water, molasses, butter or oil, sugar, salt, and cinnamon; heat until just warm, stirring occasionally. Add to dry mixture in bowl. Beat at low speed with electric mixer for 30 seconds, scraping sides of bowl constantly. Beat 3 minutes at high speed. Stir in, by hand, enough rye flour to make soft dough. Turn onto floured surface; knead until smooth, about 5 minutes. Cover; let rest 20 minutes. Punch down and divide dough in half.

Shape each half into a round loaf; place on greased baking sheet or baking sheet sprinkled with cornmeal. Brush surface of loaves with melted butter. Let rise until double, about 35 to 45 minutes. Slash tops of loaves with sharp knife forming an "X". Beat together egg white and water; brush loaves with egg white mixture and sprinkle with whole caraway seeds.

Bake at 350 degrees for 30 to 35 minutes. Remove from pan and brush with melted butter.

Crush caraway seeds in a tea cup with the back of a spoon to extract natural oils and flavor.

It's an elegant evening for dining with Fruited Snapper, bursting with fresh fruit. The two crystal goblets further set the stage for a memorable meal. They were used on the special presidential train that carried President-elect Lincoln from Troy, New York, to New York City en route to his inauguration at Washington, D.C., in 1861.

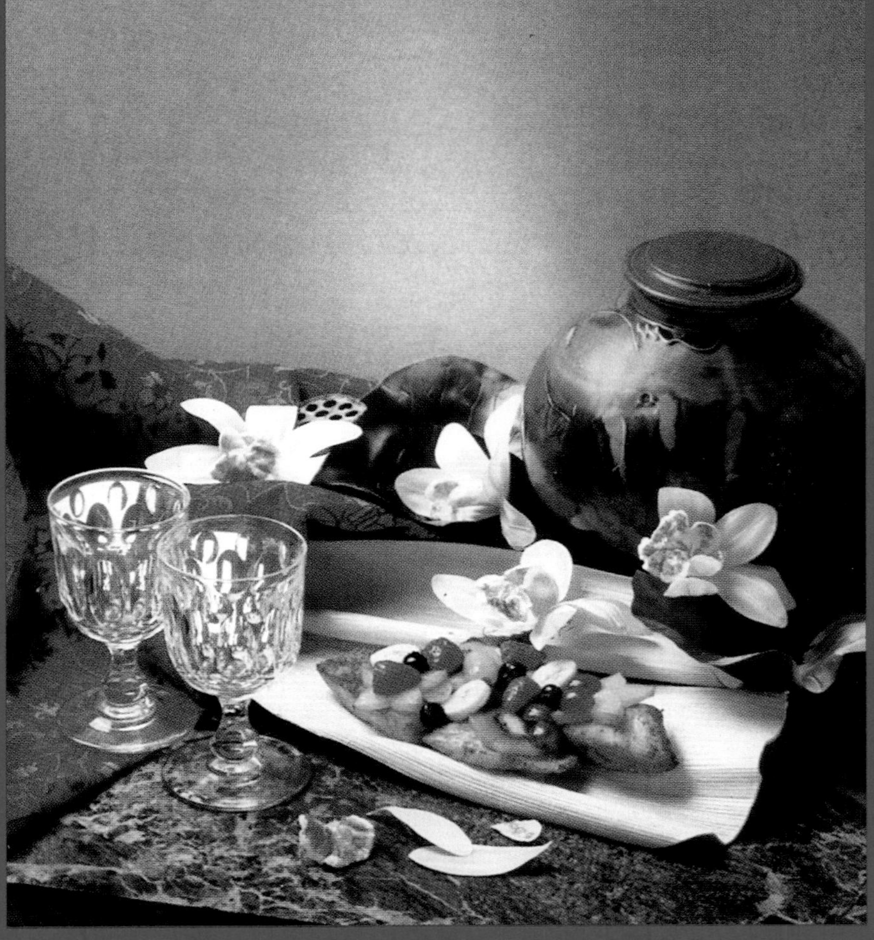

Meats and Seafood

Lincoln's Inaugural Luncheon

Menu

Mock Turtle Soup

Corn Beef and Cabbage

Blackberry Pie

Parsley Potatoes

Coffee

Although Lincoln was not known to take a great interest in food, he did plan the menu for his inaugural luncheon at the Willard Hotel in Washington on March 4, 1861. The midday meal followed the inaugural ceremonies at the Capitol. After lunch, the Lincoln's went directly to the White House, where they were to live for the next four years.

Beef Tenderloin Bordelaise

8 servings

3 pounds beef tenderloin	*2 shallots, white part only, minced*
2 tablespoons Worcestershire sauce	*2 carrots, finely diced*
½ teaspoon freshly ground black pepper	*2 tablespoons chopped fresh parsley*
4 tablespoons butter	*Pinch of rosemary*

Garnish

Sprigs of watercress	*Cherry tomatoes*
Parsley	*Ripe olives*

Brush meat with Worcestershire sauce and sprinkle with pepper. Let stand covered in refrigerator for 8 hours. Put baking pan in 400-degree oven with butter, vegetables, and herbs. When butter is melted and vegetables begin to "sizzle," add tenderloin and baste with butter mixture. Roast 35 to 45 minutes or to an internal temperature of 135 to 140 degrees for medium rare, basting meat at least twice. Remove to serving platter. Let stand 10 minutes before slicing. Garnish with sprigs of watercress or additional parsley and clusters of cherry tomatoes and ripe olives. Serve with Bordelaise Sauce.

Bordelaise Sauce

2 tablespoons butter	*1 cup red wine*
2 tablespoons flour	*¼ cup minced shallots*
1 cup beef stock or bouillon	*1 teaspoon thyme*
⅛ teaspoon freshly ground black pepper	*1 tablespoon lemon juice*
Salt	*1 tablespoon chopped parsley*

Melt butter in a heavy saucepan over low heat; stir in flour and blend well. Cook and stir for several minutes until flour is browned. Gradually add stock while stirring, and simmer for several minutes. Add pepper and salt to taste. Set aside.

Combine red wine, shallots, and thyme in a saucepan. Reduce liquid over high heat to ⅓ cup; strain. Add to brown sauce. Simmer 3 minutes; add lemon juice and parsley. Serve with Beef Tenderloin.

Bacon-Wrapped Beef Tenderloin

6 to 8 servings

3 ½ pounds beef tenderloin	*Lemon pepper*
Dijon mustard	*1 pound bacon*

Cover tenderloin with Dijon mustard. Generously sprinkle with lemon pepper. Wrap entire tenderloin with bacon strips, using toothpicks to secure.

Place on grill over drip pan filled with small amount of water. Using indirect heat, grill 50 minutes for medium doneness, 15 minutes per pound. Let cool a few minutes before slicing.

Peppered Steak

3 to 4 servings

3 to 4 New York strip steaks, 1 inch thick	*¼ cup brandy*
Freshly ground black pepper	*½ cup whipping cream*
1 tablespoon butter	*¼ teaspoon salt*

Press pepper into both sides of steaks. Let steaks stand for 1 hour or refrigerate for 30 minutes. Heat 1 tablespoon butter in skillet to sizzling but not brown. Add salt and stir. Sear steaks on each side for 3 minutes in skillet over high heat.

Remove steak to warm platter. Keep hot. Reduce heat. Stir brandy into skillet. Simmer and stir for 5 minutes. Add whipping cream. Cook and stir for 10 more minutes. Crush additional pepper over steak. Serve sauce with steak.

Steak Diane

4 servings

7 tablespoons butter or margarine (divided use)	*¼ teaspoon salt*
12 ounces fresh mushrooms, slices	*2 teaspoons Worcestershire sauce*
4 tablespoons minced onion	*1 pound beef tenderloin*
2 cloves garlic, minced	*3 tablespoons chopped parsley*

In large skillet, melt 5 tablespoons butter and add mushrooms, onion, garlic, salt, and Worcestershire sauce. Cook until tender, stirring occasionally. Stir in parsley. Spoon into side dish and keep warm. Slice beef into 8 pieces. Melt 2 tablespoons butter in same pan. Add beef slices in single layer. Cook over medium-high heat to medium doneness, approximately 4 minutes each side. Turn only once. Serve with mushroom sauce spooned over top.

This mushroom sauce would be good over chicken or other cuts of beef.

Marinated Grilled Flank Steak

3 or 4 servings

Marinade

¼ cup soy sauce	*½ teaspoon garlic powder*
1 tablespoon lemon juice	*¼ teaspoon freshly ground black pepper*
1 tablespoon Worcestershire sauce	*½ teaspoon onion salt*
3 to 4 drops hot pepper sauce	

1 pound flank steak

Combine marinade ingredients. Score meat and place in a glass dish. Pour in marinade, cover and refrigerate for 24 hours. Grill or broil to desired doneness. Slice across the grain in thin strips.

May also be sliced in thin strips across the grain, quick fried in skillet and served over rice.

Teriyaki Flank Steak

4 servings

¾ cup soy sauce
½ cup sugar
3 tablespoons ketchup
1 garlic clove, minced
3 tablespoons dry white wine or dry white vermouth
1 tablespoon freshly grated ginger (optional)
1 to 1 ½ pounds flank steak, scored
Cooked rice

Mix first six ingredients and pour over steak. Cover and marinate meat at least 8 hours or overnight in refrigerator. Drain meat and grill outdoors for 3 to 4 minutes per side. Slice flank steak on the diagonal in ¼ - to ½ - inch slices. Serve over rice.

To store fresh ginger, peel ginger root, put in glass jar, and cover with dry white wine. Lasts several months. Use liquid as a flavoring for Chinese wok cooking. Marinade may also be used on pork, chicken, or seafood.

Marinated Beef Kebabs

4 servings

➤ Enjoy this festive, economical picnic treat!

1 ½ pounds sirloin steak
½ cup oil
1 small onion, chopped
¼ cup dry red wine
1 ½ teaspoons salt
¼ teaspoon freshly ground black pepper
1 teaspoon dry mustard
1 teaspoon sugar
1 garlic clove, minced
Assorted vegetables (onion, green peppers, cherry tomatoes, mushrooms, zucchini, new potatoes), cut into 1 ½ - to 2 - inch pieces

Cut meat into 1 ½ - to 2 - inch pieces. Mix remaining ingredients except vegetables to make marinade. Cover meat with marinade and refrigerate 4 to 8 hours, turning at least once.

Skewer meat and vegetables. Grill over hot coals, turning often and brushing frequently with marinade for 10 to 20 minutes or until meat is done and vegetables are tender.

Ground Beef Roll with Mushroom Rice Filling

8 servings

2 eggs slightly beaten
1 ½ cups fresh bread crumbs
¼ cup milk
½ pound fresh mushrooms, thinly sliced
2 tablespoons butter or margarine
¾ cup finely chopped onion
2 pounds lean ground beef
¼ cup ketchup
1 ½ teaspoons salt
Freshly ground black pepper
3 tablespoons minced parsley
½ cup cooked long-grain rice, cooled
3 slices bacon

Garnish

Spiced crab apples

In large bowl, mix eggs, bread crumbs, and milk. Set aside. In skillet over medium heat, sauté mushrooms in butter until tender, about 5 minutes. Using a slotted spoon, transfer to another bowl. Sauté onion in same pan until translucent. Mix onion, beef, and ketchup with bread crumb mixture. Add salt and pepper to taste and blend gently but thoroughly.

On a sheet of waxed paper, pat out meat mixture to form a rectangle about 9x12x ¾ inches. Scatter mushrooms evenly over meat, leaving a 1-inch border of meat. Stir parsley into rice and spread over mushrooms. Roll meat as for a jelly roll by lifting and removing waxed paper, starting from shorter side. Arrange bacon slices on top. Bake uncovered at 350 degrees for 1 ¼ hours in an 8x11 inch baking dish. Let sit 5 minutes. Remove from pan to platter. Slice and serve with additional rice and parsley and crab apples for color.

Old-Fashioned Cabbage Rolls

8 servings

1 ½ pounds ground beef
2 cups cooked rice
1 cup chopped onion
2 eggs
1 teaspoon chili powder
1 teaspoon garlic powder
1 teaspoon salt
½ teaspoon freshly ground black pepper

8 large cabbage leaves, steamed
2 cups coarsely chopped tomatoes (fresh or canned)
2 8-ounce cans tomato sauce
2 cups chopped onion
4 tablespoons brown sugar
2 tablespoons vinegar

➤ This recipe came all the way to the prairie from Grodno, Poland in 1905.

Mix ground beef, cooked rice, onion, eggs, and seasonings and spoon equal amounts of mixture on cabbage leaves and roll up. Combine remaining ingredients; bring to boil and simmer for 10 minutes.

Arrange cabbage rolls in baking dish; pour sauce over top. Bake at 350 degrees for one hour. Serve immediately.

May add quartered potatoes to baking dish and bake with cabbage rolls. Meat and sauce can also be used for stuffed green peppers

Bonafide Beef Burgundy

6 servings

5 medium onions, sliced
3 to 4 strips bacon
2 pounds cubed stew meat or other beef
2 tablespoons flour
Salt
Freshly ground black pepper

2 cups beef bouillon
4 cups dry red wine
1 pound fresh mushrooms, quartered
1 to 2 tablespoons cornstarch dissolved in 1 to 2 tablespoons water
Cooked rice or noodles

In Dutch oven, brown onions and bacon. Remove onions and bacon and add beef, flour, and salt and pepper to taste. Brown the meat and add beef bouillon and wine. Let simmer 2 ½ hours. Return onions and crumbled bacon, if desired, to pan along with mushrooms. Simmer 1 more hour.

Keep meat covered with liquid. Add more bouillon and wine, in equal amounts, as needed. Thicken with cornstarch mixed with water. Thicken with more cornstarch and water if needed. Serve with rice or noodles.

Railsplitter's Beef Stew

6 servings

2 pounds cubed beef stew meat
6 carrots, sliced
1 large onion, diced
6 celery stalks, sliced
2 cups canned tomatoes
1 8-ounce can tomato sauce
½ cup water or Burgundy
4 tablespoons tapioca
1 tablespoon sugar
½ teaspoon freshly ground black pepper
1 teaspoon salt
1 garlic clove, minced
8 ounces fresh mushrooms, sliced (optional)
1 to 2 pounds small red potatoes, peeled and quartered (optional)
1 8-ounce can sliced water chestnuts, drained (optional)

Mix all ingredients in Dutch oven and cover tightly. Simmer 5 hours. Add optional ingredients during last hour of cooking.

Dilly Beef Stroganoff

6 servings

2 pounds top round steak
1 teaspoon meat tenderizer (optional)
4 tablespoons butter
1 cup chopped onion
½ teaspoon minced garlic
3 tablespoons flour
1 teaspoon Kitchen Bouquet
1 tablespoon ketchup
½ teaspoon salt
⅛ teaspoon freshly ground black pepper
10 ounces beef bouillon
1 teaspoon dill
1 10 ¾-ounce can cream of mushroom soup
8 ounces fresh mushrooms, sliced
8 ounces sour cream
Rice or noodles

Tenderize beef for 1 hour (optional). Slice beef lengthwise into thirds. Cut each slice cross grain into ½ inch strips. Melt butter in skillet; add beef and brown. Add onion and garlic; sauté 5 minutes. Remove from heat. Sprinkle on flour and Kitchen Bouquet. Add ketchup, salt and pepper; stir until smooth. Gradually add bouillon. Bring to boil, stirring constantly. Simmer on low heat 1 ½ to 2 hours. Add dill, soup, and mushrooms. Heat thoroughly. Just before serving, add sour cream and simmer until mixture thickens slightly. Serve over noodles or rice.

Big Ten Casserole

16 servings

1 ½ pounds ground beef
2 large onions, chopped
2 large green peppers, chopped
1 stalk celery, chopped
1 4-ounce jar green olives, slices
4 cups spaghetti sauce
46 ounces tomato juice
16 ounces egg noodles
16 ounces grated mild Cheddar cheese

➤ Celebrate an Illini victory with this casserole!

Brown ground beef, onions, green peppers, and celery in skillet. Cook egg noodles and drain. Combine all ingredients except cheese. Place layer of mixture in 11x13 inch baking dish and 8-inch square baking dish. Top with layer of cheese. Repeat.

Bake at 350 degrees for 45 minutes or until thoroughly heated and cheese is melted.

Madison County Meatloaf

6 servings

2 cups fresh bread crumbs
¾ cup minced onion
¼ cup minced green pepper
2 eggs, slightly beaten
2 pounds ground chuck
2 tablespoons prepared horseradish
1 ½ teaspoons salt
¼ cup milk
½ cup ketchup

➤ Inspired by our neighbors in the heart of horseradish country.

Mix onion and green pepper with bread crumbs and let stand. Add eggs and ground chuck to crumb mixture and mix well. Stir in horseradish, salt, and milk. Shape into loaf and place in 9x5 inch loaf pan. Top with ketchup. Bake at 400 degrees for 1 hour.

➤ A crowd pleaser at half-time.

Half-Time Italian Beef Sandwiches

12 to 15 servings

3 to 5 pounds sirloin or rump roast
1 teaspoon garlic powder
1 tablespoon Italian seasoning
Salt
Freshly ground black pepper
2 beef bouillon cubes
1 10-ounce jar mild pepperoncini peppers, stems removed
Water or beef bouillon

Cut roast into several chunks. Put in crock pot or slow cooker on high. Add water until meat is covered. Cook for 2 to 3 hours. Add garlic powder. Italian seasoning, salt, pepper, and bouillon cubes. Pour entire contents of pepperoncini jar into pot. Continue cooking until beef shreds easily. Add water or bouillon of needed. Serve on small buns or dinner rolls.

The longer it cooks, the better it gets. May cook in Dutch oven on stovetop over medium heat.

➤ This delicious sandwich with its spicy sauce for dipping is a specialty of Robbie McGrath of Robbie's restaurant in Decatur. The sauce is good with chicken and fish as well.

Double Tony Sandwich With Marinara Sauce

1 large sandwich

Sandwich

2 4-ounce ground chuck patties
2 sandwich-sized slices mozzarella cheese
3 slices whole wheat bread, toasted and buttered

Cook meat until medium rare or your preference. Top with cheese just prior to removing from heat.

Assemble toast, cheese and hamburger like a club sandwich and cut into quarters. Serve with Marinara Sauce for dunking.

Marinara Sauce

5 green peppers, diced
4 white onions, diced
¼ pound butter
Pinch of salt
4 tablespoons hot pepper sauce
¼ cup oregano
½ cup basil
¼ cup garlic cloves, minced
4 pounds diced tomatoes
20 ounces tomato juice

Prepare sauce by sautéing green peppers and onions in the butter until soft. Add spices and mix thoroughly. Then add tomatoes and tomato juice. Simmer for 45 minutes. Place small amount in small bowl and use as dip for sandwich.

The sauce recipe makes one gallon and is easily refrigerated or frozen for future use.

Pork Chops with Orange-Apricot Sauce

4 to 6 servings

¼ cup orange-flavored liqueur
¼ cup apricot preserves
4 tablespoons butter (divided use)
3 tablespoons lemon juice
¼ teaspoon nutmeg
4 to 6 butterfly pork chops
1 large garlic clove, crushed
2 tablespoons chopped onion
1 teaspoon poultry seasoning
1 teaspoon cornstarch
¼ cup cold water

Prepare sauce by warming liqueur and igniting, allowing flames to die out. Add preserves, 2 tablespoons butter, lemon juice, and nutmeg. Heat without boiling, blending ingredients well.

Brown pork chops in remaining butter, garlic, onion, and seasoning. Transfer chops to a covered baking dish. Pour sauce over. Bake at 300 degrees for 1 hour.

Place cooked pork chops on serving dish. Keep warm. Pour sauce from baking dish into saucepan. Heat to reduce sauce by half. Add 1 teaspoon cornstarch dissolved in ¼ cup cold water. Heat until thickened. Serve over pork chops.

Roman Pork Chops

4 servings

4 8-ounce pork chops
Flour
Oil
1 medium onion, sliced
4 cups sliced mushrooms
1 cup white wine
¼ cup sugar
3 to 4 garlic cloves, crushed
1 teaspoon freshly ground black pepper
2 to 3 cups Marinara Sauce

➤ This delicious entrée was kindly submitted to us by Kyongok Kim of Romanesque Restaurant for use in our book.

Sprinkle pork chops with flour and brown for 2 minutes on each side in a skillet. Place in large baking pan. Prepare sauce in separate pan. Sauté onion in small amount of oil until translucent. Add mushrooms and cook 1 minute more. Add wine, sugar, crushed garlic, pepper and Marinara Sauce. Cook over medium heat for 5 minutes. Pour over pork chops and cover. Bake for 1 ½ hours at 300 degrees. Serve with a thin pasta, tossed in olive oil and fresh basil or a prepared pesto sauce.

Try this with boneless chicken breasts, too.

Illini Pork Medallions

6 servings

2 large pork tenderloins (1 ¼ pounds each)
2 tablespoons oil
¼ cup butter, melted
1 medium onion, sliced
½ cup thinly sliced celery
¼ pound fresh mushrooms, sliced
1 tablespoon flour
½ cup beef stock or 1 beef bouillon cube dissolved in ½ cup hot water
½ cup white wine
1 teaspoon salt
¼ teaspoon freshly ground black pepper
Cooked rice

Garnish

Spiced crab apples
Orange slices

In hot skillet, brown meat in oil and set aside. Sauté onion, celery, and mushrooms in butter until tender. Combine flour and stock and stir into vegetables. Stir in wine. Arrange tenderloins in a 9x13 inch pan and sprinkle with salt and pepper. Pour vegetable mixture over all. Cover and bake for 1 ½ hours at 325 degrees. Cook to internal temperature of 180 degrees for fresh pork. Remove pork from pan and cut into ½-inch thick slices. Arrange on platter and serve with rice.

Pork Country Shish Kebab

2 to 6 servings

➤ A great summer dish with sliced tomatoes and corn on the cob.

3 cups pineapple juice
¼ cup soy sauce
2 slices fresh ginger root, minced, or ½ teaspoon ground
3 garlic cloves, minced
1 tablespoon oil
1 to 3 pounds pork loin or tenderloin, cubed

Mix juice, soy sauce, ginger, garlic, and oil in a shallow container and add the meat. Marinate meat for 4 to 8 hours, turning at least once.

Skewer the meat and grill over medium-hot coals for 7 to 15 minutes, turning frequently and basting with marinade as needed. Test with knife for doneness.

Butterfly, marinate, and grill an entire pork loin or tenderloin for an easy dinner for a large group.

Stir-Fry Pork with Green Beans

4 servings

2 tablespoons soy sauce

1 tablespoon sherry

2 teaspoons cornstarch

½ cup chicken stock or 1 chicken bouillon cube dissolved in ½ cup hot water

1 tablespoon peanut oil

1 medium onion, sliced

2 garlic cloves, minced

½ pound green beans, sliced diagonally in ¼-inch pieces or 1 10-ounce package frozen French-cut green beans, thawed

¾ pound boneless pork loin, sliced into ¼-inch strips

1 8 ½-ounce can water chestnuts, drained and sliced

Cooked white or brown rice

Combine soy sauce, sherry, cornstarch, and stock in small bowl; set aside. Heat oil in wok or frying pan over medium to high heat until hot but not smoking. Stir-fry onion and garlic for 1 minute. Remove from pan and set aside.

Allow oil to return to hot but not smoking. Add ½ tablespoon oil if pan is dry. Add beans and stir constantly for 2 to 3 minutes. Remove and add to onions. (If using frozen beans, thaw only and add after meat is stir-fried.) Allow oil to heat up again. Add meat and fry, stirring quickly and frequently for 3 minutes or until browned and firm. Return vegetables to pan. Add water chestnuts. Stir until mixed. Add soy sauce mixture. Stir until thick and clear and the meat and vegetables are coated. Serve with white or brown rice.

Any vegetable or vegetable combination can be used, including your favorite seasonal vegetables. If they don't have comparable cooking times, stir-fry separately. Then combine with sauce at the end. The most important point is to serve the food immediately.

Cheesy Ham-Asparagus Roll Ups

6 to 8 servings

3 tablespoons butter or margarine
3 tablespoons flour
¾ teaspoon salt
2 cups milk
1 cup shredded Swiss cheese
1 ⅓ cups white rice, cooked
8 ¼-inch thick slices cooked ham
1 ½ to 2 pounds fresh or frozen slender asparagus spears (24 to 32 spears), cooked and drained
⅓ cup freshly grated Parmesan cheese

Melt butter and blend in flour and salt. Add milk and cook, stirring constantly until thick. Add Swiss cheese and stir until melted. Blend 1 cup sauce into rice. Spoon equal amounts of rice onto each ham slice. Top with 3 or 4 asparagus spears and roll. Arrange in 8x11 inch baking dish. Pour remaining sauce over rolls. Sprinkle with Parmesan cheese. Bake, covered, at 350 degrees for 30 minutes. Uncover the last 15 minutes to brown.

You may microwave the asparagus spears in a loosely covered dish to save time. Cook just long enough to deepen in color; they will continue cooking in the oven.

Ham and Beef Loaf with Mustard Sauce

6 servings

¾ pound ground smoked ham
¾ pound ground beef
1 teaspoon dry mustard
1 small onion, chopped
1 cup quick-cooking oatmeal
1 cup milk
1 egg, beaten
¼ cup brown sugar
¼ cup vinegar

Mix thoroughly all ingredients but brown sugar and vinegar. Shape into loaf and place in greased baking dish or 9x5 inch loaf pan. Mix brown sugar and vinegar and pour over loaf. Add enough water to cover bottom of baking dish. Bake at 350 degrees for 60 minutes. Let cool slightly to slice. Serve with Mustard Sauce.

Mustard Sauce

1 cup sugar
1 tablespoon flour
1 ½ tablespoons dry mustard
2 eggs, slightly beaten
¾ cup vinegar
¼ cup water

Blend dry ingredients in bowl; stir in eggs and set aside. Mix water and vinegar and bring to simmer in saucepan. Slowly add egg mixture, stirring constantly. Cook until thickened. Serve with Ham and Beef Loaf.

Ham and Sausage Jambalaya

5 servings

¼ cup margarine
1 medium onion, chopped
½ green pepper, chopped
1 ½ large stalks of celery, chopped
½ tablespoon minced garlic
1 pound fresh sausage links, cut in 2-inch pieces
1 pound ham cubes
1 ½ cups long grain white rice
8 ounces chopped tomatoes with juice
2 ½ cups beef stock
Salt
½ teaspoon freshly ground black pepper
¼ teaspoon cayenne pepper
9 green onions, chopped

➤ Great to serve to large groups as a main dish or a side dish. This is a specialty of Gregory Cox of Cox Catering.

Garnish

Fresh parsley
Creole sauce

Melt margarine in stock pot. Add onion, green pepper, celery, and garlic; sauté until onions are translucent, about 5 minutes. Add sausage and ham; cook until browned, stirring while cooking. Add uncooked rice. Stir and brown for 5 minutes. Add tomatoes with juice. Cook a few minutes, then add stock and seasonings. Bring to a boil. Reduce heat to simmer. Cover and cook 1 hour. Sprinkle with green onions and garnish with fresh parsley and creole sauce on the side.

Hot and Spicy Pork Spareribs

4 to 6 servings

6 pounds pork spareribs
1 ½ cups chili sauce
1 cup finely chopped onion
⅔ cup light brown sugar
⅓ cup prepared mustard
1 to 2 teaspoons hot pepper sauce
2 garlic cloves, minced
1 teaspoon salt
½ teaspoon thyme

Split ribs into segments of 2 to 3 ribs each and place in shallow container. Combine all other ingredients and pour over ribs. Cover and refrigerate at least 6 to 8 hours or overnight, turning occasionally.

Grill ribs over medium coals, turning frequently and spooning sauce over ribs for 1 hour or until ribs are richly glazed and fork tender. Or bake at 350 degrees for 1 to 1 ½ hours, basting frequently.

Linguine with Sausage and Peppers

4 servings

1 ½ pounds fresh Italian sausage, cut into 2-inch slices

1 cup water

1 red pepper, julienned

1 green pepper, julienned

1 medium onion, julienned

2 carrots, julienned

½ cup red wine

1 16-ounce can tomatoes or 4 fresh tomatoes, peeled and chopped

8 ounces linguine

Garnish

Freshly ground black pepper

¼ to ½ cup freshly grated Parmesan cheese

Pierce sausage with a fork and place in large heavy skillet. Add water and cook on medium high heat, turning as needed, for 15 minutes or until water boils away. Pour off fat and excess water. Brown sausage on all sides. Remove from pan.

Add julienned vegetables and brown. Remove vegetables. Add wine and deglaze the pan. Add tomatoes and cook for 10 minutes. Add sausage, cover and simmer 15 minutes. Return vegetables to skillet and cook another 5 minutes. Cook and drain linguine. Cover with sausage, vegetables, and sauce. Serve with Parmesan cheese and black pepper.

This recipe can be prepared in advance and placed in casserole dish. Bake at 350 degrees for 30 minutes before serving.

Veal Cutlets with Artichoke Hearts

6 servings

1 ½ pounds veal cutlets
¾ cup olive oil
4 cloves garlic, minced
½ cup flour
Salt
White pepper
½ to ¾ cup dry white wine
¼ cup butter
1 14-ounce can artichoke hearts, drained and quartered
1 teaspoon basil
1 teaspoon oregano
1 pound fettuccine, cooked and drained

Garnish

Fresh parsley, chopped

Pound veal into thin scallops about ⅛-inch thick. In large skillet, heat olive oil with minced garlic to medium heat. Dredge veal in flour seasoned with salt and pepper. Sauté veal 3 to 4 minutes on each side. Remove veal and place on platter; keep warm. Increase heat slightly; add wine and butter and deglaze pan. Add artichoke hearts, herbs, and salt and pepper to taste. Simmer for 3 minutes. If sauce is too thick, add more wine. Pour sauce and artichokes over veal and serve immediately on a bed of fettuccine with chopped parsley.

Veal Roll-Ups

4 servings

4 boneless veal cutlets (about 1 pound)
1 4 ½-ounce can deviled ham
1 tablespoon chopped onion
3 ounces cream cheese
1 egg, beaten
½ cup fine dry bread crumbs
2 tablespoons butter or margarine
¾ cup water
1 envelope dry mushroom gravy mix
¼ cup dry sherry
Cooked wild rice

Pound cutlets very thin, about ⅛-inch thick. Mix ham with onions; spread on cutlets to the edges. Slice cream cheese into 12 narrow strips and place 3 strips on each cutlet. Roll cutlet jelly roll style and fasten with wooden toothpicks. Dip into beaten egg, then bread crumbs. Brown in melted butter in skillet. Remove from skillet and place in 10-inch square baking dish. Remove picks. Pour water into skillet. Add gravy mix and sherry. Cook and stir until mixture is bubbly. Pour over veal rolls and bake covered at 350 degrees for 45 minutes or until tender. Serve with wild rice.

Veal Scallopine à la Genovese

4 servings

3 tablespoons butter or margarine (divided use)	*Freshly ground black pepper*
¼ pound fresh mushrooms, thinly sliced	*Sage*
1 garlic clove	*Nutmeg*
1 pound thinly sliced veal cutlets, cut into 3-inch strips	*1 small onion, thinly sliced*
1 tablespoon flour	*½ cup sauterne or other dry white wine*
1 teaspoon salt	*1 tablespoon sliced stuffed green olives*

Sauté mushrooms in 1 tablespoon butter; set aside. Sauté garlic in 2 tablespoons butter for 3 minutes. Remove and discard garlic. In same butter, brown meat on both sides. Sprinkle flour, salt, pepper, sage, and nutmeg over meat. Add onions and wine. Cover and simmer slowly 15 minutes, turning once after 7 minutes. Add more wine if necessary. Add mushrooms and olives. Cook an additional 5 minutes.

Lamb Curry

6 to 8 servings

2 tablespoons butter	*Freshly ground black pepper*
2 tablespoons chopped onion	*Cooked rice*
2 tablespoons flour	*Chopped green pepper*
1 teaspoon curry powder	*Pineapple chunks*
2 cups chicken bouillon	*Chutney*
1 teaspoon lemon juice (optional)	*Raisins*
2 cups cubed cooked lamb	*Coarsely chopped peanuts*
Salt	

Sauté onion in butter. Stir in flour and curry powder. Add bouillon; cook over low to medium heat until slightly thickened. Add lemon juice if needed to help thicken. Add lamb. Cook until lamb is thoroughly reheated. Salt and pepper to taste. Serve over rice with chopped green pepper, pineapple chunks, chutney, raisins, or peanuts.

Lamb Curry is even better when made a day ahead and reheated.

Springfield Leg of Lamb

8 to 12 servings

1 leg of lamb

3 garlic cloves, slivered

3 tablespoons fresh rosemary or 1 tablespoon dried

Salt

Freshly ground black pepper

8 medium potatoes, peeled

8 small onions, peeled

➤ Serve with mint sauce or Peach Chutney.

Garnish

Mint sprigs

Fresh rosemary

Rinse and dry lamb. Place in large uncovered roasting pan. With a sharp pointed knife make a 1-inch deep slit into top of lamb; insert a slice of garlic. Repeat randomly over entire roast with the rest of garlic. Rub rosemary over roast. Sprinkle with salt and pepper.

Bake at 450 degrees for 45 minutes. Reduce heat to 250 degrees. Add potatoes and onions around roast, rolling them to coat with the pan drippings. Cook 1 hour and 15 minutes for medium-rare or 1 hour and 40 minutes for medium-well. Turn potatoes once or twice during cooking.

Remove meat to platter. Return potatoes and onions to oven and increase oven temperature to 350 degrees. Cook until well browned and fork tender, approximately 15 to 20 minutes longer. Carve meat and place on platter and surround with potatoes, onions, and sprigs of rosemary or mint.

Venison Steak with Pepper Sauce

6 servings

Venison

6 venison steaks
Salt
Freshly ground black pepper
4 tablespoons unsalted butter
Pepper Sauce

Sprinkle steaks lightly with salt and pepper on both sides. Melt butter in skillet and pan fry steaks, browning 6 minutes per side. Tender venison is excellent medium-rare. When the steaks are almost done, add Pepper Sauce. Reduce heat and cook for 5 minutes longer.

Pepper Sauce

⅔ cups white wine vinegar
1 ½ cups brown gravy
12 peppercorns
4 tablespoons red currant jelly
½ cup whipping cream (optional)
Freshly ground black pepper

Simmer vinegar until reduced to ⅓ cup. Add brown gravy and peppercorns and simmer gently for 20 minutes. Add jelly and stir until blended. Strain and, if you wish, add cream. Heat sauce, but do not allow to boil. Taste. It should be fairly spicy. Correct the seasoning with more pepper if needed. Serve with venison.

Sautéed Orange Roughy

2 servings

2 teaspoons margarine
½ cup white wine
1 teaspoon fresh dill or ½ teaspoon dried
½ teaspoon minced garlic
¼ cup mushrooms, chopped
½ pound orange roughy

Garnish

Lemon baskets filled with chopped fresh parsley

Heat margarine, wine, dill, garlic, and mushrooms in skillet until hot. Add fish and sauté until it flakes when tested with a fork. Turn carefully once during cooking. Remove to a platter; garnish with lemon baskets.

Marinated Grilled Halibut

4 servings

Juice of 1 lime	*2 teaspoons olive oil*
Grated peel of 1 lime	*1 ½ pounds fresh halibut*
2 tablespoons soy sauce	*1 tablespoon peanut oil*

Combine lime juice, peel, soy sauce, and olive oil. Pour over fish in a sealable container or plastic bag. Marinate for at least 1 to 2 hours, turning fish several times to redistribute the marinade. Cut fish into serving-size pieces.

Brush grill rack with peanut oil. Grill fish 2 to 3 minutes per side for each ½ inch of thickness. Fish is done when it flakes with a fork.

Any firm fish steak may be substituted for halibut. Serve with wild rice and a Caesar salad. Or try brown rice and stir-fried vegetables.

Blackened Catfish

4 servings

4 fresh catfish fillets	*¼ teaspoon ground white pepper*
½ teaspoon onion powder	*¼ teaspoon dried thyme, crushed*
½ teaspoon garlic salt	*¼ teaspoon freshly ground black pepper*
½ teaspoon ground red pepper	*⅛ teaspoon ground sage*
½ teaspoon dried basil, crushed	*¼ cup margarine, melted (divided use)*

In a small mixing bowl, combine seasonings. Brush both sides of fish with melted margarine; coat both sides with seasonings. If using a charcoal grill, remove grill rack and place an unoiled 12-inch cast-iron skillet directly on hot coals. If using a gas grill, turn to high and place skillet on the grill rack. Preheat the skillet 5 minutes or until a drop of water sizzles.

Add coated fillets to skillet. Carefully drizzle about 2 teaspoons of the melted margarine over the fish. Grill fish 2 ½ minutes or until blackened. Turn fish and drizzle with 2 teaspoons of the melted margarine. Grill 2 ½ minutes more or until blackened and fish flakes easily when tested with a fork. Transfer to serving plates. Drizzle with any remaining melted margarine.

Barbecued Salmon

5 to 7 servings

White Wine Marinade

1 ½ cups dry white wine
½ cup lemon juice
½ cup oil
1 onion, thinly sliced
3 garlic cloves, crushed
3 sprigs fresh parsley
1 teaspoon ginger
½ teaspoon thyme
¼ teaspoon hot pepper sauce
1 teaspoon salt
¼ teaspoon freshly ground black pepper

1 whole 2 to 4 pound salmon, cleaned or 5 to 7 boned baby coho salmon
1 tablespoon oil

Combine all marinade ingredients in a saucepan. Stirring occasionally, bring to a boil over high heat. Pour into non-metallic pan that is large enough to hold salmon; set aside to cool to room temperature.

If using whole salmon, score both sides of the fish by making diagonal slits with a sharp knife. If using baby coho, do not score. Place salmon in cooled marinade and turn it over to moisten evenly. Cover tightly with plastic wrap and marinate at room temperature for about 3 hours for whole salmon or 1 hour at room temperature for baby coho, turning the fish occasionally. Double marinating time if refrigerating.

Brush grill with oil. Place salmon on top of the grill and brush with remaining marinade. Grill until fish flakes with fork; turn once during cooking.

Grilled Lime Salmon

4 servings

4 fresh salmon steaks, 1 inch thick	*2 teaspoons honey*
¼ cup vegetable oil	*4 cups shredded mixed greens*
¼ cup lime juice	*½ cup shredded radishes*
1 tablespoon water	*½ cup alfalfa sprouts*
1 tablespoon soy sauce	*1 tablespoon toasted sesame seed*
2 teaspoons sesame oil	*1 canned green chili pepper, rinsed, seeded, and chopped*

Garnish

Lime slices

Place salmon in a plastic bag; set in a shallow pan. For marinade, stir together vegetable oil, lime juice, water, soy sauce, sesame oil, and honey; pour over salmon. Close bag; marinate in refrigerator 6 hours, turning bag occasionally to distribute marinade.

In large bowl, toss together remaining ingredients. Place on serving platter. Drain salmon, reserving marinade. Grill on an uncovered grill, directly over medium-hot coals for 8 to 12 minutes or until fish flakes easily when tested with a fork, turning halfway through grilling. Pour reserved marinade into a small saucepan. Place saucepan on side of grill; heat until bubbly. Pour hot marinade over greens; toss to wilt slightly. Serve grilled salmon on bed of greens. Garnish with lime slices.

Pasta With Salmon

4 to 6 servings

2 tablespoons butter or margarine	*½ teaspoon ground nutmeg*
1 cup sliced fresh mushrooms	*8 ounces spinach noodles, cooked and drained*
1 6 ½-ounce can boneless pink salmon, drained and flaked	*1 cup sour cream*
½ cup freshly grated Parmesan cheese	*Paprika*
	½ cup half and half (optional)

Melt butter in saucepan. Add mushrooms and sauté gently for 1 minute. Add salmon, cheese and nutmeg. Heat gently over low heat; add noodles and stir until hot. Fold in sour cream and add enough half and half to achieve desired consistency. Sprinkle with paprika and serve immediately.

Salmon Mushroom Duxelles with Dill Cream Sauce

1 to 2 servings

➤ Try this elegant entrée, graciously submitted by Adam Mrozowski of Baur's Restaurant.

6 mushrooms finely chopped	*1 tablespoon butter*
1 shallot, finely chopped	*2 sheets phyllo pastry*
2 tablespoons finely chopped onion	*6-ounces Alaskan King Salmon*
1 garlic clove, crushed	*Melted butter*

Sauté mushrooms, shallot, onion, and garlic in butter for 3 minutes until all liquid is absorbed. Stack phyllo sheets; place 1 tablespoon mushroom filling on center and put salmon on top; place remainder of mushroom filling on top of salmon. Brush phyllo with melted butter. Encase salmon in phyllo by making a box fold. Brush salmon-phyllo packet with melted butter. Place on waxed paper-lined baking sheet and bake at 375 to 400 degrees for 20 minutes. Serve with Dill Cream Sauce.

Dill Cream Sauce

3 ounces whipping cream	*Salt*
1 ounce fish stock	*Dash white pepper*
3 tablespoons white wine	*¼ teaspoon fresh dill*

Combine cream, stock, wine, salt to taste, and pepper in saucepan. Cook over medium heat for 10 to 12 minutes to reduce sauce. Stir often to avoid scorching. Add dill. Spoon sauce on plate and place salmon in center.

Fruited Snapper

2 to 4 servings

➤ A colorful dish that will bring raves.

2 fresh red snapper fillets	*½ cup sliced strawberries*
¼ cup lime juice	*½ sliced banana*
¼ cup butter	*½ sliced kiwi*
½ cup blueberries	

In a large oven-proof skillet, sauté fillets in lime juice and butter until done, approximately 8 minutes. Arrange fruit over fish and place under broiler for 1 to 2 minutes to heat fruit. Serve at once.

May use other fruits in season - oranges, grapes, etc. Orange roughy may be substituted for snapper.

Grilled Tuna with Pineapple-Avocado Salsa

2 servings

4 8-ounces tuna steaks	*2 jalapeño peppers, seeded and finely chopped*
Juice of 1 lemon	*Salt*
Juice of 2 limes	*Freshly ground black pepper*
¼ cup olive oil	

➤ Nancy Howard Higgins of Maldaner's Restaurant kindly submitted this spicy entrée.

Marinate tuna steaks in juices and olive oil. Add jalapeño peppers and salt and pepper to taste for 1 hour before cooking.

Salsa

2 jalapeño peppers	*1 avocado, peeled and seeded*
2 sprigs fresh cilantro	*Salt*
½ pineapple, peeled and cored	*Freshly ground black pepper*

Garnish

Mixed greens or fresh spinach	*Finely chopped tomatoes*
Sliced peppers	

For salsa, chop peppers and cilantro in a food processor until fine. Add pineapple and avocado; process until chunky. Salt and pepper to taste.

Grill tuna over hot fire about 1 ½ minutes on each side making sure not to overcook. Serve tuna on a bed of mixed greens or spinach; spoon salsa over bottom ⅓ of tuna. Garnish with sliced peppers and finely chopped tomatoes.

Horseradish Dilled Trout

3 to 6 servings

¼ cup whipping cream
2 tablespoons mayonnaise
2 ¼ teaspoons dried dill (divided use)
1 ½ teaspoons prepared horseradish (divided use)
2 tablespoons margarine, melted
¼ teaspoon seasoned salt

3 12- to 14-ounce fresh rainbow trout

For sauce, beat cream till soft peaks form. Fold in mayonnaise, 1 ½ teaspoons dill, and ½ teaspoon horseradish. Cover and chill up to 1 hour. Lightly spread remaining horseradish on insides of the fish. Sprinkle remaining dill into each cavity. In a small mixing bowl, combine margarine and salt. Brush the fish with some of the margarine mixture.

Grill fish on an uncovered grill, directly over medium-hot coals for 8 minutes. Brush with remaining margarine mixture; turn and brush other side. Grill 5 to 8 minutes more or until fish flakes easily with a fork. Serve with sauce.

Crustless Crab Quiche

6 to 7 servings

½ pound fresh mushrooms, sliced
2 tablespoons butter or margarine
4 eggs
1 cup sour cream
1 cup small curd cottage cheese
1 cup freshly grated Parmesan cheese
¼ cup flour
1 teaspoon onion powder
¼ teaspoon salt
4 drops hot pepper sauce
2 cups shredded Monterey Jack cheese
6 ounces frozen crabmeat, thawed and drained

Garnish

Tomato roses

Sauté mushrooms in butter until tender; drain. With mixer on slow or in blender, mix eggs, sour cream, cottage cheese, Parmesan cheese, flour, onion powder, salt, and hot pepper sauce. Pour into large bowl and stir in mushrooms, Monterey Jack cheese, and crabmeat. Pour into 10-inch quiche dish. Bake at 350 degrees for 45 minutes. Inserted knife should come out clean. Let stand for 5 minutes before serving. Garnish with tomato roses.

Linguine with Smoked Oysters

4 servings

1 pound linguine, cooked al dente
4 ounces dry or semi-dry white wine
2 ounces extra virgin olive oil
2 tablespoons garlic powder
4 ounces Fontina cheese, finely diced
2 3.7ounce tins smoked oysters
Freshly ground black pepper
½ to 1 tablespoon fresh, chopped parsley or ½ teaspoon dried

Rinse the pasta pot, and use to heat the wine, olive oil, and garlic powder until gently boiling (1 to 2 minutes). Reduce heat to low and stir in the cooked pasta. Immediately fold in the oysters and cheese. Cover and return to medium heat for 30 seconds. Turn off heat and leave covered 3 to 5 minutes to allow the cheese to melt. Serve hot, sprinkled with pepper and parsley.

May substitute any sharp dry white cheese - Havarti, Parmesan, or Jarlsberg - for Fontina.

Scallops in White Wine

4 servings

½ large red pepper, julienned
3 to 4 large mushrooms, thinly sliced
1 medium onion, chopped
1 tablespoon butter
1 pound bay or sea scallops
½ cup dry white wine
Salt
Freshly ground black pepper

Garnish

Snipped chives

Sauté onions, peppers, and mushrooms in butter until tender in a non-stick skillet. Add scallops with their liquid to vegetable mixture. Cook scallops until they begin to turn white, taking care not to overcook.

Remove vegetables and scallops from pan; drain in colander. Return juices to pan. Add white wine; boil until liquids are reduced by one half. Add vegetable and scallop mixture to thickened liquids. Toss together; season to taste with salt and pepper and sprinkle with chives. Serve immediately.

Bacon-Wrapped Scallops with Lemon-Chive Sauce

4 servings

2 pounds fresh or defrosted frozen sea scallops	*1 pound sliced bacon*

Lemon Chive Sauce

2 tablespoons chopped chives	*1 tablespoon olive oil*
1 garlic clove, minced	*¼ teaspoon salt*
2 tablespoons fresh lemon juice	*⅛ teaspoon freshly ground black pepper*

Drain and dry scallops. Cut bacon slices in half and wrap around scallops. Secure with a toothpick or small bamboo skewer.

Whisk remaining ingredients together in a small bowl. Grill scallops over medium-hot coals for 4 to 5 minutes. Brush scallops frequently with sauce; turn midway through cooking time. Scallops may be broiled for 10 to 15 minutes rather than grilled. Serve immediately.

Scallops Gruyère

6 servings

➤ This rich dish could serve 12 to 16 people as an appetizer.

½ cup fresh bread crumbs	*1 tablespoon chopped fresh parsley*
5 tablespoons margarine (divided use)	*1 pound sea scallops, quartered*
6 ounces shredded Gruyère cheese	*½ pound fresh mushrooms, sliced*
1 cup mayonnaise	*½ cup chopped onion*
½ cup dry white wine	

Toss bread crumbs with 1 tablespoon melted margarine; set aside. Stir together cheese, mayonnaise, wine, and parsley; set aside. In medium skillet over medium-high heat, cook scallops in 2 tablespoons margarine until opaque. Remove and drain well.

Cook mushrooms and onion in 2 tablespoons margarine for 3 minutes. Remove from heat; stir in cheese mixture and scallops. Spoon into 6 individual baking dishes or shells and sprinkle with bread crumbs. Broil 6 inches from heat source about 2 to 4 minutes or until browned. Serve immediately.

Shrimp Island Bay

2 servings

½ cup butter (divided use)
12 medium raw shrimp, peeled and deveined
6 ounces sliced fresh mushrooms
½ green pepper, julienned
1 large garlic clove, finely chopped
¼ cup dry vermouth
1 cup White Sauce
Salt
Freshly ground black pepper

➤ This delightful entrée was graciously submitted to us by Robert Snow, chef at the Island Bay Yacht Club.

Garnish

Lemon peel

Put approximately ¼ cup butter into a 12-inch heavy skillet. Allow it to melt and get hot. Add shrimp to skillet; a light sizzle sound should be heard. Sauté until the outer surface of the shrimp turns white. Remove shrimp and set aside.

Add remaining butter; allow to melt and get hot. Add mushrooms and green pepper; sauté until semi-soft. Return shrimp to skillet. Allow all ingredients to heat thoroughly, approximately 2 minutes. Do not overcook. Add garlic to taste. Add dry vermouth and allow alcohol to boil off for about 20 to 30 seconds. Add white sauce. Salt and pepper to taste. Allow mixture to thicken slightly. Serve in small individual casserole dishes, garnished with lemon peel.

White Sauce

2 tablespoons butter
2 tablespoons flour
½ teaspoon salt
½ teaspoon freshly ground black pepper
1 cup half and half

Heat butter in a saucepan. Blend in flour, salt, and pepper, stirring over heat until flour bubbles. Gradually add half and half stirring until sauce begins to thicken, approximately 2 to 5 minutes.

Make sure all ingredients are ready before beginning recipe.

Shrimp Creole

6 servings

1 cup chopped onion
1 cup chopped celery
2 garlic cloves, minced
6 tablespoons butter
2 16-ounce cans tomatoes, chopped into bite-sized pieces
2 8-ounce cans tomato sauce
1 tablespoon salt
2 teaspoons sugar
1 to 2 teaspoons chili powder
2 tablespoons Worcestershire sauce
Dash hot pepper sauce
4 teaspoons cornstarch
1 tablespoon cold water
1 ½ pounds shrimp, peeled and deveined
1 cup chopped green pepper
Cooked rice

In skillet, cook onion, celery, and garlic in butter until tender but not brown. Add tomatoes, tomato sauce and seasonings. Simmer 45 minutes. Mix cornstarch with water; stir into sauce. Cook and stir until mixture thickens and bubbles. Add shrimp and green pepper. Cover and simmer 5 minutes. Serve over rice.

Cheddar Shrimp Bake

12 to 15 servings

1 tablespoon butter or margarine
1 large onion, finely chopped
1 large green pepper, chopped
12 ounces sliced fresh mushrooms
8 ounces tomato sauce
7 ounces thin spaghetti, cooked
1 15 ½ - ounce can tomatoes, finely chopped
2 ½ cups shredded Cheddar cheese
1 cup sour cream
2 pounds cooked shrimp

In a skillet, sauté onion and green pepper in butter or margarine until slightly translucent. Add mushrooms and cook for 2 more minutes. Combine all remaining ingredients except shrimp. Add shrimp. Place in a large casserole dish. Bake at 375 degrees for 30 minutes.

Shrimp With Garlic Butter

2 servings

10 large butterflied shrimp with tails
1 cup flour
1 egg
2 tablespoons milk
½ cup fine bread crumbs
½ cup freshly grated Parmesan cheese
6 tablespoons Garlic Butter
¾ cup Hollandaise sauce

➤ This rich and elegant Shrimp de Jonghe recipe was kindly submitted to us by Chef Jim Hampton.

Flatten and pat down the butterflied shrimp. Dredge in flour. Combine egg and milk; set aside. Mix together bread crumbs and Parmesan cheese; set aside. Dip shrimp in egg wash and then into bread crumbs and cheese.

Sauté shrimp in 6 tablespoons melted Garlic Butter. Do not allow butter to brown. Cook 5 shrimp at a time and do not allow them to touch. Place in pan with tail up and press down. Sauté shrimp about 2 minutes; turn over and press down other side. Remove to plate, lined with paper towel. Add Hollandaise sauce to butter in saucepan; heat thoroughly over medium-high heat. Blend thoroughly. Arrange shrimp in a circle on plate with tails together and pour sauce around.

Garlic Butter

2 cups butter
8 to 12 garlic cloves, finely chopped
4 tablespoons fresh parsley, finely chopped
2 tablespoons green onion, finely chopped
1 teaspoon seasoned salt
½ cup Worcestershire sauce
1 tablespoon steak sauce

Allow butter to soften at room temperature for 1 hour. Beat butter, ½ cup at a time, with mixer on low speed. Add chopped garlic, parsley, onion, and seasoned salt; mix 2 minutes. Slowly add Worcestershire and steak sauces; mix 4 minutes. Store in freezer until needed.

Succulent Skewered Shrimp

6 servings

4 garlic cloves, crushed
1 cup olive oil
½ cup finely chopped fresh basil
2 tablespoons white wine vinegar
2 tablespoons Worcestershire sauce
½ teaspoon hot pepper sauce
2 pounds large fresh shrimp, peeled and deveined

➤ A flavorful dish - serve it hot or cold. Leftover shrimp can be added to a salad or pasta.

Combine all ingredients except shrimp in a shallow dish; mix well. Add shrimp, tossing gently to coat. Cover and marinate shrimp 2 to 3 hours in the refrigerator, stirring occasionally.

Remove shrimp from marinade, reserving marinade. Place shrimp on 6 14-inch skewers. Grill over medium-hot coals 3 to 4 minutes on each side, basting frequently with marinade.

The perfect still life — farm-fresh eggs and cheese, nestled among an old wooden bowl, long-handled iron spoon, firkin and "courting candle." The spiral candle holder is a reproduction, designed to establish the courting time. When the candle burned down to the metal, courting time was over. The three beautiful quilt squares were submitted in a New Salem Quilt Contest, held each June during the New Salem Quilt Show.

Poultry, Eggs, and Cheese

Once, young Lincoln was in the crowd watching a juggler and magician at Sangamontown, along the Sangamon River. When the magician asked for a hat in which to "cook" eggs, Lincoln volunteered his — after a long pause. As friend and Lincoln biographer William H. Herndon told it later, Lincoln explained why he delayed a minute: *"It was out of respect for the eggs,"* he said, *"not care for my hat."*

Champagne Chicken in Puff Pastry Shells

6 servings

➤ Excellent luncheon recipe.

6 puff pastry shells, baked	*1 ½ cups chicken broth*
2 pounds chicken breasts, split, boned, skinned, and cut into 1 inch cubes	*½ cup champagne*
1 cup sliced fresh mushrooms	*2 carrots, julienned*
2 tablespoons minced shallots	*½ teaspoon thyme*
1 garlic clove, minced	*½ cup whipping cream*
¼ cup butter	*2 tablespoons brandy*
6 tablespoons flour	*1 teaspoon salt*
	¼ teaspoon white pepper

Sauté chicken, mushrooms, shallots, and garlic in butter in large skillet until outside of chicken is no longer pink, about 4 minutes. Stir in flour. Cook, stirring constantly for 2 minutes. Stir in broth, champagne, carrots, and thyme. Heat to boiling; reduce heat. Simmer uncovered for 30 minutes, stirring occasionally.

Stir cream, brandy, salt, and pepper into chicken mixture. Place warm shell on serving plate; spoon in chicken mixture. Serve immediately.

Chicken with Orange Sauce

4 servings

➤ A colorful company dish! Easy and tastes gourmet.

2 whole chicken breasts, split, skinned, and boned (about 1 ½ pounds)	*1 cup canned condensed chicken broth*
¼ cup cornstarch	*½ orange, thinly sliced*
1 teaspoon salt	*½ green pepper, chopped*
Generous dash freshly ground black pepper	*¼ cup diced pimento*
2 tablespoons oil	*¼ pound fresh mushrooms, quartered*
½ cup orange juice	*¼ teaspoon ground ginger*

Fold chicken pieces, tucking in ends, to make 4 patty-like servings. Mix cornstarch, salt, and pepper to taste and coat chicken. Brown chicken in oil until golden in large skillet with tight-fitting lid. Drain off any excess oil. Add orange juice, chicken broth, orange slices, green pepper, pimento, mushrooms, and ginger. Cover and simmer, stirring occasionally, for 30 minutes, or until chicken is tender. Remove chicken to platter. Season sauce with salt and pepper to taste. Add a little cold water to remaining cornstarch mixture and stir until smooth. Add cornstarch mixture to skillet to thicken sauce. Pour sauce over chicken or serve on the side.

Baked Chicken and Pasta Primavera

6 servings

2 whole chicken breasts, split, boned and skinned

1 ½ garlic cloves (divided use)

1 cup flour

Salt

Freshly ground black pepper

1 tablespoon butter or margarine

2 tablespoons olive oil

1 bunch broccoli, cut into florets

1 cup whipping cream

½ cup half and half

1 cup freshly grated Parmesan cheese

½ pound fettuccine or linguine

2 to 3 tablespoons chopped fresh basil

➤ A wonderful dish for entertaining!

Pound chicken until about ¼ inch thick; cut into pieces. Season flour by combining with salt and pepper to taste. Mince ½ garlic clove and add to flour. Dip chicken into seasoned flour. Sauté chicken, a few pieces at a time, in butter and olive oil until done, approximately 5 minutes. Set aside.

Blanch broccoli for 4 minutes in boiling, salted water. Drain and rinse with cold water to refresh. Set aside. Mince remaining garlic and add to cream and half and half. Cook until creams are slightly thickened and reduced by ¼. Stir in Parmesan cheese; continue heating until cheese melts. Season to taste with salt and pepper.

Cook pasta al dente. Drain and rinse in warm water. Place pasta in baking dish. Arrange chicken and broccoli on top. Pour sauce over and sprinkle with basil. Bake at 250 degrees for 20 minutes.

Chicken and Asparagus in Wine Sauce

4 servings

1 pound fresh asparagus

2 chicken breasts, split, skinned, boned, cooked and cut into pieces

2 tablespoons butter

3 tablespoons flour

½ cup white wine

½ to 1 cup chicken broth

4 tablespoons freshly grated Parmesan cheese (divided use)

1 cup fresh sliced mushrooms

½ cup Cheddar or Swiss cheese (optional)

Cooked brown rice or fettuccine

Parboil asparagus. Drain and place in shallow baking dish. Arrange chicken pieces over asparagus. Melt butter in skillet and slowly stir in flour, wine, and chicken broth. Add 2 tablespoons Parmesan cheese, mushrooms, and Cheddar or Swiss cheese if desired. Cook, stirring constantly, until sauce thickens. Pour over chicken and asparagus. Sprinkle with remaining 2 tablespoons Parmesan cheese. Bake at 350 degrees for 20 to 30 minutes or until heated through. Serve over brown rice or fettuccine.

Apple Brandy Chicken

4 servings

- *1 3 to 3 ½ pound broiler or fryer cut up or 2 whole chicken breasts, split*
- *¼ teaspoon salt*
- *¼ teaspoon freshly ground black pepper*
- *¼ teaspoon thyme*
- *1 tablespoon oil*
- *1 large apple, cored and sliced*
- *⅔ cup apple juice*
- *½ cup chopped shallots*
- *½ cup whipping cream*
- *2 tablespoons apple brandy*

Garnish

- *Paprika*
- *Fresh parsley*

Season chicken with salt, pepper, and thyme. In large skillet, brown chicken in oil. Cover and simmer for 20 minutes. Place apple slices on top. Cover and cook 10 minutes longer or until chicken is done and apples have softened, but are not falling apart. With slotted spoon, remove chicken and apples to serving platter and keep warm.

Pour drippings into glass measure; let stand for a few minutes for the fat to rise to the top, then remove fat. Return drippings to pan. Add apple juice and shallots. Bring quickly to a boil and cook until sauce is reduced by almost half and begins to look like syrup. Stir in cream and brandy and heat until sauce starts to thicken. Spoon over chicken and apples and serve immediately. Garnish with paprika and parsley.

Chunky Pineapple Chicken

4 servings

➤ Excellent flavor!

- *1 20-ounce can pineapple chunks*
- *2 whole chicken breasts, split*
- *Salt*
- *Freshly ground black pepper*
- *1 tablespoon oil*
- *2 large garlic cloves, pressed*
- *1 teaspoon ground thyme*
- *¼ teaspoon rosemary*
- *1 tablespoon cornstarch*
- *¼ cup honey*
- *¼ cup Dijon mustard*

Drain pineapple and reserve juice. Sprinkle chicken with salt and pepper. Heat oil in frying pan. Brown one side of chicken. Add garlic, thyme, and rosemary. Brown other side. Mix 2 tablespoons pineapple juice with cornstarch; set aside. Combine honey and mustard in small bowl and mix in remaining pineapple juice. Add to skillet and spoon sauce over chicken. Cover and simmer 25 minutes. Stir cornstarch mixture into pan mixture. Add pineapple and cook, stirring until sauce boils and thickens.

Crispy Oven-Fried Chicken

6 to 8 servings

8 to 12 pieces of chicken, skinned (2 ½ to 3 pounds)
2 cups milk
1 cup crushed seasoned croutons
⅔ cup freshly grated Parmesan cheese
2 tablespoons parsley flakes, crumbled
Freshly ground black pepper

➤ The taste of fried chicken without the mess.

Place chicken pieces in shallow bowl or pan and cover with milk. Let soak 15 minutes or longer, refrigerating if necessary, to keep ingredients cold. Combine croutons, cheese, parsley flakes, and pepper in shallow bowl. Dip chicken pieces in breading mixture, coating on all sides. Place chicken on greased baking sheet. Bake at 375 degrees for 45 minutes to 1 hour. Enjoy hot or cold.

To microwave, place coated chicken pieces in glass baking dish. Microwave 20 to 25 minutes on high or until meat near bone is cooked through. Let stand 5 minutes before serving.

Homestyle Chicken and Noodles

10 servings

➤ Delicious broth!

Noodles

2 cups flour
2 teaspoons salt
3 egg yolks
1 egg
5 tablespoons water

Combine flour and salt in glass bowl. Make a well in flour and add egg. Add water, 1 tablespoon at a time. Mix with hands. Knead 10 to 12 minutes, until dough is elastic. Cover with towel for 15 minutes. Divide into 4 balls. Roll out dough ⅛ to ¼ inch thick. Cut into ½-inch strips. Dry noodles on waxed paper for 24 to 36 hours.

Broth

10 cups water
1 tablespoon garlic powder
1 teaspoon onion salt
1 teaspoon parsley flakes
1 teaspoon oregano
1 teaspoon tarragon
1 teaspoon rosemary
4 teaspoons chicken bouillon granules
1 3-pound chicken

In Dutch oven, combine water with all spices and bouillon granules. Bring to a boil. Add chicken and simmer for 3 hours. Remove from heat; skin, bone, and shred chicken. Return chicken to broth. Bring chicken and broth to boil. Slowly add noodles. Cook on low heat for an additional hour.

Swiss Chicken

8 servings

➤ Quick and easy. Make ahead, refrigerate, and bake later.

4 whole chicken breasts, split, boned, and skinned
8 sandwich slices Swiss cheese
5 tablespoons butter (divided use)
2 tablespoons flour
½ cup milk
½ cup chicken broth
Salt
Freshly ground black pepper
¼ cup white wine
1 cup dry stuffing mix

Place chicken breasts in buttered baking dish. Cover each breast with one slice of cheese. Melt 2 tablespoons butter over low heat. Add flour and blend over heat until smooth and bubbling. Slowly stir in milk and chicken broth. Season with salt and pepper to taste. Add white wine. Pour over chicken. Mix stuffing mix with 3 tablespoons melted butter. Spread over top of chicken. Bake at 350 degrees for 45 to 60 minutes.

Great Grilled Chicken

8 servings

➤ Wonderful summertime recipe. This is especially juicy and worth the long marinating time.

1 cup plain yogurt
¼ cup dark brown sugar
4 large garlic cloves
3 tablespoons cider vinegar
2 teaspoons Worcestershire sauce
2 dashes hot pepper sauce
3 pounds chicken parts

Blend all ingredients except chicken in food processor or blender. Arrange chicken in single layer in shallow dish and pour marinade evenly over top. Cover and refrigerate up to 48 hours, turning occasionally.

Remove chicken from marinade. Grill over slow fire for about 1 hour or until done, turning often and basting frequently with marinade.

Barbecued Teriyaki Chicken

6 servings

1 ¼ cups brown sugar
1 cup soy sauce
½ teaspoon minced fresh ginger root
3 garlic cloves, crushed
1 ½ to 2 cups crushed pineapple, undrained
2 ½ to 3 pounds chicken, cut up

➤ Easy, do-ahead barbecued chicken.

Combine all ingredients except chicken in 9x13 inch baking dish. Add chicken and bake at 400 degrees for 40 minutes. Remove chicken from oven; turn over to coat with marinade. Cover and refrigerate for 4 to 12 hours.

Over medium to hot coals, barbecue chicken 3 to 5 minutes per side or until heated through. Brush with marinade frequently.

Use chicken breasts cut into small pieces for a tasty appetizer.

Chicken with Horseradish Cream

8 servings

4 tablespoons flour
1 teaspoon salt
½ teaspoon freshly ground black pepper
4 whole chicken breasts, split, boned, and skinned
3 tablespoons butter
1 garlic clove, crushed
1 cup sliced fresh mushrooms
½ cup Horseradish Cream
1 cup whipping cream
2 tablespoons chopped parsley
Cooked wild rice

Combine flour, salt, and pepper in a plastic bag. Add pieces of chicken and coat well. Melt butter in large skillet. Sauté chicken pieces in butter on low heat, turning to brown on both sides. Cook 20 to 30 minutes, or until tender. Remove to heated platter or warming oven. Add garlic and mushrooms to drippings in pan. Cook for 2 minutes. Stir in Horseradish Cream and whipping cream. Bring to a boil, stirring constantly until sauce slightly thickens. Return chicken to sauce, turning to coat. Heat through; stir in parsley. Serve over wild rice.

Horseradish Cream

½ cup whipping cream
¼ cup mayonnaise
1 to 2 tablespoons prepared mustard
1 heaping tablespoon prepared horseradish
½ teaspoon lemon juice
½ teaspoon Worcestershire sauce
¼ teaspoon seasoned salt
⅛ teaspoon white pepper

Whip cream until stiff. Fold in remaining ingredients. Chill 8 hours or before serving.

Cashew Chicken

4 servings

➤ Wonderful flavor, mildly sweet.

3 tablespoons soy sauce (divided use)
2 tablespoons sherry wine (divided use)
2 tablespoons water
1 tablespoon cornstarch
2 whole chicken breasts, split, skinned, boned, and cut in strips
2 to 3 tablespoons peanut oil (divided use)
2 dried whole hot red peppers
2 to 3 teaspoons finely chopped fresh ginger root
1 cup coarsely chopped fresh mushrooms
1 green pepper, cut in strips
4 green onions, cut in ½-inch pieces, tops included
2 stalks celery, cut diagonally in ½-inch pieces
¼ cup sugar
¼ teaspoon freshly ground black pepper
2 teaspoons vinegar
1 cup unsalted cashews
Cooked rice

Mix marinade of 1 tablespoon soy sauce, 1 tablespoon sherry, water, and cornstarch. Add chicken strips to marinade. Let set for 20 minutes or more.

Heat 1 to 2 tablespoons peanut oil in skillet or wok. Add whole red hot peppers and fry 1 minute. Discard peppers. Add chicken, ginger root, mushrooms, green pepper, onion, and celery. Stir fry approximately 5 minutes.

Combine 1 tablespoon sherry, 2 tablespoons soy sauce, sugar, pepper, vinegar, and 1 teaspoon peanut oil. Pour over chicken mixture. Add cashews and cook an additional 2 to 3 minutes. Serve over hot rice.

Add red pepper strips for more color.

Bates Avenue Chicken

8 servings

➤ Quick and easy!

1 16-ounce can whole berry cranberry sauce
1 8-ounce bottle Russian salad dressing
1 package dry onion soup mix
¼ teaspoon salt
Freshly ground black pepper
4 whole chicken breasts, split, skinned and boned
Cooked rice or noodles

Combine cranberry sauce, salad dressing, soup mix, salt, and pepper to taste. Arrange chicken in 3-quart baking dish; pour sauce over top. Cover and bake at 325 degrees for 1 hour. Remove cover; bake 15 minutes more or until brown. Serve over rice or noodles.

Chicken Enchiladas

8 servings

1 ¾ cups shredded Monterey Jack or mozzarella cheese
1 ¾ cups shredded Cheddar cheese
3 ounces cream cheese
1 ½ cups mild picante sauce
2 cups chopped or shredded cooked chicken
½ cup diced red pepper
¼ cup diced green onion
1 teaspoon cumin
8 flour tortillas
Shredded lettuce
Chopped tomatoes
Sour cream (optional)

➤ Spice up this tasty Mexican dish even more with medium or hot picante sauce. Easy and delicious!

Combine 1 cup Monterey Jack, 1 cup Cheddar, cream cheese, ¼ cup picante sauce, chicken, red pepper, green onions, and cumin. Spoon equally in center of each tortilla — roll and place seam side down in greased 9x13 inch pan. Spoon remaining picante sauce over tortillas. Cover with remaining cheese.

Bake at 350 degrees for 20 to 30 minutes or until hot. Top with lettuce and tomatoes. May serve with sour cream.

Nutty Chicken

6 servings

3 whole chicken breasts, split, boned, and skinned
4 teaspoons ginger
1 teaspoon salt
2 tablespoons oil
½ cup chopped onion
2 medium tomatoes, peeled and chopped
1 small garlic clove, minced
1 to 2 small hot chili peppers, seeded and chopped
½ cup crunchy peanut butter
½ cup water
6 fresh or frozen okra pods, cut into ½-inch pieces
Cooked brown rice

➤ Children love the milder version of this, made with only one pepper.

Garnish

Cocktail peanuts
Pineapple chunks
Avocado slices
Sliced green onions

Dredge chicken breasts in mixture of ginger and salt. In a skillet, brown chicken in oil. Remove chicken and drain off oil.

Add remaining ingredients except rice to skillet and stir until peanut butter is smooth. Return chicken to skillet. Cover and cook until chicken is tender, about 20 minutes. Serve with brown rice and garnish with peanuts, pineapple chunks, avocado slices, or sliced green onions.

CHICKEN CACCIATORE

6 to 8 servings

➤ A nice buffet dish. Serve with rotini, cavatelli, or bow-tie pasta.

1 tablespoon olive oil	*½ cup dry red or white wine*
2 whole chicken breasts, split, boned, and skinned	*½ cup chicken broth*
6 mild Italian sausages, cut into 1-inch pieces	*2 16-ounce cans tomatoes*
1 to 2 carrots, julienned	*1 teaspoon oregano*
1 cup chopped onion	*1 tablespoon basil*
1 green pepper, cut into ½-inch strips	*1 tablespoon fresh chopped parsley*
1 garlic clove, minced	*Freshly ground black pepper*
	¼ to ½ teaspoon red pepper (optional)

In large skillet, heat oil and brown chicken on both sides until golden. Remove chicken. Brown sausage in skillet; remove. Add carrots, onions, peppers, and garlic. Sauté until onions are translucent; pour off fat. Move vegetables to one side, add wine, and deglaze the skillet. Add rest of ingredients; return meats to pan; stir to blend. Cook over high heat for 5 minutes, stirring occasionally. Cover and reduce heat to medium-low and cook for 15 minutes. Remove cover. If sauce is too thin, increase hat and continue cooking, stirring often, until sauce is thickened.

CHICKEN CORDON BLEU

2 servings

2 whole chicken breasts, split, boned, and skinned	*½ cup flour*
1 2-ounce slice Swiss cheese	*¼ cup butter*
2 1-ounce slices thinly sliced ham	*½ cup dry white wine*
Salt	*Pinch of sage*
Freshly ground black pepper	*Pinch of basil*
	¼ cup whipping cream

Put each piece of chicken between 2 sheets of waxed paper. Pound with meat mallet until chicken is doubled in length and width and is very thin. Cut cheese slice in half. Lay each half on one slice of chicken. Cover each slice of cheese with a slice of ham. Top each with remaining pieces of chicken and press together firmly; pound lightly so they stay together.

Sprinkle lightly with salt and pepper and roll in flour. Heat butter in skillet. Brown meat on both sides over high heat until golden. Cook 3 to 4 minutes more on each side. Remove to warm serving plates and keep warm. Add wine to skillet and reduce to one half. Add sage, basil, and cream. Stir until smooth and brownings from skillet are dissolved in sauce. Pour over chicken and serve.

Chicken Florentine

6 servings

- *1 10-ounce package frozen chopped spinach, cooked and drained*
- *3 ounces cream cheese, room temperature*
- *3 whole chicken breasts, split*
- *2 tablespoons butter*
- *2 tablespoons Madeira wine*
- *¾ cup plus 2 tablespoons water (divided use)*
- *1 teaspoon salt (divided use)*
- *Freshly ground black pepper*
- *1 tablespoon cornstarch*

In medium bowl, mix cooked spinach, cream cheese, and ½ teaspoon salt. Push fingers between skin and meat on chicken to form pocket. Spoon of spinach mixture ⅙ into each pocket. Melt butter in 12-inch skillet over medium-high heat. Add chicken and cook, skin side down, 5 minutes or until well browned. Turn once. Add wine, ¾ cup water, ½ teaspoon salt and pepper to taste. Heat to boiling; reduce heat to low. Cover and simmer for 20 to 25 minutes, or until chicken is tender.

Remove chicken to platter or individual plates. Mix cornstarch and 2 tablespoons water together. Stir into pan drippings and cook 1 to 2 minutes on medium-high heat until thick. Pour glaze over chicken. Serve immediately.

Oven Chicken Kiev with Sauce

8 servings

- *4 whole chicken breasts, split, boned, and skinned*
- *4 tablespoons chopped fresh chives or 4 teaspoons dried*
- *6 ounces Monterey Jack cheese, cut into 8 strips*
- *¾ cup fine dry bread crumbs*
- *⅓ cup freshly grated Parmesan cheese*
- *1 teaspoon seasoned salt*
- *¼ teaspoon freshly ground black pepper*
- *10 tablespoons butter (divided use)*
- *2 tablespoons flour*
- *½ cup milk*
- *½ cup chicken broth*
- *Salt*
- *Freshly ground black pepper*
- *Cooked rice*

Pound breasts to ¼-inch thickness. Place ½ tablespoon fresh chives or ½ teaspoon dried chives and 1 strip of cheese in the center of each breast. Roll breasts from split end to pointed end and secure with toothpicks.

Combine bread crumbs, Parmesan cheese, salt, and pepper. Melt 8 tablespoons butter. Dip each breast into melted butter and then roll in crumb mixture. Place chicken rolls seam down in 9x13 inch baking dish. Drizzle with remaining melted butter. Cover and chill 4 hours or overnight.

Bake uncovered at 400 degrees for 20 minutes. Melt 2 tablespoons butter over low heat; add flour and blend until smooth and bubbling. Slowly stir in milk and chicken broth. Season with salt and pepper to taste. Spoon sauce over chicken and bake 15 minutes more. Serve with rice.

Fancy Prairie Turkey

8 to 10 servings

➤ Too elegant to be considered leftovers. Great for brunch, luncheon, or a buffet.

2 to 3 pounds turkey breast, cooked and cut into large pieces
½ cup margarine
⅓ cup flour
2 ⅓ cups milk
1 ⅓ cups shredded Cheddar cheese
2 ounces Gruyere cheese, grated
4 ounces tomato sauce
1 garlic clove, crushed
¾ teaspoon monosodium glutamate (optional)
1 teaspoon salt
½ teaspoon cayenne pepper
10 ounces fresh mushrooms, halved
2 14-ounce cans artichoke hearts, drained

Make cream sauce by melting margarine in saucepan, adding flour and cooking until well blended. Stir constantly. Add milk, stirring until sauce thickens. Melt cheeses with tomato sauce in a small pan. Add garlic, monosodium glutamate, salt, and cayenne. Combine cheese sauce with cream sauce. Arrange artichoke hearts, turkey, and mushrooms in shallow, buttered 3-quart baking dish. Pour sauce over and bake at 350 degrees for 40 minutes.

Stuffed Cornish Hens with Cherry Sauce

4 servings

➤ This stuffing is a wonderful accompaniment for beef, pork or other poultry dishes.

1 6-ounce box wild rice with seasonings
¼ cup butter
1 medium onion, chopped
½ pound fresh mushrooms, sliced, or 1 4-ounce can sliced mushrooms, drained
1 8-ounce can sliced water chestnuts
⅓ cup sliced almonds
4 Cornish hens
1 ½ tablespoons cornstarch
4 tablespoons sugar
¼ tablespoon salt
¼ teaspoon dry mustard
½ tablespoon ginger
1 16-ounce can water-packed, pitted, sour red cherries
½ cup orange juice
¼ cup currant jelly
2 tablespoons dry sherry

Cook rice according to package directions. Sauté onion, mushrooms, and water chestnuts in butter for 5 minutes, or until onions are translucent. Stir in sliced almonds; drain. Add rice. Stuff cavities of hens with rice mixture and lace with string and skewers. Roast hens at 350 degrees for 1 ¼ hours, or until brown and tender.

In saucepan, combine cornstarch, sugar, salt, mustard, and ginger. Drain cherries, reserving liquid. Add cherry liquid to cornstarch mixture; add orange juice and currant jelly. Cook, stirring constantly, until mixture thickens. Add drained cherries and sherry. Spoon over Cornish hens and serve with extra stuffing.

These Cornish hens are also excellent with Sour Cherry Chutney.

Pheasant with Sauerkraut and White Wine

8 servings

2 cups white stock or chicken consommé
1 cup dry white wine
4 pheasants
Salt
Freshly ground black pepper
4 tablespoons unsalted butter, melted
Braised Sauerkraut

Simmer white stock or consommé and white wine together until reduced to 1 ½ cups. Split pheasants along the back. Open and flatten them gently. Sprinkle lightly with salt and pepper. Brush birds with butter and place in a roasting pan. Baste with wine sauce. Broil for 5 minutes on each side or until birds are nearly browned.

Layer Braised Sauerkraut in a large casserole. Place pheasants on top. Cover and bake at 325 degrees for about 30 minutes. Pheasants are ready when flesh has lost its pink color. Do not overcook.

Place pheasant halves on large platter and surround with Braised Sauerkraut. Pour remaining wine sauce over birds and serve.

Braised Sauerkraut

2 quarts sauerkraut
6 small white onions, sliced
3 carrots, finely sliced
¾ pound thick-sliced bacon, blanched and cut into ½-inch pieces
6 tablespoons unsalted butter
6 fresh parsley sprigs
2 bay leaves
12 peppercorns
1 ½ cups dry white wine
⅓ cup gin
3 cups chicken consommé
Salt
Freshly ground black pepper

Wash sauerkraut in cold water several times to remove brine. Drain and squeeze out as much water as possible. In a Dutch oven, sauté onions, carrots, and blanched bacon with butter until vegetables are nearly tender, but not browned. Add sauerkraut and stir. Cover and simmer for 15 minutes.

Add parsley, bay leaves, peppercorns, wine, gin, and enough consommé to cover sauerkraut. Cover and bake at 300 degrees for 4 hours or until all liquid has been absorbed. If sauerkraut dries out during baking, add more consommé. Remove bay leaves. Season to taste with salt and pepper; serve with pheasant.

Roast Duck with Liver Stuffing and Black Cherries

4 servings

➤ Peter Duer of the Sangamo Club contributed this unique and excellent recipe.

1 duck liver	*½ cup half and half*
5 to 6 chicken livers	*3 cups French bead cubes*
3 tablespoons butter or margarine	*1 4-5 pound duck*
Salt	*2 tablespoons flour*
Freshly ground black pepper	*1 ½ cups stock, made from neck and gizzard*
Thyme	*½ cup cherry juice*
Pinch of chopped parsley	*1 cup black cherries*
1 egg	
1 ½ cups white wine (divided use)	

Sauté livers lightly in butter; chop coarsely. Add salt, pepper, and thyme to taste. Add parsley, egg, ½ cup wine, and half and half; mix. Add bread cubes and mix. If dressing seems dry, add more wine and half and half.

Stuff duck and close with needle and thread. Salt outside of duck and place breast side up on rack in shallow pan. Roast at 375 degrees for 2 hours, or until meat thermometer reads 170 degrees when inserted in middle of stuffing. Baste frequently with pan drippings.

For crisp skin, place duck under broiler for 10 minutes. Remove to warm platter and cover. Save drippings from pan; remove duck fat.

To the drippings, add flour and stir until smooth. Add stock, cherry juice, and remaining wine. Cook and reduce to a light consistency. Add salt and pepper to taste. Add black cherries and glaze duck lightly with sauce. Serve extra sauce on side.

Wild Duck with Currant Sauce

4 servings

1 large apple, chopped	*Freshly ground black pepper*
1 medium white onion, chopped	*4 to 6 strips bacon*
1 large orange	*Bacon grease or oil*
1 4-ounce can pineapple chunks	*1 10-ounce jar currant jelly*
2 mallard ducks	*1 ounce sherry*

Combine apple and onion in bowl. Cut two thin slices from the middle of the orange and save. Peel the rind from the remaining orange and save for sauce. Chop the remaining orange and add to apples and onion. Add pineapple chunks and reserve juice.

Lightly grease outside and cavity of ducks with bacon grease or oil. Stuff cavity of ducks with chopped apple mixture. (Not all will be used). Place ducks in large baking dish, breast up; sprinkle lightly with pepper. Add 1 inch of water to pan.

Wrap bacon strips over breasts and anchor with toothpicks. Place orange slices on top and anchor. Add remaining chopped apple mixture to dish around duck. Pour pineapple juice over ducks. Cover baking dish and roast in oven at 275 degrees for 1 hour and 30 minutes. Do not overcook. Remove ducks and discard all stuffing ingredients.

Combine currant jelly, sherry, and orange rind in blender. Process until smooth. Serve with duck. This keeps in refrigerator for several months.

If ducks have been frozen, thaw in refrigerator for 24 hours before cooking. Cooking ducks at a low temperature results in a moist and tender dish. No need to baste or turn the ducks during cooking

Quail with Cream Sauce

6 servings

3 tablespoons safflower oil	*½ teaspoon dried rosemary, crumbled*
Flour	*1 cup chicken broth*
9 quail (breasts, legs, and thighs)	*Salt*
½ tablespoon minced onion	*Freshly ground black pepper*
2 tablespoons snipped parsley	*1 cup hot cream or milk*

In skillet, dredge quail in flour and brown in hot oil on both sides. Use paper towels to absorb excess grease. Place in large casserole. Add onion, parsley, rosemary, and chicken broth. Cover. Cook at 300 degrees for 2 hours, or until tender. Check occasionally and add small amounts of water, as needed.

About 15 to 20 minutes before completely cooked, add 1 cup hot cream. Return to oven.

Quail is a very delicate meat. Be sure it is kept moist while cooking, but do not have moisture standing when you add the hot cream. If the cream is not hot, it will curdle.

Herbed Chicken Bake

12 servings

➤ Prepare this tasty casserole a day ahead for a quick and easy brunch.

4 cups herb-seasoned bread cubes
1 cup plus 2 tablespoons water
¼ cup butter, melted
3 cups cubed cooked chicken
½ cup butter
½ cup flour
4 cups chicken broth
¼ teaspoon salt
6 eggs, slightly beaten

Garnish

Cinnamon apple rings

Mix bread cubes, water, and melted butter; spread in bottom of 9x13 inch pan. Layer cooked chicken over stuffing. In saucepan, melt ½ cup butter and blend in flour. Add chicken broth and salt. Cook and stir mixture until it thickens. Add half the hot mixture to the eggs and blend. Pour in the remaining hot mixture and blend. Pour egg mixture over chicken and stuffing. Bake at 325 degrees for 50 to 60 minutes or until set. Garnish with apple rings.

Try serving with Mouselline Broccoli Sauce, using half the amount of mushrooms and replacing 3 cups cream with 4 cups half and half.

Artichoke Pie

6 to 8 servings

2 9-ounce packages frozen artichoke hearts
4 tablespoons butter or margarine
¼ cup chopped onion
1 tablespoon flour
½ cup half and half
½ cup sour cream
4 eggs, beaten
Salt
Freshly ground black pepper
¼ teaspoon grated nutmeg
2 teaspoons minced parsley
1 baked 9-inch pie shell
½ cup shredded Cheddar cheese
½ cup shredded Swiss cheese
½ cup freshly grated Parmesan cheese

Cook artichoke hearts as directed; drain, slice, and set aside. Melt butter and sauté onion until translucent. Stir in flour until well blended; add half and half and stir until thickened. Combine sour cream, eggs, nutmeg, parsley, and salt and pepper to taste. Add egg mixture to thickened onions; set aside.

Place a layer of artichoke hearts in bottom of pie shell and sprinkle Cheddar cheese over it. Add another layer of artichoke hearts and top with Swiss cheese. Pour egg mixture over layered artichokes and cheese; top with Parmesan cheese. Bake at 350 degrees for 45 minutes or until center is set.

Cheese Strata with Lemon Mushroom Sauce

4 to 6 servings

> ➤ Delightfully different!

1 cup scalded milk	*Freshly ground black pepper*
1 cup soft white bread cubes	*¼ teaspoon dry mustard*
1 ½ cups grated Cheddar cheese	*3 egg yolks, slightly beaten*
2 tablespoons butter or margarine	*3 egg whites, whipped to form soft peaks*
Salt	

Lemon Mushroom Sauce

½ pound fresh mushrooms, sliced	*1 ½ tablespoons lemon juice*
3 tablespoons butter or margarine (divided use)	*1 ½ tablespoons, cornstarch dissolved in 1 tablespoon water*
1 cup chicken broth	

Pour scalded milk over bread cubes in 2-quart baking dish. Add cheese and 2 tablespoons butter; add salt, pepper, and dry mustard. Stir well. Slowly add beaten egg yolks. Fold in the whipped egg whites. Place dish in pan of hot water. Bake at 325 degrees for 45 minutes.

Sauté mushrooms in 2 tablespoons butter. Bring chicken broth to a boil. Add remaining tablespoon butter, lemon juice, and mushrooms. Thicken with cornstarch mixture. Serve sauce over individual portions of Cheese Strata.

Deep Dish Ham and Broccoli Pie

6 to 8 servings

> ➤ Delicious for a summer dinner.

1 9-inch deep dish pie shell	*½ teaspoon salt*
1 cup fresh broccoli florets	*¼ teaspoon freshly ground black pepper*
½ pound cubed ham or cooked bacon	*¼ teaspoon tarragon*
2 to 4 tablespoons peeled and chopped tomato	*⅛ teaspoon nutmeg*
1 cup shredded Swiss cheese	*1 scant cup scalded whole milk*
¼ cup chopped onion	*4 eggs, slightly beaten*

Blanch broccoli in 2 cups salted water. Drain well; pat dry with paper towel and chop. Bake pie shell at 450 degrees for 4 minutes. Remove from oven; reduce oven temperature setting to 350 degrees. Layer broccoli, ham, tomato, and cheese in pie shell. Add more grated cheese if desired. Sprinkle onion over top and set aside. Mix seasonings, milk, and eggs. Pour into pie shell. Bake 30 to 40 minutes until set. Remove from oven and let stand a few minutes before serving.

Spinach and Ricotta Pie

6 to 8 servings

1 10-ounce package frozen spinach, thawed	*¼ cup finely chopped onion*
2 cups ricotta cheese	*2 teaspoons prepared mustard*
½ cup shredded Swiss cheese	*¼ teaspoon oregano*
½ cup grated Parmesan cheese	*¼ teaspoon salt*
½ cup sliced fresh mushrooms	*1 egg, slightly beaten*
	Pastry for two-crust pie

Drain spinach; press out water. Blend spinach with cheese, mushrooms, onion, mustard, oregano, and salt. Stir in egg.

Roll out half of pastry and line 9-inch pie pan. Spread filling on pastry. Roll out remaining pastry for top crust. Place on filling. Trim and flute edge and prick top with fork. Bake at 425 degrees for 35 minutes or until crust is browned. Serve hot with Herb Tomato Sauce

Herb Tomato Sauce

1 15-ounce can tomato sauce	*Salt*
½ teaspoon garlic powder	*Freshly ground black pepper*
1 teaspoon Italian seasoning	

Heat tomato sauce on stove or in microwave oven. Add garlic powder, Italian seasoning, and salt and pepper to taste. Heat and serve.

Lasagne Rollatine

8 servings

Tomato Sauce

1 ½ teaspoons olive oil
1 28-ounce can plum tomatoes
1 6-ounce can tomato paste
1 large garlic clove minced
1 teaspoon sugar
1 teaspoon oregano
1 bay leaf

Heat oil in heavy saucepan. Add garlic and sauté for one minute. Do not brown garlic. Add other ingredients, breaking up tomatoes with a spatula. Simmer, stirring often to prevent burning, for 1 ½ hours. Remove bay leaf before serving.

Mornay Sauce

½ cup butter
½ cup flour
3 cups milk
1 teaspoon salt
⅛ teaspoon freshly ground black pepper
2 egg yolks
½ cup freshly grated Parmesan cheese

Melt butter and stir in flour; gradually add milk and cook, stirring until thickened. Add salt and pepper. Beat egg yolks and add to mixture in pan. Heat until thickened. Add cheese and remove from heat.

1 pound lasagna (18 unbroken noodles), cooked and drained
3 10-ounce packages frozen chopped spinach, cooked and drained
16 ounces ricotta cheese
1 cup freshly grated Parmesan cheese
½ cup butter
¼ teaspoon nutmeg
¼ teaspoon salt
⅛ teaspoon freshly ground black pepper

Combine spinach with cheeses and butter. Season with nutmeg, salt, and pepper. Place a thin layer of tomato sauce in bottom of 9x13 inch baking dish. Spread about ¼ cup spinach filling along each noodle. Roll up noodles and place them in baking dish. Top with Mornay Sauce and then top with remaining Tomato Sauce. Bake at 350 degrees for 45 to 50 minutes.

Manicotti

6 to 8 servings

2 medium onions, finely chopped
2 garlic cloves, chopped
2 tablespoons oil
1 29-ounce can whole peeled tomatoes, drained and cut up
2 4-ounce cans tomato sauce
1 6-ounce can tomato paste
2 4-ounce cans mushrooms, drained
2 teaspoons Italian seasoning
1 ¼ teaspoons salt (divided use)
¾ teaspoon freshly ground black pepper (divided use)
1 12-ounce package frozen chopped spinach, cooked and drained
8 ounces ricotta cheese
½ cup freshly grated Parmesan cheese
1 ½ cups shredded mozzarella cheese (divided use)
1 egg
6 to 8 manicotti shells, cooked and drained

Sauté onions and garlic in oil until onions are translucent. Add tomatoes, tomato sauce, tomato paste, mushrooms, Italian seasoning, 1 teaspoon salt, and ½ teaspoon pepper. Simmer at least 30 minutes.

Combine spinach, ricotta, Parmesan, 1 cup mozzarella, ¼ teaspoon salt, ¼ teaspoon pepper and egg. Mix well. Fill shells with mixture. Pour half of the sauce in 9x13 inch baking dish. Place shells in dish. Cover with remaining sauce. Sprinkle with remaining ½ cup mozzarella. Bake at 350 degrees for 25 to 30 minutes.

You may want to cook additional shells in case they break during preparation.

Austrian-Style Scrambled Eggs

2 large servings

➤ A fast and delicious dish for two.

2 to 3 strips uncooked bacon, chopped
1 small or ½ medium onion, minced
Rendered bacon grease or vegetable oil (optional)
½ green pepper, chopped
½ cup any mild cheese, cut into small cubes
5 large eggs
Sliced or diced tomato (optional)
Salt and freshly ground black pepper

In skillet, heat chopped bacon until it begins rendering fat. Add minced onion and sauté until bacon is crisp and onion is golden. Add more bacon grease or vegetable oil if needed. Add chopped green pepper and sauté until heated through and softened. Add eggs and cheese cubes; stir to combine well. When eggs are set and cheese has melted, add salt and pepper to taste. To serve, spoon eggs on two warm plates. Top with tomato if desired.

Any mild cheese may be used such as Edam, Gouda, Swiss, Monterey Jack, Brick, or Muenster.

Ham and Cheese Buffet

8 to 10 servings

5 eggs
2 cups milk
16 ounces baked ham, diced into ¼-inch cubes
1 ½ cups grated Cheddar cheese
1 8-ounce can sliced mushrooms, drained
8 slices toasted bread, crusts removed and cubed
¼ cup butter or margarine, melted

Beat eggs with milk. Add ham, cheese, mushrooms, and bread cubes. Pour into 9x13 inch greased pan. Pour melted butter over the top. Bake at 325 degrees for 1 hour.

Egg Sausage Brunch

8 to 10 servings

3 cups shredded Cheddar (divided use)
1 dozen eggs
Salt
Freshly ground black pepper
⅔ cup whipping cream
1 pound sausage, browned and well drained

Sprinkle half the cheese in bottom of buttered 9x13 inch baking dish. Beat eggs and pour over cheese; add salt and pepper to taste. Add cream, sprinkle sausage over all, and top with remaining cheese. Bake at 350 degrees for 30 minutes.

➤ This simple casserole may be prepared ahead and baked just before serving.

Bacon-Cheese Bake

8 to 10 servings

2 cups sliced fresh mushrooms
¼ cup chopped onion
2 tablespoons butter
1 dozen eggs
8 ounces grated Cheddar cheese
1 cup cottage cheese
1 pound bacon, cooked and crumbled

Sauté mushrooms and onion in butter. Beat eggs; add grated cheese, cottage cheese, sautéed mushrooms and onion, and most of bacon. Pour into greased 9x13 inch pan and sprinkle rest of bacon on top. Bake at 425 degrees for 15 minutes; lower heat to 325 degrees and bake for another 15 minutes or until done.

Crabby Eggs

6 to 8 servings

➤ A delightful alternative to an old favorite!

6 eggs, hard boiled
6 ounces fresh crabmeat, shredded
3 tablespoons mayonnaise
1 teaspoon Worcestershire sauce
⅛ teaspoon hot pepper sauce
Fresh dill

Cut eggs in half, remove yolks. Mash egg yolks and mix with shredded crabmeat. Add mayonnaise, Worcestershire sauce and hot pepper sauce. Fill egg whites with mixture and sprinkle with dill.

Easy Spinach Soufflé

12 servings

16 ounces creamed cottage cheese
6 eggs
2 tablespoons butter or margarine, melted
8 ounces American cheese, cubed
6 tablespoons flour
1 10-inch package frozen chopped spinach, thawed
⅛ teaspoon salt

Beat eggs in large bowl. Add cottage cheese and mix together. Add melted butter and cheese; mix. Add flour, spinach, and salt; blend together. Pour into ungreased 9x13 inch baking pan. Bake at 350 degrees for 60 minutes.

4-Way Egg Bake

12 servings

1 dozen eggs
4 tablespoons margarine, melted
8 ounces sour cream
16 ounces Cheddar cheese, cubed
1 ½ cups chopped and drained tomatoes
1 small green pepper, diced
1 pound ham, diced (optional)
1 pound sausage, cooked and crumbled (optional)
1 10-ounce package frozen spinach, cooked and chopped (optional)
1 10-ounce package frozen, chopped broccoli, cooked (optional)

Beat eggs well. Beat in melted margarine and sour cream. Fold in cheese, tomatoes, and green pepper. Add any optional ingredients desired. Pour into 8x11 inch or 9x13 inch baking dish and bake at 350 degrees for 1 hour.

Mexican Strata

6 servings

- *6 slices firm white bread, crusts removed*
- *Butter*
- *2 cups shredded sharp Cheddar cheese*
- *2 cups shredded Monterey Jack cheese*
- *1 4-ounce can mild green chilies, chopped and drained*
- *6 eggs, beaten*
- *2 cups whole milk*
- *1 teaspoon salt (optional)*
- *2 teaspoons paprika*
- *1 teaspoon oregano*
- *½ teaspoon freshly ground black pepper*
- *¼ teaspoon garlic powder*
- *¼ teaspoon dry mustard*

Butter one side of each slice of bread; place slices buttered side down in 7x11 inch baking dish. Top with shredded Cheddar cheese, followed by Monterey Jack cheese. Scatter green chilies over cheese. Combine eggs, milk, and remaining ingredients; beat until well blended. Pour over cheese. Refrigerate overnight. Bake uncovered in 325 degree oven for 50 minutes or until nicely browned and firm. Let sit 10 minutes before serving.

Ham and Egg Scramble

6 to 8 servings

- *1 cup cubed Canadian bacon or ham*
- *¼ cup chopped green onion*
- *9 tablespoons butter or margarine (divided use)*
- *1 dozen eggs, beaten*
- *1 cup sliced fresh mushrooms*
- *2 tablespoons flour*
- *2 cups milk*
- *½ teaspoon salt*
- *⅛ teaspoon freshly ground black pepper*
- *2 cups shredded sharp Cheddar cheese*
- *2 ½ cups fresh bread crumbs*
- *Paprika*

➤ This cheesy dish works well for supper or brunch.

In large skillet, sauté cubed Canadian bacon and green onion in 3 tablespoons butter until onion is tender. Add eggs and cook over medium high heat, stirring to form large, soft curds. When eggs are set, stir in mushrooms.

Melt 2 tablespoons butter in heavy saucepan over low heat. Blend in flour and cook 1 minute. Gradually add milk until mixture thickens, stirring constantly. Add salt, pepper, and cheese, stirring until cheese melts and mixture is smooth. Stir sauce into egg mixture.

Spoon into greased 7x11 inch baking dish. Melt remaining butter and combine with crumbs; mix well. Spread crumbs evenly over egg mixture. Sprinkle with paprika. Cover and refrigerate overnight. Uncover and bake at 350 degrees for 30 to 40 minutes, or until heated through.

Three-quarters cup seasoned bread crumbs may be substituted for fresh bread crumbs.

Legend has it that Mary Todd learned many cooking lessons from books like the one here by Mrs. Leslie. The Royal Crown Derby teapot, featuring her favorite flower, the violet, was part of a set of china used in Springfield and selected to go with the family to the White House. The Sweet and Sour Green Beans and Capital City Cranberries complete the scene.

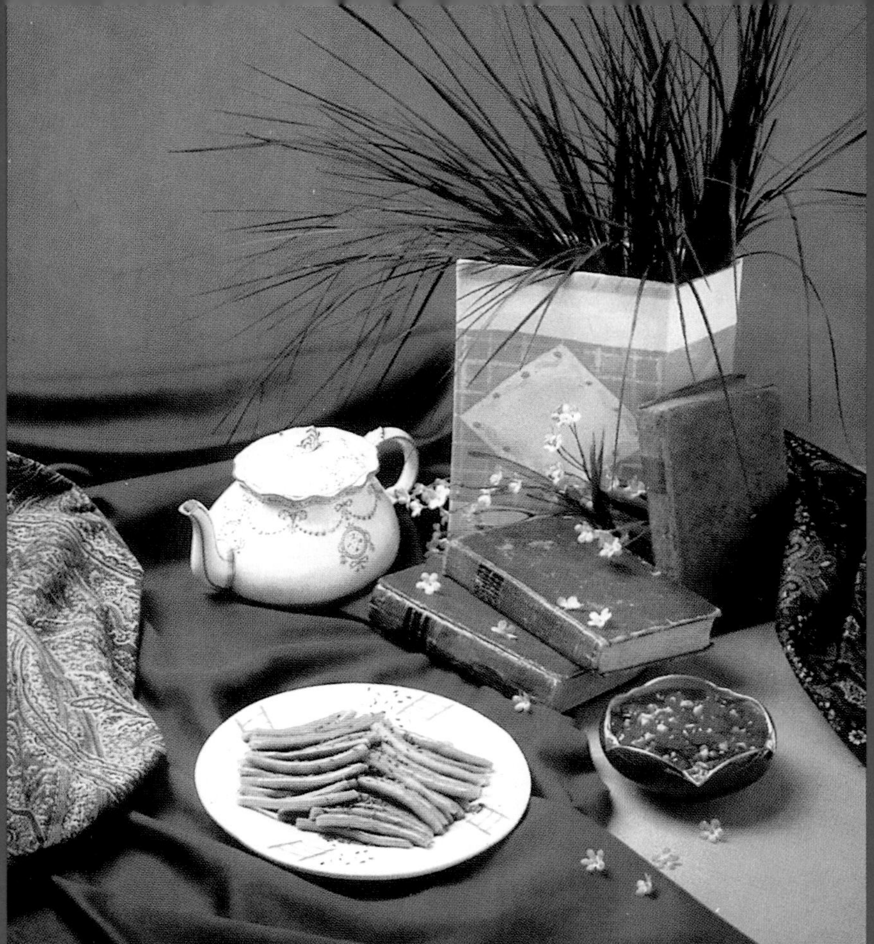

Vegetables and Accompaniments

While Lincoln was serving in Congress from 1847-49, he, Mary and the children lived in the boardinghouse of Mrs. Julia Spriggs in Washington, D.C. Another boarder, Mr. Theodore Weld, wrote of the great quantities of graham bread and corn bread spread on the long boardinghouse table with huge pitchers of milk. *"Mush we have always once and generally twice a day,"* he wrote. *"At dinner potatoes, turnips, parsnips, spinnage (sic) with eggs, almonds, raisins, figs and bread; the puddings, pies, cakes, etc."*

Asparagus Almondine

4 to 6 servings

4 tablespoons olive oil (divided use)	*4 tablespoons sliced almonds*
2 quarts water	*3 tablespoons butter or margarine*
2 pounds fresh asparagus, cleaned and cut into 1-inch pieces	*1 garlic clove, minced*
	1 tablespoon fresh lemon juice

Add 2 tablespoons olive oil to water; bring to boil. Add asparagus and cook for 2 minutes. Drain and rinse under cold water for 1 minute. Keep in cold water until ready to use.

Sauté almonds in butter until lightly browned. Set aside. In a large skillet, sauté garlic in remaining olive oil. Do not let garlic brown. Add drained asparagus and stir-fry until hot, approximately 2 minutes. Add sautéed almonds and lemon juice and stir to mix. Serve immediately.

Artichokes Florentine

8 to 12 servings

➤ This is an elegant dish that is deceptively easy to prepare. Very rich, it goes well with grilled or broiled meats, or may be used as an appetizer.

2 14-ounce cans artichoke bottoms	*2 tablespoons butter or margarine*
1 10-ounce package frozen creamed spinach, thawed	*½ cup sour cream*
	½ cup mayonnaise
12 fresh mushrooms, sliced	*2 tablespoons lemon juice*
Garnish	
Tomato roses	*Red pepper slices*

Drain artichoke bottoms; fill with creamed spinach. Sauté mushrooms in butter. Spoon mushrooms over spinach. Place in shallow 7x11 inch baking dish. Combine sour cream, mayonnaise, and lemon juice. Pour over artichokes. Bake at 375 degrees for 15 minutes or until heated thoroughly. Serve hot, garnished with tomato roses or red pepper slices.

Prairie Schooner Baked Beans

12 to 15 servings

1 cup brown sugar
½ up cider vinegar
½ teaspoon dry mustard
¼ teaspoon garlic powder
1 pound uncooked bacon, diced
2 medium yellow onions, sliced in rings
1 16-ounce can lima beans, drained
1 16-ounce can red kidney beans, drained
1 16-ounce can giant butter beans, drained
2 16-ounce cans baked beans in molasses

Simmer brown sugar, vinegar, mustard, and garlic powder in saucepan over low heat for 20 minutes. Fry bacon until crisp; remove from pan. Sauté onions in bacon grease until soft, but not browned. Remove from pan. Combine all beans, onions, and bacon in 3-quart casserole. Pour sauce over and mix well. Cover and bake at 350 degrees for 1 hour.

Sweet and Sour Green Beans

6 to 8 servings

¼ cup vinegar
⅓ cup sugar
2 tablespoons oil
1 teaspoon celery seed
1 teaspoon caraway seed
1 ½ pounds fresh green beans or 16 ounces frozen green beans, cooked

➤ This is very easy and very delicious.

In small saucepan, combine vinegar, sugar, oil, celery seed, and caraway seed; stir over medium heat until sugar dissolves. Pour over hot, drained beans. Serve immediately.

Jeweled Beets

6 servings

1 tablespoon vinegar
4 tablespoons butter or margarine
1 teaspoon sugar
Salt (optional)
Pinch of nutmeg
1 cup sour cream
8 to 10 small beets, cooked, skinned, and sliced

Combine all ingredients except beets in saucepan over low heat. Add beets and combine well. Cook over medium heat until hot. Do not let boil. Serve immediately.

Blue Ribbon Broccoli

8 servings

2 tablespoons butter or margarine
2 tablespoons flour
1 cup milk
2 tablespoons chopped mushrooms
2 eggs, well beaten
½ cup mayonnaise
¼ cup finely chopped onion
1 ½ cups grated sharp Cheddar cheese
20 ounces broccoli, cooked, drained and chopped
Salt
Freshly ground black pepper
¼ cup finely crushed buttery cracker crumbs

Melt butter over low heat. Blend in flour, stirring constantly until mixture is smooth. Slowly add milk, stirring constantly until thickened, about 5 minutes. Remove from heat and stir in mushrooms.

Combine eggs, mushroom sauce, mayonnaise, onion, and grated cheese. Stir in broccoli. Add salt and pepper to taste. Pour into greased 2-quart baking dish. Top with crushed crackers. Bake at 350 degrees for 30 minutes or until bubbly.

An easy substitution for mushroom sauce is a can of cream of mushroom soup.

Mousseline of Broccoli with Mushroom Sauce

8 servings

½ pound fresh broccoli, stems peeled	*Lemon juice*
½ cup whipping cream	*White pepper*
4 eggs	*Nutmeg*
Salt	

➤ This rich dish is a specialty of local chefs Cissy Bunn and Carol Fraase from Another Cooking School.

Butter 8 ½-cup custard cups or molds. Cook broccoli until tender. Rinse with cold water to stop cooking and retain bright green color. Purée broccoli in food processor. Add cream and eggs, one at a time, processing after each addition. Season to taste with salt, pepper, and lemon juice. Fill custard cups; cover with buttered foil or waxed paper. Place cups in shallow baking pan; fill pan with boiling water so that water reaches ½ way up sides of cups. Bake at 375 degrees for 25 to 30 minutes or until mousseline is set. Unmold onto serving plates and spoon on Mushroom Sauce.

Mousseline can be cooked in one mold but allow extra cooking time.

Mushroom Sauce

2 tablespoons butter	*3 cups whipping cream*
2 ounces dried mushrooms, soaked in warm water (optional)	*Salt*
1 ½ pounds fresh mushrooms, cut in quarters or eighths	*White pepper*
2 large shallots, finely chopped	*Lemon juice*
1 cup dry vermouth	*2 tablespoons butter (optional)*

Drain dried mushrooms, reserving liquid, and cut into smaller pieces than fresh mushrooms. Melt butter in saucepan, cook mushrooms and shallots together over medium-high heat until liquid evaporates. Add vermouth and cook over high heat until reduced by half. Add cream and cook until sauce is thickened. Season to taste with salt, white pepper, and lemon juice. For richer sauce, whisk in 2 tablespoons butter. For stronger mushroom flavor, add some of the reserved mushroom liquid. Serve over Mousseline of Broccoli.

This thick, rich Mushroom Sauce also makes an excellent filling for pastry shells.

Ginger-Sweet Carrots

5 servings

¼ teaspoon salt
1 tablespoon sugar
¼ teaspoon ground ginger
Pinch of nutmeg
½ teaspoon cornstarch
2 tablespoons margarine
¼ cup orange or pineapple juice
5 medium carrots, peeled, sliced in ¼-inch pieces, cooked and drained.

Microwave method: Combine all dry ingredients in a small microwave-safe container. Add margarine and juice. Cook in microwave oven for 30 seconds on high or until sauce is boiling; cook an additional 10 seconds.

Stovetop method: Combine sugar, salt, ginger, nutmeg, and cornstarch in small saucepan. Add juice and cook until mixture boils. Boil 1 minute. Stir in margarine.

Pour sauce over carrots and stir. Serve immediately.

Sunshine Carrots

8 servings

➤ This delicious casserole can be put together early in the day and refrigerated until cooking time. It's even better the second day!

1 6-ounce package dried apricots
1 12-ounce an apricot nectar
2 16-ounce cans tiny whole carrots, drained
¾ cup brown sugar
2 tablespoons butter or margarine
½ cup slivered or sliced almonds

Soak the apricots in the nectar overnight. Place 1 can carrots in greased 2-quart baking dish. Top with half the apricots and nectar. Sprinkle with half the brown sugar and dot with half the butter. Sprinkle with half the almonds. Repeat layers. Bake at 350 degrees for 30 to 40 minutes or until bubbly.

Nutty Cheese Cauliflower

6 to 8 servings

1 head fresh cauliflower	*3 tablespoons chopped walnuts*
3 tablespoon butter	*¾ to 1 cup pasteurized cheese spread*
3 tablespoons fine dry bread crumbs	

Cut off stalks and outer leaves of cauliflower and wash in cold water. Place whole cauliflower in saucepan and add 1 inch salted water. Cover and bring to a boil; cook 20 to 25 minutes or until tender. Mix butter, bread crumbs, and nuts in small saucepan, stirring over medium heat until lightly browned. Place cauliflower in shallow baking dish. Spread with cheese. Sprinkle with bread crumb mixture. Bake in 350 degree oven for 12 to 15 minutes until browned.

New Salem Corn Casserole

10 to 12 servings

1 16-ounce can whole kernel corn, drained	*½ cup margarine, melted*
1 16-ounce can cream style corn	*1 cup sour cream*
2 eggs, slightly beaten	*1 8 ½-ounce box corn muffin mix*
½ teaspoon salt	*1 to 2 cups graded Cheddar cheese (optional)*

Mix together all ingredients except cheese. Add 1 cup Cheddar cheese if desired. Pour into greased 9x13 inch pan. Bake at 350 degrees for 40 minutes or until set. If more cheese is desired, add additional ½ to 1 cup Cheddar cheese on top of casserole when set. Bake another 5 minutes or until cheese melts.

Each year, sweet corn is celebrated at the Chatham Sweet Corn Festival just outside of Springfield. Over 10,000 ears of butter-slathered corn are consumed during the event.

Corn Pudding

8 servings

5 to 6 ears fresh sweet corn
3 eggs, beaten
2 tablespoons flour
1 cup half and half
Salt
Freshly ground black pepper
1 tablespoon butter, melted

Scrape corn from cobs. Mix corn with eggs, flour, and half and half. Salt and pepper to taste. Pour into buttered 1 ½-quart baking dish. Drizzle top with melted butter. Bake at 325 degrees for 1 hour or until knife inserted in center comes out clean. Serve immediately.

Eggplant Rollantini

6 to 8 servings

➤ This meatless main dish was graciously submitted by local chef Gloria Schwartz.

2 eggplants, about 1 pound each
Salt
6 tablespoons olive oil
1 15-ounce container ricotta cheese
½ cup freshly grated Romano cheese (divided use)
1 garlic clove, minced
1 tablespoon fresh basil, chopped or 1 teaspoon dried
¼ teaspoon freshly grated nutmeg or ⅛ teaspoon dried
¼ teaspoon fresh oregano or ⅛ teaspoon dried
1 ½ cups Tomato Sauce

Peel eggplants. Slice lengthwise into ¼- to ½-inch slices. Salt and drain on paper towels for 30 minutes. Arrange slices in single layer on greased shallow baking pan. Brush liberally with olive oil. Broil 5 inches from heat for 5 to 6 minutes or until browned and soft. Turn slices, brush with more oil and broil 5 to 6 minutes more. Remove and let cool.

In a large bowl, combine ricotta, ¼ cup Romano cheese, garlic, basil, nutmeg, and oregano. Spread some of this mixture evenly over each eggplant slice. Roll each slice, starting at narrow end. Arrange rolls in a single layer in a greased shallow 3- to 4-quart baking dish. Pour Tomato Sauce over rolls and sprinkle with remaining ¼ cup Romano cheese.

Bake at 350 degrees for 20 to 30 minutes or until bubbly.

Italian Eggplant

8 to 10 servings

1 large eggplant, approximately 2 pounds	*¼ to ½ cup olive oil*
Salt	*3 cups Tomato Sauce*
Freshly ground black pepper	*8 ounces mozzarella cheese, thinly sliced*
3 eggs, slightly beaten	*1 15-ounce container ricotta cheese*
1 cup fine dry bread crumbs	*1 teaspoon Italian seasoning*
	½ cup freshly grated Parmesan cheese

Peel eggplant. Cut in ½-inch slices. Sprinkle with salt and pepper to taste. Dip slices into egg and then bread crumbs. Cook eggplant without crowding in large skillet over medium-high heat, adding oil as needed. When browned, drain eggplant thoroughly on paper towels.

Grease 9x13 inch baking dish. Line bottom with half the eggplant slices. Cover with half the Tomato Sauce. Layer half the mozzarella slices. Cover with half the ricotta cheese mixed with the Italian seasoning. Repeat layers. Sprinkle with Parmesan cheese. Bake at 350 degrees for 30 minutes or until top is lightly browned and bubbly.

Mouthwatering Mushrooms

6 servings

1 pound fresh mushrooms, stems removed	*¼ cup chicken or beef broth*
⅓ cup butter or margarine	*Dash of freshly ground black pepper*
2 tablespoons flour	*½ cup fresh fine bread crumbs*
½ cup half and half	*½ cup freshly grated Parmesan cheese*

Arrange mushrooms, stem side down, in greased 7x11 inch baking dish. Melt butter in a small saucepan over low heat. Increase heat to medium high and blend in flour. Cook 3 minutes, stirring constantly. Slowly pour in half and half and bring to a boil. Mix in broth and pepper and return to a quick boil. Remove from heat. Pour sauce evenly over mushrooms. Sprinkle with bread crumbs. Bake at 350 degrees for 30 minutes. Sprinkle with cheese. Bake another 5 minutes, until cheese melts. Serve immediately.

Onion Pie

6 to 8 servings

30 saltine crackers, crushed
¾ cup butter or margarine (divided use)
3 cups thinly sliced onion
½ pound sharp Cheddar cheese, grated
1 ½ cups scalded milk
3 eggs beaten

Garnish

Cherry tomatoes
Red onion flowers

Mix crackers and ½ cup melted butter; press into 8-inch square pan to form crust. Sauté onion in ¼ cup butter until golden brown. Place onion in crust and sprinkle cheese over top. Add milk to eggs. Pour over onions and cheese. Bake at 350 degrees for 30 minutes. Slice and garnish with cherry tomatoes or red onion flowers.

May use 9-inch pie pan and ¼ cup to ½ cup less crust.

Satisfying Spinach

4 to 5 servings

1 10-ounce package frozen chopped spinach
1 tablespoon minced onion
2 eggs, beaten
½ cup sour cream
1 cup freshly grated Parmesan cheese
1 tablespoon flour
2 tablespoons butter, melted
Salt
Freshly ground black pepper

Heat spinach with onion until spinach thaws. This may be done in a microwave oven or add a small amount of water to spinach in saucepan on stove. Drain and set aside.

Mix eggs, sour cream, Parmesan cheese, flour, melted butter, salt, and pepper. Stir in spinach-onion mixture. Pour into greased 1-quart baking dish. Bake at 350 degrees for 25 to 30 minutes, or until center is set. Do not overcook or it will separate.

Triple Cheese Tomatoes

8 servings

1 large ripe tomato, preferably beefsteak
1 large slightly green tomato
1 cup mayonnaise
1 cup freshly grated Parmesan cheese
¼ teaspoon garlic powder
¼ cup grated sharp Cheddar cheese
¼ cup grated mozzarella cheese

➤ Excellent with grilled beef or chicken.

Slice tomatoes ¼-inch thick. Combine mayonnaise, Parmesan cheese, and garlic powder. Arrange a layer of tomato slices, overlapping slightly, in a greased 9-inch pie pan. Spread a layer of mayonnaise mixture evenly over tomatoes. Repeat, ending with mayonnaise layer. Combine grated cheddar and mozzarella and sprinkle over top. Bake at 350 degrees for 30 minutes or until cheese has melted and is slightly brown. Do not overbake. Serve immediately.

This dish can be baked and reheated, or frozen, thawed and reheated.

Mushroom-Stuffed Tomatoes

6 servings

6 medium firm tomatoes
1 pound fresh mushrooms, coarsely chopped
2 tablespoons lemon juice
3 green onions, minced
¼ cup butter
Salt
Freshly ground black pepper
3 egg yolks, slightly beaten
½ cup fresh bread crumbs
1 tablespoon melted butter or margarine

Cut tops from tomatoes; remove pulp and drain upside down. Mix chopped mushrooms with lemon juice. Sauté mushrooms and green onions in butter in large skillet. Add salt and pepper to taste. Blend a small amount of mushroom mixture with egg yolks. Gradually add egg yolks to mushrooms in skillet. Continue cooking, stirring constantly until mixture thickens. Arrange tomatoes in a shallow, greased pan. Fill each tomato with mushroom mixture. Toss bread crumbs with 1 tablespoon melted butter. Top each tomato with bread crumbs. Bake at 350 degrees for 20 minutes.

Zucchini Luxe

6 to 8 servings

➤ This dish was created by a penny-wise graduate student for an all-zucchini potluck. The dishes went all the way from appetizers to desserts - even a beverage!

- *½ cup minced onion*
- *4 cups shredded, unpeeled zucchini*
- *¼ cup plus 2 tablespoons butter or margarine*
- *8 ounces cream cheese, softened*
- *2 eggs, separated*
- *Salt*
- *Freshly ground black pepper*
- *Pinch of nutmeg*
- *1 cup finely crushed herb-seasoned stuffing*

Sauté onion and zucchini in 2 tablespoons butter until volume of vegetables is reduced by half or all liquid has been evaporated. Mix together cream cheese, egg yolks, salt, pepper, and nutmeg. Add cream cheese mixture to zucchini and onion; mix well. Beat egg whites until stiff but not dry; fold into zucchini mixture. Pour into greased shallow 1 ½-quart baking dish. Mix remaining butter with stuffing and sprinkle on top. Bake at 375 degrees for 30 minutes or until puffy and top is slightly brown.

Zucchini Supreme

6 servings

- *4 cups zucchini, sliced in ¼-inch rounds*
- *2 cups boiling water*
- *2 eggs, well beaten*
- *1 onion, coarsely chopped*
- *1 cup freshly grated Parmesan cheese*
- *1 cup mayonnaise*
- *Salt*
- *Freshly ground black pepper*
- *¼ cup cracker or dry bread crumbs*
- *2 tablespoons butter or margarine, melted*

Cook zucchini in boiling water for 5 minutes. Drain well and blot with paper towel. In large bowl, combine eggs, onion, Parmesan cheese, and mayonnaise. Add salt and pepper to taste. Add zucchini and mix lightly. Pour into greased 1 ½-quart baking dish. Mix crumbs with melted butter; sprinkle over zucchini. Bake at 350 degrees for 30 minutes or until bubbly.

Mixed Grill

4 to 6 servings

½ small green cabbage, sliced in narrow wedges

2 peppers (red, yellow, or orange), slice in wedges

2 cups fresh broccoli florets or fresh snow peas or green pepper wedges

2 tablespoons olive oil

Garlic powder

Freshly ground black pepper

➤ The combinations are endless. Start with these suggestions or pick your favorite fresh vegetables - the more colorful the better!

Toss vegetables in oil; add garlic powder and pepper to taste. Add more oil if needed to lightly coat vegetables. Loosely wrap vegetables in heavy aluminum foil. Place foil packet on moderately hot grill with seam side up. Cook for 20 to 30 minutes, gently shaking packet several times to prevent scorching. When firmest vegetable is fork-tender, serve.

Italian Vegetable Platter

8 servings

Italian Marinade

¾ cup oil

⅓ cup vinegar

1 garlic clove, quartered

1 tablespoon coarsely chopped onion

½ teaspoon salt

⅛ teaspoon basil

⅛ teaspoon rosemary

¼ teaspoon oregano

Dash cayenne pepper

➤ This versatile dish may also be chilled and served as an antipasto salad.

Vegetables

3 cups fresh broccoli florets, ¾- to 1-inch diameter

1 ½ cups fresh cauliflower florets

1 cup thinly sliced carrot rounds

1 tablespoon chopped red pepper or pimento

12 to 15 whole pitted ripe olives

In blender, combine marinade ingredients; blend until garlic and onion are liquefied. Arrange vegetables on plate or platter with broccoli surrounding cauliflower and carrots in center. Scatter pepper over all. Spoon ¾ cup marinade evenly over vegetables. Cover with plastic wrap and cook in microwave oven on high for 4 to 5 minutes. Add olives to platter and serve hot. Or let cool, uncovered, and serve at room temperature as an antipasto.

Cinnamon Apples

6 servings

➤ Best if made a day ahead. Good hot for breakfast or chilled as a side dish. Serve with beef or pork.

1 cup water
1/4 cup sugar
1/8 teaspoon salt
1/2 cup red cinnamon candies
8 to 10 small apples, peeled and sliced

Combine water, sugar, salt, and cinnamon candies in large saucepan. Cook, stirring, until candies are completely dissolved. Add apples; simmer uncovered for 20 minutes or until apples are soft. Uncover and let simmer until apples are translucent, about 10 more minutes. Serve hot or cold.

Capital City Cranberries

8 to 10 servings

➤ Serve this versatile dish over cream cheese as an appetizer, ice cream as a dessert, or with a turkey at holiday time.

1 pound fresh cranberries
2 1/2 cups sugar
Grated peel of 1 orange
3/4 cup light rum
1/2 cup crushed walnuts (optional)

Wash and drain cranberries. Put cranberries in 2-quart casserole dish with sugar and grated orange peel. Bake in 350 degree oven for 45 minutes or until cranberries have popped. Add rum and bake cranberries 15 more minutes. Sprinkle crushed walnuts on top.

Cranberries can be cooked in microwave oven.

Pineapple Soufflé

6 servings

- *1 20-ounce can crushed pineapple in juice*
- *3 eggs slightly beaten*
- *½ cup sugar*
- *2 tablespoons flour*
- *½ teaspoon salt*
- *4 slices white bread, with crusts, cubed*
- *½ cup butter, melted*

➤ A delightful and simple side dish for pork or lamb.

Mix pineapple, eggs, sugar, flour, and salt together. Spread pineapple mixture into greased 9x5 inch loaf pan or 2-quart casserole dish. Toss bread cubes in melted butter. Spread bread cubes on top of the pineapple mixture. Bake at 350 degrees for 40 to 45 minutes. Let set before serving.

Chili Cheese Hominy

8 servings

- *¼ cup chopped onion*
- *2 tablespoons margarine, melted*
- *2 15 ½-ounce cans hominy, drained*
- *2 4-ounce cans chopped green chilis, drained*
- *1 cup sour cream*
- *1 teaspoon chili powder*
- *1 teaspoon salt*
- *⅛ teaspoon freshly ground black pepper*
- *1 ½ cups shredded Cheddar cheese (divided use)*

➤ This unusual side dish may be prepared in advance, just ready to pop in the oven.

Sauté onion in margarine in large skillet for 5 minutes. Add hominy, chilis, sour cream, chili powder, salt, pepper, and ½ cup cheese. Mix well. Pour into lightly greased 2-quart baking dish. Recipe can be refrigerated up to 8 hours at this point. Bake at 400 degrees for 20 minutes. If refrigerated, add 10 minutes to baking time. Sprinkle remaining 1 cup cheese over top and bake 5 more minutes.

Company Pasta

10 to 12 servings

1 cup frozen chopped broccoli
1 cup frozen snow peas
1 cup sliced fresh zucchini
1 cup baby peas
1 9-ounce package frozen artichoke hearts
1 tablespoon olive oil
12 fresh mushrooms, sliced
2 tomatoes, chopped
½ cup fresh chopped parsley
4 teaspoons minced garlic
1 pound linguine or fettuccine, cooked
1 cup whipping cream
½ cup freshly grated Parmesan cheese
½ cup butter
⅓ cup fresh chopped basil

Garnish

Red pepper strips
Carrot curls

Blanch broccoli, snow peas, zucchini, peas, and artichokes in boiling water for 3 to 4 minutes. Rinse in cold water; drain and set aside.

Heat olive oil in medium skillet and sauté mushrooms 2 to 3 minutes. Add tomatoes, parsley, garlic, and sauté an additional 2 to 3 minutes. Set aside.

Drain cooked pasta. Add whipping cream, Parmesan cheese, butter, and basil. Toss well, mixing thoroughly. Add blanched vegetables and mushroom mixture and toss gently. Garnish with red pepper strips or carrot curls for color. Serve immediately.

Fettuccine Alfredo

6 to 8 servings

16 ounces fettuccine
2 tablespoons butter
1 ½ cups half and half
⅓ cup freshly grated Parmesan cheese
1 teaspoon garlic salt
1 teaspoon chopped fresh parsley
Freshly ground black pepper

Boil fettuccine in large pot until tender. Drain well; add butter and half and half, stirring constantly. Add Parmesan cheese, garlic salt, parsley, and pepper to taste. Toss thoroughly and serve immediately.

Olive Walnut Pasta

4 servings

⅔ cup chopped walnuts
½ cup chopped ripe olives
½ cup chopped pimento
⅓ cup chopped parsley
2 tablespoons fresh chopped basil or ¾ teaspoon dried
2 to 3 teaspoons olive oil
1 garlic clove, minced
8 ounces linguine, cooked and drained
Salt
Freshly ground black pepper

➤ Pasta lovers will appreciate this quick and easy dish that is prepared in a microwave oven.

Combine first 7 ingredients in microwave-safe 1-quart dish; cook on high 1 minute. Pour over pasta and toss to mix; salt and pepper to taste. Serve immediately.

Pasta with Artichoke Hearts

10 to 12 servings

2 6-ounce jars marinated artichoke hearts
2 garlic cloves, crushed
1 tablespoon olive oil
1 tablespoon butter or margarine
1 ½ cups sliced onion
2 teaspoons dried basil
1 cup sour cream
1 cup cottage cheese
Salt
Freshly ground black pepper
Cayenne pepper
Parmesan cheese
1 pound spaghetti or fettuccine, cooked and drained

Drain marinade from artichoke hearts into skillet. Add crushed garlic, olive oil, and butter; heat. Add onion and sauté about 5 minutes or until translucent. Cut artichoke hearts into bite-sized pieces; add to onion mixture and sauté for 3 to 5 more minutes. Remove from heat and stir in basil, sour cream, and cottage cheese. Add salt, pepper, cayenne, and Parmesan cheese to taste. Toss with pasta. Serve immediately.

Pasta with Asparagus

6 to 8 servings

½ cup butter
1 medium onion, minced
2 to 3 garlic cloves, minced
1 pound fresh asparagus, cut diagonally
8 ounces fresh mushrooms, sliced
1 carrot, sliced
1 cup half and half
½ cup chicken stock
2 teaspoons basil
½ cup chopped green pepper
½ cup chopped red pepper
12 ounces fettuccine, cooked
Salt
Freshly ground black pepper
1 cup freshly grated Parmesan cheese

Heat a large skillet over medium heat; add butter, onion, and garlic. Sauté until onion is translucent. Mix in the asparagus, mushrooms, and carrots. Sauté for 5 to 10 minutes, stirring frequently. Increase heat to high and add half and half, chicken stock, and basil. Let mixture boil until liquid begins to reduce. Stir in the peppers and cook 2 to 3 more minutes. Add drained fettuccine, salt and pepper to taste, and cheese. Heat thoroughly and serve immediately. Top with additional Parmesan cheese if desired.

Cream of the Crop Potatoes

12 servings

➤ Excellent for buffet dinners. The extra effort is worth it!

½ teaspoon minced garlic
2 green onions, chopped
½ teaspoon cayenne pepper
3 tablespoons butter
1 ¼ cups milk
1 ½ cups whipping cream
½ teaspoon salt
¼ teaspoon freshly ground black pepper
2 ½ pounds red potatoes, unpeeled and cut in 1/8-inch slices
1 cup shredded mozzarella cheese
¼ cup freshly grated Parmesan cheese

Sauté garlic, onion, and cayenne in butter in large saucepan for 2 minutes. Add milk, cream, salt, and pepper, stirring well. Add potatoes. Bring mixture to a boil over medium heat, stirring occasionally. Spoon mixture into a lightly greased 9x13 inch baking dish. Sprinkle with mozzarella cheese and Parmesan cheese. Bake at 350 degrees for 45 minutes or until bubbly and golden brown. Let stand 30 minutes before serving.

Crab-Stuffed Potatoes

6 servings

6 medium baking potatoes, cleaned and rubbed with vegetable oil
½ cup chopped shallots
2 tablespoons butter
1 cup sour cream
¾ cup shredded Cheddar cheese
¼ cup Parmesan cheese
1 teaspoon salt
½ teaspoon freshly ground black pepper
4 tablespoons cooked crabmeat
Paprika

Garnish

Cooked, crumbled bacon

➤ Make several potatoes and freeze them for those times when you want something convenient but special. May use larger potatoes and extra bacon or crabmeat for main dish.

Bake potatoes at 400 degrees for 1 hour. Cool. Slice each potato lengthwise across the top, making an opening large enough to remove the pulp. Remove pulp without breaking potato skins. Sauté shallots in butter. Pour over potato pulp. Add sour cream, Cheddar cheese, Parmesan cheese, salt, pepper, and crabmeat.

Beat with mixer until well blended. Stuff potato skins. Sprinkle top with paprika. Garnish with cooked, crumbled bacon.

If baking immediately, place on baking sheet and bake at 350 degrees for 15 minutes. Potatoes may be refrigerated up to 2 days, but add 15 minutes to baking time. Potatoes may be wrapped in foil and frozen up to 3 months. To bake frozen potatoes without thawing, cook foil-wrapped potatoes at 350 degrees for 30 minutes. Unwrap and bake 30 minutes more or until thoroughly heated.

May substitute 8 slices of cooked, crumbled bacon for crabmeat.

Hearty Cheese Potatoes

6 servings

➤ Great recipe to use when you need to prepare potatoes in advance. Combine with ham chunks for a main-dish casserole.

5 medium potatoes
½ teaspoon salt
2 tablespoons butter
2 tablespoons flour
1 ½ cups hot milk
½ cup shredded Cheddar cheese
¼ cup grated Parmesan cheese
1 garlic clove, minced
Salt
Freshly ground black pepper

Topping

¼ cup shredded Cheddar cheese
¼ cup grated Parmesan cheese
Paprika

Garnish

Crumbled cooked bacon
Chopped chives

Boil unpeeled potatoes in salted water until tender. Cool slightly. Peel and cut into ¼-inch slices. Layer slices in greased 9x13 inch casserole dish.

Melt butter in saucepan and stir in flour until smooth. Gradually add hot milk, stirring constantly. Stir in cheeses and garlic until cheese is melted; season to taste with salt and pepper. Pour sauce over potatoes. Top with extra cheeses. Sprinkle paprika on top. Bake uncovered at 350 degrees for 30 minutes or until bubbly. If desired, place under broiler at end of baking to brown top. Garnish with chopped chives or crumbled cooked bacon.

Recipe may be refrigerated up to 2 days before baking, but increase baking time 10 minutes.

Pineapple Sweet Potatoes

10 servings

2 ½ pounds sweet potatoes, cooked
1 8-ounce can crushed pineapple in juice
1 16-ounce can chunk pineapple in juice
½ teaspoon cinnamon
½ teaspoon cloves
Juice of 1 orange
Grated peel of 1 orange
¼ cup dark brown sugar

Topping

4 tablespoons butter, melted
1 cup chopped walnuts or pecans
½ cup brown sugar

➤ A great time-saver for holiday meals and a wonderful side dish for ham or turkey.

Slice cooled and peeled potatoes into ½-inch rounds. Mix crushed and chunk pineapple, cinnamon, cloves, orange juice, grated peel, and brown sugar. Combine with potatoes and put in greased 2-quart casserole.

Mix topping ingredients. Pour over sweet potato mixture. Bake covered at 375 degrees for 30 minutes or until golden brown.

May be refrigerated 24 hours in advance of baking; increase baking time 10 minutes.

Crunchy Sesame Fries

5 Servings

5 medium baking potatoes
1 ½ tablespoons melted margarine
1 teaspoon soy sauce
½ teaspoon garlic salt
2 tablespoons sesame seed
Salt
Freshly ground black pepper
Apricot Sweet and Sour Sauce or soy sauce

➤ A low-fat alternative to French fries.

Scrub potatoes well. Leaving skins on, cut into ¾-inch strips. Spray 2 baking sheets with vegetable oil spray. Spread potatoes on the sheets. Combine margarine and soy sauce. Drizzle over potatoes and mix lightly. Sprinkle garlic salt and sesame seed on the potatoes. Salt and pepper to taste.

Bake at 450 degrees for 15 minutes. Turn potatoes over and continue baking for 15 more minutes. Watch carefully during last 10 minutes, as potatoes burn easily. Serve hot with Apricot Sweet and Sour Sauce or soy sauce.

May prepare up to 4 hours prior to baking.

Apricot Sweet and Sour Sauce

1 cup

➤ This sauce is delicious on chicken, ham, or egg rolls.

½ cup brown sugar
1 tablespoon cornstarch
½ teaspoon ground ginger
1 tablespoon lemon juice
5 ½ ounces apricot nectar

Combine brown sugar and cornstarch in microwave-safe bowl. Stir in ginger, lemon juice, and nectar. Cook in microwave oven on high 4 minutes or until sauce is thick and translucent, stirring several times.

Béchamel or White Sauce

2 cups

➤ Try one of these easy sauces for broiled or poached fish fillets.

3 tablespoons butter
3 tablespoons flour
1 cup milk or cream
1 cup warm chicken or fish stock
Salt
White pepper

Melt butter over low heat. Stir in flour and cook for 2 minutes. Gradually add liquid, stirring constantly until sauce thickens. Season to taste with salt and pepper.

Variations:

Mornay Sauce - Add ½ cup grated Cheddar, Swiss, or Gruyère cheese and a pinch of nutmeg or cayenne pepper to prepared Béchamel. Whisk until smooth.

Shrimp Sauce - Add ½ cup chopped, cooked shrimp.

Mushroom Sauce - Add ½ cup sautéed sliced mushrooms. Simmer 5 minutes.

Vegetable Sauce - Add ½ cup sautéed onions, celery, or green pepper.

All sauces may be made 5 to 6 hours in advance.

Tomato Sauce

3 cups

1 ½ teaspoons olive oil
2 garlic cloves, chopped
1 28-ounce can plum tomatoes
1 6-ounce can tomato paste
1 teaspoon sugar
1 teaspoon oregano
1 bay leaf

In a heavy 3-quart saucepan, heat oil; add garlic and sauté for 1 minute. Do not let garlic brown. Add remaining ingredients. Break apart tomatoes with a wooden spoon.

Simmer slowly for 1 ½ hours, stirring often to prevent scorching. Remove bay leaf before serving.

➤ Local chef Gloria Schwartz contributed the recipe for this wonderfully versatile tomato sauce.

Zesty Zucchini Tomato Sauce

6 servings

1 large onion, cut in eighths
3 garlic cloves
¼ cup butter
2 medium zucchini, cut in chunks
1 carrot, cut in chunks
2 stalks celery, cut in chunks
1 16-ounce can stewed tomatoes
1 6-ounce can tomato paste
1 tablespoon sugar
1 tablespoon fresh basil or 1 teaspoon dried
Salt
Freshly ground black pepper

With steel blade in food processor, mince onion and garlic. Sauté onion and garlic in butter in pan. Process zucchini, carrot and celery until minced. Add vegetables to sauté pan and cook until tender and some of the liquid is reduced. Whirl stewed tomatoes and paste in processor. Add tomato mixture, sugar, basil, salt, and pepper to pan. Simmer 10 minutes.

➤ This heart-healthy sauce is a great way to use fresh vegetables from the garden. It can be made in advance, then refrigerated or frozen. It may be reheated in the microwave oven.

Confetti Rice

8 servings

1 cup chopped onion
½ cup chopped green pepper
1 garlic clove, minced
3 tablespoons butter
1 ½ cups uncooked rice
2 cups beef broth, boiling hot
1 ½ teaspoons salt
¼ teaspoon freshly ground black pepper
½ teaspoon basil
3 medium tomatoes, each cut into 8 wedges

In skillet, sauté onion, green pepper, and garlic in butter until tender. Add rice and cook 2 minutes longer. Turn into a shallow 2-quart casserole; stir in broth and seasonings. Arrange tomato wedges on top of rice. Cover tightly and bake at 350 degrees 35 to 40 minutes or until rice is tender and liquid is absorbed.

Raisin and Nut Rice

6 to 8 servings

➤ Graciously submitted by professional cook Gloria Schwartz.

¼ cup butter or margarine
¼ cup chopped onion
¼ cup slivered almonds or pine nuts
¼ cup golden raisins
3 cups hot cooked rice

Melt butter in large saucepan. Add the onions and almonds and lightly brown. Add the raisins and cook until slightly puffed. Add the cooked rice and gently mix. Serve hot.

Spirited Rice

4 to 6 servings

➤ This light and easy dish is especially good with chicken.

2 ½ cups chicken broth
½ cup white wine
¼ cup butter or margarine
1 cup converted rice
1 teaspoon salt

Bring broth and wine to boil. Add butter, rice, and salt. Stir. Pour into greased 8-inch square or 1 ½- to 2-quart baking dish. Cover and bake at 350 degrees for 1 hour.

Kiwi Chutney

2 quarts

12 ripe kiwi, peeled and sliced
3 medium onions, finely chopped
1 lemon, sliced very thin, seeds removed
2 to 3 tablespoons crystalized ginger
1 teaspoon ground ginger
1 cup raisins
½ teaspoon salt
½ teaspoon cayenne pepper
2 pounds brown sugar
½ cup vinegar

➤ This zippy chutney may be canned or frozen. Try it over cream cheese as an appetizer. This makes a welcome gift.

Combine all ingredients in a large saucepan. Simmer for 2 hours, stirring frequently to break down kiwis. Pour into shallow pan and cool completely. Refrigerate or place in sterile jars and seal. Serve cold.

Sour Cherry Chutney

1 quart

2 garlic cloves, minced
3 to 3 ½ cups chopped pitted dark cherries
½ cup raisins
1 ½ cups brown sugar
3 ounces cider vinegar
½ tablespoon salt
⅛ teaspoon ground cloves
⅛ teaspoon cayenne pepper

➤ Show off this sweet-and-sour relish in a crystal bowl.

Combine first 5 ingredients in large saucepan and bring to a boil. Lower heat and simmer uncovered for 1 hour and 20 minutes, stirring occasionally. During last 40 minutes, add salt, cloves, and pepper. Cool and refrigerate or store in sterilized jars. Serve chutney cold with steak, beef roast, pork chops, or Cornish hen.

The amount of garlic may be varied according to preference. May substitute same amount of tomatoes for cherries.

Peach Chutney

4 ½ cups

➤ A wonderful tangy flavor to accompany game or lamb. Or try it on Brie or cream cheese as an appetizer.

1 ½ cups cider vinegar
1 ¼ cups sugar
1 ¼ cups light brown sugar
3 ½ cups chopped peaches
½ cup golden raisins
1 tablespoon lemon juice
1 teaspoon minced fresh ginger root
1 teaspoon cinnamon
¾ teaspoon salt
¾ teaspoon dry mustard
½ teaspoon minced garlic
¼ to ½ teaspoon cayenne pepper

Bring vinegar and sugar to a boil. Reduce heat and add remaining ingredients. Simmer until mixture thickens slightly, about 25 minutes. Cool and refrigerate or store in sterilized jars.

Garden Bounty Relish

6 servings

5 medium tomatoes, peeled, seeded, and chopped
1 medium green pepper, finely chopped
1 medium onion, finely chopped
1 stalk celery, finely chopped
1 tablespoon prepared horseradish
2 teaspoons salt
⅔ cup vinegar
½ cup sugar
1 teaspoon mustard seed
⅛ teaspoon ground cloves
Freshly ground black pepper

Combine tomatoes, other chopped vegetables, horseradish, and salt. Cover, let stand for 2 hours at room temperature. Drain thoroughly.

Stir remaining ingredients into vegetable mixture. Chill in covered container at least 24 hours before serving.

Tangy Mustard Ring

12 servings

4 eggs	*¼ cup water*
1 tablespoon dry mustard	*1 tablespoon unflavored gelatin*
½ teaspoon salt	*¼ cup hot water*
¾ cup sugar	*1 cup whipping cream*
¾ cup cider vinegar	

➤ A treat for mustard lovers, this is great with ham or roast beef!

Garnish

Cherry tomatoes	*Fresh parsley*

Beat eggs. Add mustard, salt, sugar, vinegar, and ¼ cup water. Dissolve gelatin in hot water. Mix egg mixture with gelatin mixture. Cook in double boiler until thickened. Let cool. Meanwhile, whip cream. Fold into cooled egg mixture. Lightly oil a 5-cup mold or ring. Do not use a vegetable oil spray. Pour mixture into mold and refrigerate at least 3 hours.

When ready to serve, dip mold in warm water for 10 seconds, being careful not to let water go over rim. Place serving dish on top of mold and invert. Shake gently to release ring from mold. If ring does not unmold, repeat process. Fill center of ring with cherry tomatoes and garnish outer edge with fresh parsley.

May be made 3 to 24 hours prior to serving. Unmold just before serving.

Even though Mr. Lincoln supposedly could not resist Mary Todd's White Cake, he probably would not have been able to refuse a piece of this elegant Victorian Sandwich Cake. Completing the picture are Lincoln's kid gloves; a hand tooled leather copy of Edward and Mary Bod's The Man in the White House, highlighting Lincoln's trials as a wartime leader; Mary Todd Lincoln's book of sheet music, and silver ice tongs, a gift to the Lincolns while living in Springfield.

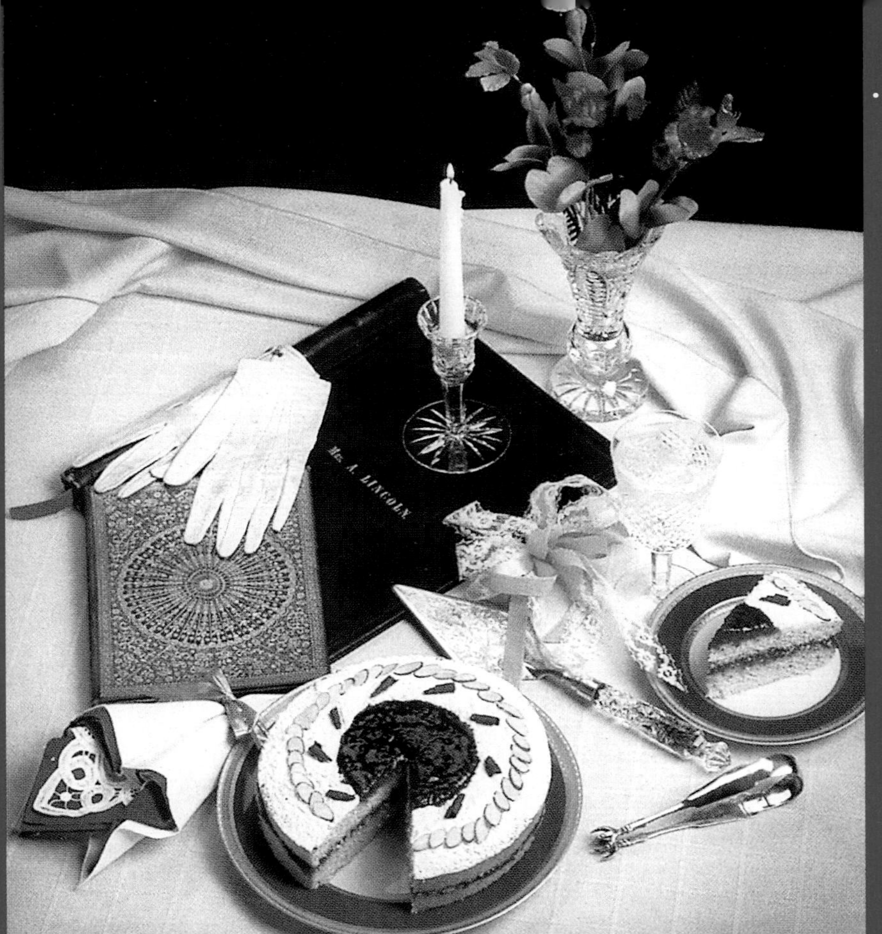

DESSERTS

Lincoln enjoyed a strong cup of coffee. Once, after being served an unidentified, steaming beverage he said to the waiter: ***"If this is coffee, please bring me a cup of tea, but on the other hand, if this is tea, please bring me a cup of coffee."***

The Ultimate Chocolate Cake

12 servings

➤ The cake lives up to its name.

2 ½ cups flour	*2 eggs*
1 ¾ teaspoons baking soda	*3 ounces unsweetened chocolate, melted*
1 ¼ teaspoons baking powder	*1 teaspoon vanilla*
⅔ cup butter	*1 ½ cups buttermilk*
1 ¾ cups sugar	*Cocoa*

Sift together flour, baking soda, and baking powder; set aside. Cream butter until fluffy; add sugar and cream well. Add eggs, one at a time, beating well after each addition. Add chocolate and vanilla. Add dry ingredients alternately with buttermilk. Mix well. Grease two 8- or 9-inch round cake pans; dust pans with cocoa. Pour batter into pans. Bake at 350 degrees for 25 to 30 minutes or until cake tests done. Let layers cool in pans for 10 minutes; remove from pans and finish cooling on racks. Assemble layers and frost with The Ultimate Chocolate Icing.

Substitution for buttermilk: Combine 1 ½ tablespoons vinegar to enough milk to make 1 ½ cups. Let stand for 10 minutes or until it curdles.

The Ultimate Chocolate Icing

4 ounces unsweetened chocolate	*1 teaspoon vanilla*
⅓ cup butter	*⅓ cup plus 2 tablespoons evaporated milk, heated*
3 cups sifted powdered sugar	
⅛ teaspoon salt	

Melt chocolate and butter together in top of double boiler or slowly in microwave oven. In bowl, combine sugar, salt, vanilla, and evaporated milk. Add melted chocolate mixture. Beat until icing thickens. Cool to room temperature before spreading on The Ultimate Chocolate Cake.

Fresh Apple Cake with Carmel Sauce

12 to 16 servings

2 eggs, beaten
2 cups sugar
½ cup oil
2 cups flour
2 teaspoons cinnamon
1 ½ teaspoons baking soda
1 teaspoon salt
2 cups broken pecans or walnut pieces
4 cups peeled and sliced apples

➤ This was the favorite apple cake during recipe testing.

Beat together eggs, sugar, and oil in large bowl. In another bowl, combine flour, cinnamon, baking soda, and salt. Add dry ingredients to sugar mixture. Batter will be thick. Stir in nuts and apples. Spread batter into greased and floured 9x13 inch baking pan. Bake at 350 degrees for 50 minutes. Serve warm with Caramel Sauce.

Carmel Sauce

½ cup butter
1 tablespoon flour
½ cup brown sugar
½ cup white sugar
½ cup evaporated milk
1 teaspoon vanilla

Combine butter, flour, sugars, and evaporated milk in saucepan. Bring mixture to a boil for 1 to 2 minutes, stirring constantly. Remove from heat. Stir in vanilla; cool. Serve on warm Fresh Apple Cake.

Lizzie Cake

6 to 9 servings

¼ cup butter
¾ cup sugar
2 eggs
1 egg yolk
1 cup flour
½ teaspoon grated lemon peel
1 cup blueberries
3 ounces semi-sweet chocolate

➤ This unusual cake will disappear quickly.

Garnish

Sweetened whipped cream

Cream butter; add sugar and beat. Add eggs and egg yolk. Mix well. Add flour and lemon peel; mix. Pour batter into greased and floured 8-inch square pan. Sprinkle blueberries on top. Bake at 325 degrees for 45 minutes. Remove from oven and let cool 10 minutes. Remove from pan and finish cooling on rack with blueberries on top.

Melt chocolate. Invert cake. Spread with chocolate. Let cool and harden. Invert again so blueberries are on top. Serve with sweetened whipped cream.

Art Fair Sunshine Cake

10 to 12 servings

➤ A refreshing cake for spring — or whenever you want springtime flavor.

½ cup butter	*1 teaspoon baking powder*
1 cup sugar	*1 cup sour cream*
1 egg	*1 cup chopped nuts*
1 ¾ cups flour	*Grated peel of 1 lemon*
1 teaspoon baking soda	*Grated peel of 1 orange*

Cream butter, sugar, and egg. Add flour, baking soda, baking powder, sour cream, chopped nuts, and grated peels. Mix well. Spoon into greased and floured bundt pan. Bake at 350 degrees for 40 minutes. Remove from oven. Let cool 10 minutes and remove from pan.

Citrus Glaze

1 cup sifted powdered sugar	*Juice of 1 orange*
Juice of 1 lemon	

Mix powdered sugar with juices. Stir well. Slowly spoon glaze over warm cake.

Cinnamon Pudding Cake

6 to 9 servings

➤ Something wonderful for the family on a winter evening.

1 ¾ cups brown sugar	*½ teaspoon salt*
1 ½ cups water	*2 ½ teaspoons cinnamon*
4 tablespoons butter (divided use)	*1 cup sugar*
2 cups flour	*1 cup milk*
2 teaspoons baking powder	*½ cup chopped pecans*

Garnish

Sweetened whipped cream

In a small pan, bring to a boil brown sugar, water and 2 tablespoons butter and set aside. Mix together flour, baking powder, salt, cinnamon, 2 tablespoons melted butter, sugar, and milk. Pour into greased 9-inch square pan. Pour brown sugar mixture over cake. Sprinkle chopped pecans over top. Bake at 350 degrees for 30 minutes. Serve warm with sweetened whipped cream.

Victorian Sandwich Cake

8 to 10 servings

➤ An elegant cake to serve at tea time.

1 cup butter	*1 ½ teaspoons baking powder*
1 ⅓ cups sugar	*½ teaspoon salt*
4 eggs	*Powdered sugar*
2 cups flour	*Lemon Curd*

Garnish

Slivered almonds	*Chocolate curls*

In a bowl, cream together butter and sugar until mixture is light and fluffy. Add eggs, one at a time, beating well after each addition. In another bowl, stir together flour, baking powder, and salt. Slowly add dry ingredients to butter mixture; mix well. Pour batter into 2 greased 9-inch round cake pans. Bake at 375 degrees for 15 to 20 minutes or until inserted toothpick comes out clean. Cool layers in pans for 10 minutes; cool completely on racks.

Place 1 layer on serving plate; spread Lemon Curd on top. Place 2nd layer on top. Dust top with powdered sugar. Carefully spread Lemon Curd in 4-inch circle on center of top layer. Garnish with almonds and chocolate curls.

Lemon Curd

½ cup butter	*Juice of 3 large lemons*
3 eggs	*Grated peel of 1 lemon*
3 egg yolks	*¼ teaspoon salt*
1 ½ cups sugar	

Melt butter in top of double boiler. Beat eggs and yolks together; add sugar, lemon juice, grated peel, and salt. Add to melted butter. Cook over simmering water, stirring constantly, until mixture is shiny and thickened. Cool completely. Lemon Curd will continue to thicken as it cools.

For a different taste, try raspberry or apricot jam instead of Lemon Curd.

Aunt Belle's Prune Cake

10 servings

➤ Sweet and spicy, this moist cake elegantly combines old-fashioned flavors.

15 prunes
1 ½ cups sugar
3 eggs
1 cup oil
1 cup buttermilk
2 cups flour
1 teaspoon baking powder
1 teaspoon baking soda
1 teaspoon cinnamon
1 teaspoon nutmeg
½ teaspoon salt

In a saucepan, cover prunes with water and simmer 10 minutes or until tender. Drain. Remove pits and chop.

Mix sugar, eggs, oil, and buttermilk until well blended. Combine flour, baking powder, baking soda, cinnamon, nutmeg, and salt in a separate bowl. Add prunes to sugar mixture. Blend in dry ingredients. Pour batter into 2 greased and floured 8-inch round cake pans. Bake at 375 degrees for 20 to 22 minutes. Remove from oven, cool in pans 15 minutes, then remove from pans and finish cooling on racks. Frost with Coffee Icing.

Coffee Icing

⅓ cup butter, softened
3 cups powdered sugar
½ teaspoon vanilla
1 tablespoon very strong coffee
1 tablespoon milk

Blend butter and sugar. Add vanilla, coffee, and milk. Beat until smooth.

Lincoln Park Pound Cake

12 to 16 servings

➤ This cake is wonderful plain or topped with fruits, ice cream, or Caramel Sauce.

1 ½ cups butter, softened
3 cups sugar
1 teaspoon vanilla
1 teaspoon lemon juice
5 eggs
3 cups flour
1 cup evaporated milk

Combine butter, sugar, vanilla, and lemon juice. Beat well. Add eggs, beating well after each one. Beginning and ending with flour, add flour and evaporated milk alternately. Pour into greased and floured bundt pan or 10-inch tube pan. Bake at 300 degrees for 1 hour 45 minutes. Cool before removing from pan.

Sweet Rhubarb Cake

12 to 16 servings

½ cup butter
1 ½ cups brown sugar
2 eggs
2 cups flour
1 teaspoon baking soda
½ teaspoon salt
1 cup buttermilk
1 teaspoon vanilla
2 cups chopped fresh or frozen rhubarb

Topping

⅓ cup sugar
¼ teaspoon cinnamon
½ cup chopped nuts
1 cup flaked coconut

➤ A delight served with homemade vanilla ice cream.

Cream butter and brown sugar. Add eggs and beat until creamy. In another bowl, stir dry ingredients together and add buttermilk. Mix into brown sugar mixture. Stir in vanilla and rhubarb. Spoon into greased and floured 9x13 inch pan.

Mix all topping ingredients together. Sprinkle on cake. Bake at 350 degrees for 50 minutes.

Date Chocolate Chip Cake

12 to 16 servings

1 cup chopped dates
1 ½ cups boiling water
½ cup butter or margarine
1 ½ cups sugar (divided use)
1 ½ teaspoons baking soda (divided use)
2 eggs, well beaten
1 ¾ cups flour
¼ teaspoon salt
1 cup chocolate chips, semi-sweet or milk chocolate
½ cup chopped nuts

Garnish

Sweetened whipped cream

➤ This attractive cake has a delicious and unusual flavor.

Combine dates and boiling water. Set aside to cool. Cream butter with 1 cup sugar and ¾ teaspoon baking soda. Add eggs. Sift together flour, salt, and remaining ¾ teaspoon baking soda. Add flour mixture and date mixture alternately to creamed mixture. Batter will be thinner than most cake batter. Pour into greased 9x13 inch pan. Sprinkle with chocolate chips, nuts, and ½ cup sugar. Bake at 350 degrees for 35 minutes. Serve with sweetened whipped cream.

Best Blueberry Spice Cake

9 servings

½ cup shortening	*½ teaspoon salt*
1 cup plus 3 tablespoons sugar (divided use)	*1 teaspoon cinnamon (divided use)*
1 egg	*¼ teaspoon ginger*
3 tablespoons molasses	*¼ teaspoon cloves*
2 cups flour	*1 cup buttermilk*
1 teaspoon baking soda	*2 cups blueberries*

Topping

1 cup whipping cream	*2 tablespoons honey*

Cream shortening with 1 cup sugar and egg. Beat in molasses. Sift flour, baking soda, salt, ½ teaspoon cinnamon, ginger, and cloves into another bowl. Add the dry ingredients and buttermilk alternately to the creamed mixture. Mix thoroughly. Gently fold in blueberries. Pour into greased and floured 9-inch square baking pan. Mix together 3 tablespoons sugar and ½ teaspoon cinnamon. Sprinkle over the top. Bake at 350 degrees for 50 to 60 minutes or until golden brown.

Whip together cream and honey until soft peaks form. Place a dollop on each serving.

Lemon Sauce

2 cups

➤ Try this refreshing sauce with Fresh Apple Cake, Lincoln Park Pound Cake or Best Blueberry Spice Cake.

¾ cup sugar	*1 ½ cups water*
1 tablespoon plus 1 ½ teaspoons cornstarch	*¼ cup lemon juice*
1 egg, beaten	*2 teaspoons grated lemon peel or very thin strips (optional)*

Combine sugar and cornstarch in saucepan. Slowly stir in egg and water. Bring to boil, stirring constantly. Cook for 1 minute. Remove from heat. Add lemon juice and peel. Chill.

Black Walnut Cake

12 to 16 servings

2 cups sugar
½ cup shortening or butter
2 egg whites
1 teaspoon baking soda
1 teaspoon vanilla
1 ¾ cups buttermilk
2 ¾ cups cake flour
1 cup coarsely chopped black walnuts

➤ Enjoy this flavorful cake topped with fresh whipped cream or sliced like tea bread with a swirl of soft butter or cream cheese.

Cream sugar, butter, and egg whites for 5 minutes. Stir baking soda and vanilla into buttermilk. Add flour and buttermilk mixture alternately to creamed mixture, beginning and ending with flour. Fold in nuts. Pour into greased and floured 9x13 inch pan or two 9x5 inch loaf pans. Bake at 350 degrees for 30 to 40 minutes or until toothpick inserted in center comes out clean.

Pineapple Sheet Cake

24 servings

2 cups flour
2 cups sugar
2 teaspoons baking soda
2 eggs, beaten
1 teaspoon vanilla
1 20-ounce can crushed pineapple with juice
1 cup chopped nuts (optional)

➤ A quick and easy cake for potlucks or picnics.

Combine all ingredients for cake. Pour into greased and floured 10x16 inch sheet cake pan. Bake at 350 degrees for 25 to 30 minutes or until cake begins to brown. Remove from oven and frost with Cream Cheese Icing. Cool and serve.

Cream Cheese Icing

8 ounces cream cheese, softened
2 tablespoons butter
2 cups powdered sugar
1 teaspoon vanilla
½ cup chopped nuts (optional)

Combine cream cheese, butter, powdered sugar, and vanilla. Mix well. Spread icing on warm cake. If desired, sprinkle with nuts.

Pumpkin Walnut Log

12 servings

➤ A beautiful holiday dessert.

3 eggs, room temperature	*½ teaspoon nutmeg*
1 cup sugar	*½ teaspoon cloves*
⅔ cup canned pumpkin	*½ teaspoon salt*
1 teaspoon lemon juice	*1 cup walnuts, finely chopped*
¾ cup flour	*Powdered sugar*
1 teaspoon baking powder	*1 cup whipping cream*
2 teaspoons cinnamon	*2 tablespoons honey*
¾ teaspoon ginger	

Beat eggs on high speed for 5 minutes; gradually beat in sugar. Stir in pumpkin and lemon juice. In separate bowl, combine flour, baking powder, cinnamon, ginger, nutmeg, cloves, and salt. Fold pumpkin mixture into dry ingredients. Spread batter in greased and floured 10x15 inch jelly roll pan. Top with walnuts. Bake at 350 degrees for 12 to 15 minutes. Remove from oven and immediately turn cake out on cloth towel sprinkled with powdered sugar. Starting at narrow end, roll up cake together with towel. Let cool completely.

Whip cream with honey until soft peaks form. Carefully unroll cooled cake; spread whipped cream over cake. Roll up again. Chill until ready to serve.

Election Night Rum Cake

12 to 16 servings

1 cup chopped pecans	*4 eggs*
1 18 ½-ounce yellow cake mix, without pudding	*½ cup cold water*
1 3-ounce package instant vanilla pudding	*½ cup oil*
	½ cup rum

➤ An easy dessert for any celebration.

Sprinkle pecans on bottom of 10-inch greased tube pan or 12-cup bundt pan. Mix remaining cake ingredients with electric mixer. Blend thoroughly. Pour mixture into pan over pecans. Bake at 350 degrees for 1 hour. Remove from oven and cool on rack. Invert onto serving plate. Prick top of cake with toothpick. Spoon warm Rum glaze over cake.

Rum Glaze

½ cup butter	*1 cup sugar*
¼ cup water	*½ cup rum*

Melt butter in saucepan. Stir in water and sugar. Boil 5 minutes while stirring constantly. Remove saucepan from heat and stir in rum.

Banana and Sour Cream Cake

12 servings

½ cup unsalted butter	*½ teaspoon baking powder*
1 ½ cups sugar	*½ teaspoon salt*
2 eggs	*1 cup sour cream*
2 cups sifted cake flour	*1 cup mashed ripe bananas*
1 teaspoon baking soda	*1 teaspoon vanilla*

Cream butter with sugar. Add eggs and blend well. Combine and sift dry ingredients; add alternately with sour cream and mashed bananas to creamed mixture. Add vanilla. Spread in 2 greased and floured 9-inch round cake pans. Bake at 350 degrees for 40 minutes. Test for doneness with toothpick inserted in center. Remove from oven, cool in pans 10 minutes, then remove from pans and finish cooling on racks. Frost with Orange Icing.

Orange Icing

⅓ cup butter, softened	*Grated peel of 1 orange*
3 cups powdered sugar	*2 to 3 tablespoons orange juice*
1 teaspoon vanilla	

Cream butter and beat in sugar. Add vanilla, orange peel and 2 tablespoons orange juice. Beat well. Add more orange juice if needed for desired spreading consistency.

GRAPE PECAN TORTE

10 servings

➤ This elegant dessert is a Christmas tradition for one Springfield family.

6 egg whites, room temperature	*2 tablespoons orange-flavored liqueur or 1 teaspoon grated orange peel*
⅛ teaspoon salt	*2 1-ounce squares semi-sweet chocolate, shaved into curls*
1 ½ cups sugar	*2 cups seedless green grapes, halved*
1 teaspoon vinegar	*2 cups seedless red grapes, halved*
½ teaspoon vanilla	*¾ cup broken pecans*
1 ½ cups whipping cream	
¼ cup powdered sugar	

Draw two 9-inch circles on waxed paper and place on baking sheets. In large bowl, beat egg whites and salt until foamy. Beat in sugar, 2 tablespoons at a time, until all is added and egg whites are stiff. Beat in vinegar and vanilla. Spread half of mixture on each waxed paper circle. Bake at 250 degrees for 1 hour or until hard. Cool completely.

Combine whipping cream, sugar, and liqueur or orange peel; beat until stiff. Place 1 meringue circle on serving plate. Spread with half of whipped cream. Sprinkle with half of green and red grapes, nuts, and chocolate. Top with second meringue circle and repeat. Refrigerate up to 4 hours.

Other fresh fruits, such as peaches, may be used.

SWEETWATER STRAWBERRY SHORTBREAD

8 servings

½ cup butter	*1 cup whipping cream*
½ cup brown sugar (divided use)	*1 teaspoon vanilla*
1 cup chopped nuts	*¼ cup sugar*
1 cup flour	*4 cups chopped strawberries, drained*

Combine butter, ¼ cup brown sugar, nuts, and flour. Press into 9-inch springform pan. Bake at 350 degrees for 25 minutes. Cool.

Combine cream, vanilla, sugar, and remaining brown sugar. Beat until fluffy. Fold in strawberries. Spread over shortbread. Refrigerate several hours. Remove from springform pan and serve.

May be frozen, but thaw before serving.

Cheesecake with Chocolate Crust and Raspberry Sauce

12 servings

Crust

7 ounces thin chocolate wafer cookies, crushed

¼ cup butter, melted

Filling

24 ounces cream cheese, room temperature

½ cup sugar

4 eggs, room temperature

1 tablespoon vanilla

Sauce

1 tablespoon cornstarch

3 tablespoons sugar

10 ounces frozen raspberries

For crust, combine butter and cookie crumbs. Press in bottom of 9-inch springform pan. Bake at 375 degrees for 15 minutes. Cool.

For filling, beat cream cheese until fluffy, gradually adding sugar. Add eggs, 1 at a time, beating just until incorporated. Stir in vanilla. Pour over cooled crust and bake at 350 degrees for 40 minutes until almost firm. Turn off oven; leaving door ajar, let cheesecake cool until room temperature. Refrigerate at least 6 hours.

For sauce, mix cornstarch and sugar in saucepan. Force berries through a sieve to remove seeds. Add berry juice to cornstarch mixture. Bring to a boil, stirring constantly, for 1 minute. Remove from heat and cool. Spoon over cheesecake when ready to serve.

Strawberry Pecan Cheesecake

12 servings

Crust

¾ cup coarsely ground pecans	*3 tablespoons butter, melted*
¾ cup finely crushed graham cracker crumbs	*1 tablespoon sugar*

Filling

32 ounces cream cheese	*1 tablespoon lemon juice*
4 eggs	*1 teaspoon grated lemon peel*
1 ¼ cups sugar	*2 teaspoons vanilla*

Topping

1 ½ cups sour cream	*1 teaspoon vanilla*
3 tablespoons sugar	

Strawberry Glaze

1 quart strawberries	*¼ cup orange-flavored liqueur*
2 tablespoons cornstarch	*¼ cup water*
12 ounces strawberry, raspberry, or red currant jelly	

To make crust, combine pecans, graham cracker crumbs, butter and sugar. Press in bottom of buttered 9- or 10-inch springform pan.

Using an electric mixer, beat cream cheese until smooth. Add eggs, sugar, lemon juice, lemon peel, and vanilla; beat on low speed until mixed. Spoon filling over crust. Place pan on baking sheet and bake at 350 degrees for 45 to 50 minutes. Remove cheesecake from oven and let stand on cooling rack for 15 minutes.

While cake is baking, prepare topping by combining sour cream, sugar, and vanilla; mix well. Cover and refrigerate until ready to use. Spoon topping on top of cooled cheesecake, spreading ½ inch from edge. Return cheesecake to oven and bake at 350 degrees for 5 minutes. Remove from oven and cool. Refrigerate up to 3 days before serving.

Prepare the glaze the day the cheesecake is served. Hull, wash, dry, and halve strawberries. Combine 4 ounces of jelly with cornstarch in saucepan; blend well. Add remainder of jelly, orange-flavored liqueur, and water. Cook over medium heat, stirring frequently until thick and clear, about 5 to 10 minutes. Cool to lukewarm. Arrange strawberries on top of cheesecake; spoon glaze over berries. Refrigerate until topping is set.

Grand Cheesecake

12 servings

24 ounces creamed cottage cheese, at room temperature	*⅓ cup cornstarch*
16 ounces cream cheese, softened	*1 cup egg yolks*
½ cup plus 2 tablespoons butter, softened	*½ cup sour cream*
1 ¾ cups sugar	*2 teaspoons vanilla*
	1 ½ teaspoon salt

➤ This beautiful golden-topped cheesecake is wonderful with your favorite fruit topping.

Cream cottage cheese and cream cheese together in blender or food processor. Pour into large mixing bowl. Add butter, sugar, and cornstarch; blend until smooth. Add egg yolks, sour cream, vanilla, and salt. Blend well. Pour into buttered and floured deep 10-inch springform pan. Bake at 375 degrees for about 1 hour or until set. Knife will come out clean when inserted in center. Turn off oven and allow cake to remain in oven with door ajar until cooled to room temperature. Refrigerate several hours. Serve.

Mini Cheesecakes

2 dozen

9 ounces cream cheese, softened (divided use)	*⅓ cup sugar*
½ cup butter, softened	*1 teaspoon grated lemon peel*
1 cup flour	*1 egg*

Topping

12 strawberries, halved (optional)	*Strawberry jam or jelly, warmed slightly*

Beat 3 ounces cream cheese and butter. Add flour and mix well. Shape dough into 24 balls and place into mini-cupcake pans. Press dough onto bottoms and sides to line cups.

Combine 6 ounces cream cheese, sugar, grated lemon peel, and egg. Beat well. Fill pastry-lined cups ¾ full. Bake at 350 degrees for 30 minutes. Let cool in pans. If desired, top each with strawberry half. Spoon a little jam or jelly on each as a glaze.

Upside Down Date Pudding

9 servings

1 cup pitted dates
2 ½ cups boiling water (divided use)
2 cups brown sugar (divided use)
½ cup granulated sugar
1 egg
2 tablespoons butter, melted
1 ½ cups flour
1 teaspoon baking soda
½ teaspoon baking powder
½ teaspoon salt
1 cup walnuts
1 tablespoon butter

Garnish

Sweetened whipped cream

Combine dates and 1 cup boiling water; set aside. Mix together ½ cup brown sugar, granulated sugar, egg, and melted butter. Sift together flour, baking soda, baking powder, and salt; add to sugar mixture. Stir in nuts and dates with water. Pour into 7x11 inch baking dish.

Combine 1 ½ cups brown sugar, remaining butter and 1 ½ cups boiling water. Pour over date batter. Bake at 375 degrees for 40 minutes. Cut into 9 servings; invert onto serving plates. Garnish with sweetened whipped cream.

Genuine Lemon Custard

4 servings

1 tablespoon butter
¾ cup sugar
2 tablespoons flour
⅛ teaspoon salt
2 eggs, separated
1 cup milk
¼ cup lemon juice
1 ½ tablespoons grated lemon peel

Cream butter and sugar. Add flour and salt. Beat egg yolks; add milk, lemon juice, and lemon peel. Add to butter mixture. Beat egg whites until stiff and fold whites into lemon mixture. Pour into buttered 8-inch square baking dish; place dish in pan of hot water. Bake at 350 degrees for 30 minutes or until custard is set. Spoon into serving bowls.

A roasting pan works well to hold water and baking dish. Heat water in pan while preheating oven.

Never Enough Peach Cobbler

12 servings

1 ½ cups sugar (divided use)
1 cup flour
2 teaspoons baking powder
½ cup milk
1 tablespoon oil
2 29-ounce cans sliced peaches
1 tablespoon butter
½ teaspoon almond extract
1 tablespoon lemon juice

➤ Just like Grandma used to make.

Stir together ½ cup sugar, flour, baking powder, milk, and oil in order listed. Pour batter into ungreased 9x13 inch baking dish. Drain 1 can of peaches. Mix drained and undrained peaches, butter, and 1 cup sugar in large saucepan. Bring to boil and cook until sugar dissolves. Remove from heat. Add almond extract and lemon juice. Pour immediately over batter. Bake at 375 degrees for 45 minutes.

Summer Fruit Cobbler

9 servings

1 cup flour
1 tablespoon brown sugar
¼ teaspoon cinnamon
½ teaspoon baking powder
⅜ teaspoon salt (divided use)
⅓ plus 1 tablespoon shortening
3 tablespoons milk
1 cup plus 1 teaspoon sugar (divided use)
2 tablespoons quick cooking tapioca
4 cups fresh fruit (sliced peaches or blueberries, or 3 cups peaches and 1 cup blueberries)
⅓ cup water
1 tablespoon lemon juice
1 teaspoon grated lemon peel
3 tablespoons butter
⅛ teaspoon cinnamon

➤ A warm and homey dessert.

Mix flour, brown sugar, baking powder, cinnamon, and ⅛ teaspoon salt. Cut in shortening and add enough milk to form a soft dough. Pat or roll out dough on floured pastry cloth to fit 7x11 inch or 9-inch square baking dish. Set aside.

Mix 1 cup sugar, tapioca, and ¼ teaspoon salt. Stir in fruit, water, lemon juice, and peel. Pour into greased baking dish. Dot with butter. Cover fruit with pastry crust and cut 4 slits on top. Mix 1 teaspoon sugar and cinnamon; sprinkle over crust. Bake at 375 degrees for 40 minutes.

Sautéed Apples with Rum Sauce

8 servings

➤ This grown-up comfort food combines down-home flavors in an elegant manner.

Rum Sauce

6 egg yolks, slightly beaten
1 cup whipping cream
1 cup milk, heated
½ cup sugar
3 tablespoons dark rum
2 teaspoons vanilla

Combine egg yolks, cream, milk, and sugar in top of double boiler. Cook over simmering water, stirring frequently until sauce thickens, about 30 minutes. Remove from heat and stir in rum and vanilla. Chill.

3 tablespoons butter
10 cups Golden Delicious apples, peeled and thickly sliced
¾ cup raisins
⅓ cup sugar
1 teaspoon grated lemon peel
½ teaspoon cinnamon
¼ teaspoon nutmeg

Garnish

Toasted pecan pieces

Melt butter in large skillet. Add remaining ingredients, except nutmeg. Sauté over medium heat until apples are soft, about 10 minutes. Sprinkle with nutmeg. Serve warm with chilled Rum Sauce. Sprinkle with pecans.

Apple Cheddar Pie

8 servings

8 cups sliced, pared apples
2 tablespoons lemon juice
¼ cup flour
⅓ to ½ cup brown sugar
⅛ teaspoon nutmeg
1 teaspoon cinnamon
1 10-inch unbaked pie shell
6 ounces sharp Cheddar cheese, shredded

Streusel Topping

⅔ cup flour
½ cup brown sugar
⅓ cup butter

Combine apples with lemon juice in a large bowl. Mix together ¼ cup flour, ⅓ cup to ½ cup brown sugar, nutmeg, and cinnamon in a separate bowl. Add to apples and mix. Place in pie shell. Top with Cheddar cheese.

For topping, mix ⅔ cup flour and ½ cup brown sugar; cut in butter until mixture is crumbly. Spoon streusel topping over shredded cheese, making sure cheese is completely covered so it will not burn. Bake at 425 degrees for 30 to 35 minutes or until bubbly and golden brown.

This pie is at its best when served warm.

Pie with Pizazz

8 servings

3 eggs, beaten
1 cup sugar
½ cup light corn syrup
¼ cup butter, softened
¼ cup flour
2 tablespoons bourbon or brandy
½ cup semi-sweet chocolate chips
¾ cup large pecan pieces
1 9-inch unbaked pie shell

➤ Great plain or topped with whipped cream!

Mix eggs, sugar, and corn syrup. Add butter and mix. Stir in flour. Mix in bourbon or brandy, chocolate chips, and pecans. Pour into pie shell. Bake at 350 degrees for 1 hour and 10 minutes.

Pineapple Meringue Pie

8 servings

➤ Even an inexperienced baker can have beautiful results with this attractive pie.

⅓ cup plus 1 tablespoon cornstarch
1 ¼ cups sugar (divided use)
½ teaspoon salt
2 20-ounce cans unsweetened crushed pineapple, undrained
4 eggs, separated and at room temperature
2 tablespoons lemon juice
1 teaspoon grated lemon peel
1 teaspoon grated orange peel (optional)
1 10-inch baked pie shell

Combine cornstarch, ¾ cup sugar, and salt in saucepan. Stir in pineapple. Cook over low heat, stirring constantly, until clear and thickened. Beat egg yolks; stir a little hot mixture into yolks. Add egg yolks and lemon juice, lemon peel, and orange peel to hot mixture. Cook for 1 minute. Cool thoroughly. Pour filling into pie shell. Beat egg whites while slowly adding remaining ½ cup sugar; continue beating until meringue stands in stiff peaks. Swirl meringue on pie, covering entire surface to pastry rim. Bake at 425 degrees for 4 minutes or until meringue browns. Let cool and chill. Serve.

Orange Dream Pie

8 servings

Crumb Crust

½ cup butter, melted
1 ⅓ cups gingersnap or vanilla wafer crumbs
¼ cup flaked coconut

Combine butter, cookie crumbs, and coconut. Press into 9-inch pie pan. Bake at 375 degrees for 12 minutes. Cool.

Filling

1 ½ quarts vanilla ice cream, softened
1 6-ounce can frozen orange juice concentrate, thawed
¼ cup flaked coconut, toasted

Place baked pie crust in freezer for a few minutes. Remove and spread ⅓ of ice cream on crust. Drizzle ⅓ cup orange juice concentrate on top. Repeat 2 more times. Sprinkle toasted coconut over top. Freeze until ready to serve.

May substitute 9-inch baked pie shell for crumb crust.

Caramel Pecan Pie

8 servings

½ cup butter	*1 teaspoon vanilla*
1 cup light corn syrup	*⅛ teaspoon salt*
1 cup sugar	*1 cup pecan halves*
3 eggs, beaten	*1 9-inch unbaked pie shell*
1 teaspoon lemon juice	

Brown butter in large saucepan over medium heat, stirring constantly. Remove from heat. Add corn syrup, sugar, eggs, lemon juice, vanilla, salt, and pecans. Mix well; pour into pie shell. Bake at 425 degrees for 10 minutes. Reduce heat to 325 degrees and bake an additional 40 minutes. Let cool before serving.

For a crisp crust, serve soon after preparing.

Two Crust Lemon Pie

8 servings

Pastry dough for double crust 9-inch pie	*¼ cup butter, softened*
1 ½ cups sugar	*3 eggs*
2 tablespoons flour	*1 medium lemon*
⅛ teaspoon salt	*½ cup water*

➤ This unique pie is even better with vanilla ice cream.

Topping

2 teaspoons sugar	*¼ teaspoon cinnamon*

Line 9-inch pie pan with pastry dough; set aside. Combine sugar, flour, and salt. Blend in butter. After reserving 1 teaspoon egg white, beat eggs. Add eggs to sugar mixture; mix until smooth. Grate 1 teaspoon lemon peel from lemon. Then peel and cut whole lemon into paper-thin slices, about ⅓ cup. Remove seeds. Add ½ cup water, grated lemon peel, and lemon slices to sugar mixture; mix well. Pour into pie crust. Cover with top crust. Cut slits in top crust. Seal and flute edge. Brush top with egg white. Mix together topping ingredients and sprinkle over pie. Bake at 400 degrees for 30 to 35 minutes.

Peanut Butter Pie

8 servings

➤ This pie will receive rave reviews.

1 cup plus 3 tablespoons powdered sugar (divided use)

½ cup creamy peanut butter

1 9-inch baked pie shell

⅔ cup sugar

¼ cup cornstarch

⅛ teaspoon salt

2 cups milk, scalded

3 egg yolks, beaten

2 tablespoons butter

1 teaspoon vanilla

1 cup whipping cream

2 tablespoons chopped peanuts

Blend 1 cup powdered sugar with peanut butter until mixture resembles tiny pellets. Cover bottom of pie shell with ½ of mixture. Combine sugar, cornstarch, and salt in top of double boiler. Slowly pour scalded milk into egg yolks while stirring or whisking. Then slowly pour egg-milk mixture into double boiler, stirring or whisking. Stirring constantly, cook until pudding is smooth and thick.

Remove from heat. Add butter and vanilla. Working quickly, so that warm pudding will partially melt the peanut butter, pour ½ of pudding into pie shell. Cover with remaining peanut butter mixture. Top with remaining pudding. Cover and chill for several hours.

Combine whipping cream and 3 tablespoons powdered sugar. Whip until soft peaks form. Spoon sweetened whipped cream over pie. Sprinkle with peanuts.

Apple Creek Turnovers

12 servings

Pastry

2 cups flour
¼ teaspoon salt
1 cup butter, chilled and cut into pieces
⅔ cup sour cream

➤Serve with butter brickle ice cream.

Filling

3 tablespoons flour
⅛ teaspoon salt
½ cup to ⅔ cup sugar
½ teaspoon cinnamon
¼ teaspoon cloves
¼ teaspoon nutmeg
5 cups apples, peeled and thinly sliced

Mix together 2 cups flour and ¼ teaspoon salt. Cut in butter with pastry cutter or 2 knives until mixture has texture of coarse meal. Mix in sour cream. Pat into ball. Refrigerate until well chilled, at least 8 hours.

Mix together 3 tablespoons flour, ⅛ teaspoon salt, sugar (adjust amount of sugar to tartness of apples), and spices. Combine with apples. Divide dough into 4 portions. On well-floured pastry cloth, roll out dough into circle about ⅛ -inch thick. Spread ¼ of apple mixture on circle. Fold top over filling and seal edge with fork. Repeat with remaining dough and filling. Cut small slits in turnover tops to allow steam to escape during baking. Bake at 350 degrees for 30 to 40 minutes or until crust is golden brown.

Glaze

¼ cup butter, melted
1 ½ cups powdered sugar
1 teaspoon vanilla
1 to 2 tablespoons hot water

Combine butter, powdered sugar, vanilla, and enough water to make glaze. Drizzle over top of turnovers.

Lebkuchen

3 dozen cookies

➤ A traditional German Christmas cookie.

½ cup honey
½ cup molasses
¾ cup brown sugar
1 tablespoon grated lemon peel
1 tablespoon lemon juice
1 egg, slightly beaten
3 cups flour
½ teaspoon baking soda
1 teaspoon cinnamon
1 teaspoon allspice
½ teaspoon cloves
½ teaspoon nutmeg
1 cup finely chopped citron and/or nuts

Topping

Multi-colored candy sprinkles

Bring honey and molasses to a boil. Let cool. Add sugar, lemon peel, lemon juice, and egg. Sift together flour, baking soda, and spices. Add flour mixture and citron and/or nuts to honey mixture. Mix well. Chill dough at least 12 hours.

Working with half the dough, roll out to about ¼-inch thickness on floured surface. Cut into 2x3 inch bars. Place on greased baking sheet. Bake at 350 degrees for 10 to 12 minutes. Let cool. Spread Lemon Icing on bars and top with multi-colored candy sprinkles.

Lemon Icing

3 tablespoons butter, softened
1 ½ cups powdered sugar
2 tablespoons lemon juice

Mix butter and powdered sugar. Beat in lemon juice. Spread on Lebkuchen.

Rich Mint Brownies

8 dozen bars

Brownies

- *1 cup sugar*
- *1 cup flour*
- *16 ounces chocolate syrup*
- *½ cup butter, melted*
- *4 eggs*

Mint Frosting

- *½ cup butter, softened*
- *1 pound powdered sugar*
- *¼ cup milk*
- *2 teaspoons peppermint extract*
- *10 drops green food coloring*

Chocolate Glaze

- *½ cup butter or margarine*
- *12 ounces semi-sweet chocolate chips*

➤ A colorful addition to a dessert buffet.

Mix together Brownie ingredients. Pour into greased 11x16 inch baking pan or jelly roll pan. Bake at 350 degrees for 20 minutes. Cool completely.

Beat together Mint Frosting ingredients. Spread mixture evenly over cooled Brownies. Refrigerate for at least 20 minutes.

Melt together Chocolate Glaze ingredients. Spread on top of Mint Frosting. Refrigerate until firm. Cut into small squares, cleaning knife after each cut.

Simple Sesame Cookies

4 dozen cookies

- *2 cups butter, softened*
- *1 ½ cups sugar*
- *3 cups flour*
- *1 cup sesame seed*
- *2 cups flaked coconut*
- *½ cup almonds, finely chopped*

➤ A unique refrigerator cookie.

Cream butter, add sugar and mix well. Add flour. Stir in sesame seed, coconut, and almonds. Divide dough into thirds. Place one third on waxed paper. Roll into a 2-inch diameter log. Repeat with other thirds. Wrap and chill until cold. Cut into ¼-inch slices. Bake on ungreased baking sheet at 300 degrees for 30 minutes or until lightly browned.

State Fair Cheese-Date Fold Overs

2 ½ to 3 dozen cookies

➤ This Blue Ribbon winner of the 1979 Illinois State Fair Bake-Off was created 35 years ago and has been a favorite ever since!

Pastry

½ cup butter

4 ounces finely grated American or Cheddar cheese

1 ⅓ cups sifted flour

¼ teaspoon salt

2 tablespoons ice water

Date Filling

1 cup chopped pitted dates

½ cup brown sugar

¼ cup water

Cream butter and cheese until well mixed. Combine flour and salt; blend into cheese mixture. Add ice water and mix well. Chill 1 hour or longer.

Combine dates, sugar, and water. Cook over medium heat, stirring constantly, until filling is the consistency of jam. Cool slightly. Roll dough ⅛-inch thick on well-floured surface. Cut with a 2 ½- or 2 ¾-inch round cutter. Place 1 to 1 ½ teaspoons of date mixture on half of each circle. Fold in half and press edges together; press edges with tines of fork to seal in filling. Bake on ungreased baking sheet at 375 degrees for 10 to 12 minutes. Cool slightly; remove from pan.

Chewy Peanut Bars

3 dozen bars

➤ Easy, quick, and tasty.

⅔ cup butter

2 ¼ cups light brown sugar

3 eggs

1 teaspoon vanilla

2 ¼ cups flour, sifted

½ teaspoon salt

2 ½ teaspoons baking powder

1 ½ cups chocolate-covered peanuts

Melt butter. Add sugar and stir to blend thoroughly. Add eggs, one at a time, beating after each addition. Stir in vanilla. Mix together dry ingredients; stir into butter mixture until well blended. Stir in chocolate covered peanuts. Spread in greased 11x16 inch baking pan. Bake at 350 degrees for 30 minutes or until lightly browned and cookie comes away from edges of pan. Let cool. Cut into bars.

Old-Fashioned Sugar Cookies

4 dozen cookies

1 cup butter
1 ½ cups sugar
2 eggs
1 tablespoon vanilla

3 ½ cups flour
2 ½ teaspoons baking powder
½ teaspoon salt

➤ For the holidays, top cookies with colored sugar.

Beat butter, sugar, eggs, and vanilla until light and fluffy. Sift together flour, baking powder, and salt. Add dry ingredients gradually to butter mixture.

Roll dough into 1-inch balls. Place on greased baking sheet 2 inches apart. Butter bottom of a glass, dip in sugar and flatten cookies. Bake at 375 degrees for 10 minutes.

Blue Ribbon Apricot Bars

1 ½ dozen cookies

⅔ cup chopped dried apricots
1 ¼ cups sifted flour
¼ cup sugar
½ cup margarine
2 eggs

1 cup brown sugar
½ teaspoon salt
½ teaspoon baking powder
½ teaspoon vanilla

Garnish
Sliced almonds

➤ Best cookie at the 1987 Illinois State Fair.

Rinse apricots and cover with water in a saucepan. Simmer for 10 minutes. Drain and cool.

Mix together flour, sugar, and margarine until crumbly. Press into ungreased 9-inch square pan. Bake in 350 degree oven for 20 minutes.

Blend together eggs, brown sugar, salt, baking powder, and vanilla. Stir apricots into blended mixture. Spread on top of baked crust. Return to oven and bake 30 to 35 more minutes. Remove from oven; cool in pan on rack.

Cut in 3x1 ½ inch bars. Top each bar with five almond slices placed in flower design.

Glazed Apple Bars

16 servings

➤ These make great tailgate fare.

4 cups flour	*2 eggs, slightly beaten*
2 ⅓ cups sugar (divided use)	*5 to 8 apples, peeled and thinly sliced*
½ teaspoon salt	*¾ teaspoon cinnamon*
1 ½ cups butter	

Combine flour, 2 cups sugar, and salt. Cut in butter and add eggs. Mix well. Crumble ¾ of mixture in bottom of 11x16 inch pan. Pat down gently. Top with apple slices arranged neatly in rows. Combine remaining ⅓ cup sugar with cinnamon. Sprinkle over apples. Crumble remaining dough evenly over top. Bake at 350 degrees for 40 to 50 minutes. Cool before drizzling glaze over top. Cut into bars.

Glaze

1 cup sifted powdered sugar	*1 ½ teaspoons almond extract*
1 tablespoon water	

Blend powdered sugar, water, and almond extract to make glaze.

Funk's Grove Maple Syrup Bars

2 dozen cookies

½ cup butter
¼ cup sugar
1 cup flour
¾ cup brown sugar
⅓ cup maple syrup
1 tablespoons butter
1 egg
½ teaspoon vanilla
⅓ cup chopped pecans

➤ These chewy bars have a wonderful maple aroma.

Cream butter and sugar in food processor. Add flour and process until just blended. Dough does not form ball. Pat into bottom of greased 9-inch square pan. Bake at 350 degrees for 25 minutes or until lightly browned.

Beat brown sugar, syrup, and butter to blend. Beat in egg and vanilla. Pour over shortbread. Sprinkle with nuts. Bake 25 minutes or until set. Cool and cut into bars.

Keepsake Brownies

2 dozen cookies

4 ounces unsweetened baking chocolate
1 cup butter
2 cups sugar
3 eggs, beaten
1 teaspoon vanilla
1 cup flour
¼ teaspoon salt
1 cup walnuts, coarsely chopped

➤ A rich brownie for chocolate lovers.

Carefully melt chocolate and butter. Stir. Mix in sugar. Mix in eggs and vanilla. Gradually add flour and salt. Stir in nuts. Pour into greased and floured 9-inch square pan. Bake at 350 degrees for 50 to 60 minutes.

Cranberry Gems

6 dozen cookies

½ cup butter, softened
¾ cup brown sugar
1 cup sugar
⅓ cup plain yogurt
2 tablespoons orange juice
1 tablespoon grated orange peel
2 egg whites
3 cups flour
1 teaspoon baking powder
½ teaspoon allspice
¼ teaspoon salt
¼ teaspoon baking soda
½ cup chopped nuts
2 ½ cups coarsely chopped cranberries
Powdered sugar

Cream butter and sugars together. Beat in yogurt, orange juice, orange peel, and egg whites. Sift together flour, baking powder, allspice, salt, and baking soda. Blend dry ingredients into sugar mixture. Stir in chopped nuts and cranberries. Drop by teaspoonfuls onto greased baking sheets. Bake at 375 degrees for 12 to 15 minutes. Let cool. Dust with powdered sugar.

Refrigerator Shortbread

4 dozen cookies

➤ A buttery, crisp cookie.

1 cup butter
½ cup plus 2 tablespoons sugar
2 ½ cups flour

Cream butter and sugar. Mix in flour. Form into 2 rolls, each 6 inches in length. Wrap in waxed paper. Chill thoroughly.

Slice about ¼-inch thick. Place on ungreased baking sheets. Sprinkle with additional sugar. Bake at 350 degrees for 15 minutes.

These cookies change little in size or shape and remain light in color.

Nut Fingers

2 dozen cookies

2 cups finely chopped walnuts	*1 cup sugar*
1 ½ teaspoons cinnamon	*1 tablespoon fresh lemon juice*
1 pound phyllo pastry	*⅓ cup honey*
½ cup butter, melted	*½ cup water*

➤ An elegant cookie of Greek origin.

Combine walnuts and cinnamon. Place stack of phyllo pastry between sheets of plastic wrap. Remove top sheet from stack and place on work surface. Brush half of sheet with melted butter. Fold other half over buttered half. Brush top with butter. Sprinkle 1 ½ tablespoons nut mixture down the center. Fold in thirds lengthwise. Roll into 3-inch finger. Place on ungreased baking sheet. Repeat with other phyllo sheets. Bake at 350 degrees for 25 minutes or until golden brown. Cool to room temperature.

In saucepan, combine sugar, lemon juice, honey, and water. Simmer for 10 minutes. Soak fingers in warm syrup for 5 minutes. Drain on rack.

Chewy Fudge Drops

3 dozen cookies

9 ounces semi-sweet chocolate chips	*1 14 ½ ounce can sweetened condensed milk*
2 tablespoons butter	*1 cup chopped pecans*
1 cup flour	*1 teaspoon vanilla*

➤ Easy to make and delightful to eat.

Melt chocolate chips and butter in saucepan over very low heat. Add remaining ingredients and mix well. Drop by rounded teaspoonfuls onto lightly greased baking sheet. Bake at 350 degrees for 8 to 10 minutes.

Butterscotch Icebox Cookies

6 dozen cookies

➤ German in origin, this cookie has been the favorite of one Springfield family since 1935.

2 cups dark brown sugar	*1 teaspoon baking soda*
¾ cup butter	*1 teaspoon cream of tartar*
2 eggs	*¼ teaspoon salt*
3 cups flour	*4 ounces pecan halves*

Cream brown sugar and butter. Add eggs one at a time, beating well after each addition. Sift together dry ingredients; gradually add to creamed mixture. Shape into 2 rolls, each 2 inches in diameter. Wrap in waxed paper and refrigerate overnight. Slice ⅛-inch thick and place on lightly greased baking sheet. Place a pecan half on each slice. Bake at 350 degrees for 10 to 15 minutes or until golden brown.

Kolachky

3 dozen cookies

➤ A rich, filled cookie.

1 cup butter, softened	*1 ½ cups flour*
8 ounces cream cheese, softened	*½ teaspoon baking powder*
1 tablespoon milk	*1 12-ounce can pastry filling (apricot, almond, strawberry, or raspberry)*
1 tablespoon sugar	*Powdered sugar*
1 egg yolk, beaten	

Cream butter, cream cheese, milk, and sugar. Add egg yolk. Beat well. Combine flour and baking powder. Add dry ingredients to creamed mixture. Refrigerate dough overnight.

Roll out dough ¼-inch thick on floured surface. Cut into 2-inch rounds and place onto ungreased baking sheet. Depress dough in center with thumb. Fill depression with 1 teaspoon pastry filling. Bake at 400 degrees for 10 to 15 minutes. Place on rack to cool. Dust with powdered sugar.

Cinnamon Pinwheels

4 dozen cookies

1 cup butter
1 ⅔ cups flour
½ cup plus 1 tablespoon sour cream
¼ cup sugar
2 teaspoons cinnamon or cardamom

Glaze

3 tablespoons sugar
1 tablespoon water

➤ An attractive, dainty cookie.

Cut butter into flour with pastry blender. Stir in sour cream. Cover and refrigerate overnight.

Mix sugar and cinnamon. Working with half the dough, roll into a 7x20 inch rectangle on well-floured surface. Sprinkle with half the cinnamon-sugar mixture. Roll up tightly, beginning with shorter side. Wrap and refrigerate about 1 hour. Repeat with remaining dough.

Cut roll into ¼-inch slices. Place about 2 inches apart on ungreased baking sheet. Combine glaze ingredients and brush glaze over cookies. Bake at 350 degrees for 20 minutes or until golden brown.

Pepparkakar

8 dozen cookies

1 cup butter
1 ½ cups sugar
1 egg, beaten
2 tablespoons light corn syrup
3 cups flour
2 teaspoons baking soda
1 teaspoon ginger
1 teaspoon cardamom
1 teaspoon cinnamon
1 teaspoon cloves
Colored sugar sprinkles

➤ A colorful, Swedish Christmas cookie.

Cream together butter, sugar, egg, and syrup. Sift together dry ingredients and add to creamed mixture. Refrigerate overnight. Divide dough into fourths. Roll out dough very thin on well-floured surface. Cut with cookie cutter. Top with colored sugar sprinkles. Bake on ungreased baking sheet at 375 degrees for 6 minutes.

Microwave Carmel Corn

4 quarts

➤ Easy to make and wonderful to eat.

1 cup brown sugar	*½ teaspoon salt*
½ cup margarine	*½ teaspoon baking soda*
¼ cup corn syrup	*4 quarts popped popcorn*

In a large microwave-safe bowl, combine sugar, margarine, syrup, and salt; cook in microwave oven for 2 minutes on high. Add baking soda and stir well. Spray vegetable cooking spray on inside large paper bag; add popcorn. Pour syrup over popcorn; fold down bag top and cook on high for 1 ½ minutes. Shake bag well. Cook for 1 ½ minutes more. Shake bag and cook for an additional 30 seconds. Open bag and spread hot caramel corn on waxed paper to cool. Store in air-tight container.

Spiced Pecans

1 pound

➤ Spiced pecans make wonderful gifts.

1 egg white	*¼ teaspoon cinnamon*
2 tablespoons water	*¼ teaspoon cloves*
½ cup sugar	*¼ teaspoon allspice*
½ teaspoon salt	*3 cups pecan halves*

In medium bowl, whisk egg white until frothy. Blend in water, sugar, salt, cinnamon, cloves, and allspice. Add pecan halves and toss until pecans are well coated. Spread on foil-covered baking sheet. Bake at 250 degrees for 45 minutes, stirring every 15 minutes. Spread on waxed paper to cool. Store in an air-tight container.

Indian Summer Caramels

96 one-inch caramels

2 cups sugar	*3 cups whipping cream (divided use)*
1 ½ cups light corn syrup	*½ cup chopped nuts (optional)*

In large pan, mix together sugar, syrup, and 1 cup cream. Bring to a boil over medium-high heat until syrup reaches 234 degrees (soft ball) on candy thermometer. Syrup must be stirred constantly throughout cooking time to avoid scorching. Add 1 cup cream; continue cooking until temperature again reaches 234 degrees. Add remaining cup of cream; cook until syrup temperature is 234 degrees for third time. Remove from heat; add chopped nuts, if desired. Pour caramel into well-buttered 9x13 inch pan. Let cool. Cut and wrap individually in waxed paper.

Kiwi Ice

6 servings

6 kiwi, peeled and chopped
1 cup orange juice
3/4 cup light corn syrup

➤ A great palate cleanser.

Puree kiwi and strain to remove seeds. Blend kiwi juice, orange juice, and corn syrup; pour in freezer container. Freeze for 3 hours. Place kiwi ice in mixing bowl; beat until fluffy. Return to freezer until firm. To serve, let stand at room temperature for a few minutes. Spoon into individual serving bowls.

Belle Orange

4 servings

1 cup sugar
1/2 cup water
2 large navel oranges
1/3 cup orange-flavored liqueur

Garnish

Sweetened whipped cream
Toasted slivered almonds

➤ A dressy make-ahead dessert.

Mix sugar and water in saucepan. Boil for 3 minutes; let syrup cool. Peel oranges, removing all white pith. Pull sections apart and cut each section into 3 or 4 pieces. Combine oranges, syrup, and liqueur. Marinate in refrigerator for 2 hours or more. Serve in individual bowls or shallow champagne glasses. Top with whipped cream and almonds.

Orange Brandy Freeze

6 servings

➤ Attractive when served in hollowed-out orange shells or chocolate shells.

1 quart vanilla ice cream, softened

1 6-ounce can frozen orange juice concentrate, partially thawed

⅓ cup brandy

1 teaspoon lemon juice

2 drops red food coloring (optional)

8 drops yellow food coloring (optional)

Garnish

Toasted flaked coconut

Toasted slivered almonds

In bowl, combine ice cream, orange juice, brandy, lemon juice, and food coloring, if desired. Stir until completely mixed. Cover bowl tightly; freeze for up to 1 week. Garnish with toasted coconut or almonds when serving.

For a Lime Rum Freeze; substitute frozen limeade concentrate for orange concentrate, rum for brandy, and 8 drops of green food coloring for red and yellow food colorings.

Pecan Nut Crunch

8 servings

3 egg whites

1 cup sugar

½ teaspoon baking powder

¾ cup graham cracker crumbs

1 cup chopped nuts

¾ cup flaked coconut (optional)

Vanilla ice cream or sweetened whipped cream

Beat egg whites until frothy with electric mixer. Gradually add sugar; beat until stiff and glossy. Fold in baking powder, graham cracker crumbs, nuts, and coconut. Press mixture into 8-inch pie pan; smooth top. Bake at 325 degrees for 40 minutes. Refrigerate for at least 3 hours. Serve with ice cream or whipped cream.

To make bars, use a 9-inch square pan and bake for 35 minutes.

Frozen Cocoa-Nut Bars

16 servings

15 ounces cream-filled chocolate sandwich cookies, crushed
½ cup butter, melted
½ gallon ice cream, softened
1 ½ cups salted peanuts
2 cups powdered sugar
1 12-ounce can evaporated milk
1 6-ounce package semi-sweet chocolate chips
¼ cup butter

➤ A treat for all ages.

Mix cookie crumbs with melted butter. Press into ungreased 9x13 inch pan. Chill. Spread ice cream over crust. Sprinkle with peanuts. Freeze while preparing chocolate topping.

Mix powdered sugar and evaporated milk in saucepan. Stirring mixture, bring to boil for 1 minute. Remove from heat; add chocolate chips and butter. When chocolate and butter is melted, whisk mixture. Cool and spread over frozen dessert. Return to freezer until firm. Cut into bars to serve.

Frosty Pumpkin Squares

18 to 24 servings

2 cups whipping cream
3 cups graham cracker crumbs
1 cup coarsely chopped nuts
1 teaspoon vanilla
3 tablespoons powdered sugar
1 16-ounce can pumpkin
1 cup brown sugar
2 teaspoons cinnamon
1 teaspoon nutmeg
1 teaspoon salt
½ gallon vanilla ice cream, softened

Garnish

Whipped cream
Chopped nuts or pecan halves

Whip cream; combine with crumbs, nuts, vanilla, and powdered sugar. Spread in 9x13 inch pan. Place in freezer while preparing filling.

Combine pumpkin, brown sugar, cinnamon, nutmeg, and salt; mix until blended. Blend pumpkin mixture into softened ice cream. Spread over crust; cover and return to freezer. Freeze until firm, about 3 hours. Cut into squares and serve with whipped cream. Sprinkle with chopped nuts or pecan halves.

The Junior League of Springfield, Inc. gratefully acknowledges those who have supported this project by providing financial assistance and professional expertise.

The Franklin

Robert's Seafood Center
Famous-Barr
Bergner's
Marianna Munyer, Illinois Historic Preservation Agency
Dan Egler
Carlberg Grafix
Security Federal Savings and Loan
New Salem Lincoln League
Judy Winkelman, Lincoln Home
Wayne Temple, Illinois State Archives
Micro Age Computers
Thomas Schwartz, Illinois State Historical Library
Randy Vereen
Jim Helm
Dan Ortgessen
Eileen Actig
Jim Hickey
Quilt Block Makers from New Salem Contest:
Peace Basket, Donna Walzer
Tulip Time, Marcella Woods
Whig Rose, Cynthia Zoesch
New Salem State Historic Site
Illinois State Historic Library
Tom and Karen Paisley, owners and operators, Underfanger Mayflower Moving and Storage, Inc.
Holiday Inn East
Springfield Convention & Visitors Bureau
Metropolitan Life Insurance Company
Lou Holden, Mary Todd Lincoln Home
Robert Morris College
Tobin Jewelers
Craig Burkhardt of Sorling, Northrup, Hanna, Cullen and Cochran, Ltd.
Afar
Regina Santarelli
George S. Grimmett & Co.
Aletha Robinson Soule
Seasons
Stout and Lauer Jewelers

Honest to Goodness **Committee Chairs**

1989-90
Susan Helm

1990-91
Cathy Slater

1991-92
Susie Fairfield
Valerie Presney

1992-93
Suzie Pettyjohn

1993-94
Diana Auxier Brennan

1994-95
Bonnie Matheis

1995-96
Carol Beck

1996-97
Nysha Drennan

1997-98
Mysti Grant

1998-99
Jamie Stone

1999-2000
Kelli Gidcumb

2000-01
Tiffani Hamerlinck

2001-02
Mimi Power

2002-03
Karen Kloppe

2003-04
Ruth Hanken

2004-05
Tanya DeSanto

2005-06
Brandy Cathers

Honest to Goodness **Committee**

Marketing Chairman
Cathy Slater

Administrative Staff
Mary Beth Roland
Debbie Sidener

Treasurers
Jane Hasselbring
Julia Ferner

Testing Coordinators
Trish Egler
Suzie Pettyjohn

Recipe Collection Coordinators
Cindy Simmons
Jane Novotny

Graphic Design Liaisons
Shirley Lampros
Tara McVary

Production Coordinator
Suzette Engerman

Market Research Chairman
Julie Kellner

Public Relations Chairs
Linda Warmoth
Shelly Andrews
Karen Korsgard

Advisors
Florence Lee Wellons
Char Barker

Reprint Editor 2004-05
Tanya DeSanto

We salute the following members of the Junior League of Springfield who gave countless hours of recipe collection, testing, research, writing, editing, proofing, and love to make Honest to Goodness a reality. We apologize for anyone we might have missed.

Test Team Captains

Jan Andersen
Helen Appleton
Carla Barrios
Erin Bauman
Jane Bussing
Tiss Cullen
Beryl Feldman
Mary Gail Galle
Jeannette Hassebrock
Pat Huff
Gloria Lamb
Sandy Megginson
Catherine Meyer
Julie Noonan
Cindy Spengler
Sharon Turner
Florence Lee Wellons
Pat Wheat
Dottie Willard

Lisa Ahlenius
Juanita Akers
Karen Anderson
Linda Anderson
Marcia Anderson
Shelley Andrews
Jane Arbuthnot
Joanne Ashford
Mary Beth Awerkamp
Patti Backs
Patricia Bally
Karen Barber
Mary Barber
Char Barker
Sherri Barry
Susan Bauersachs
Molly Becker
Nancy Becker
Sandra Becker
Taylor Becker
Sandy Bellatti
Victoria Benn
Gina Bennett
Paula Bensko
Fran Bernard
Terri Benson
Fran Bernard
Carolyn Berning
Elizabeth Bettendorf
Lori Blankenhorn
Betty Blythe
Linda Bohan
Susan Boor
Paula Borah
Camille Bourisaw
Susan Bown
Caren Boyd
Susan Braasch
Phyllis Brissenden
Kathleen Britton
Sherrie Broughton
Cathy Brown
Mary Ellen Brown
Kathy Bruns
Barbara Burkhardt
Ann Burton
Lois Burton
Amy Butler
Anne Capestrain
Camille Carr
Lois Carroll
Rambha Chaudhary
Marita Child
Stephanie Chipman
Bert Clarke
Phoebe Clarke
Joan Colangelo
Gretchen Cooley
Diane Corcoran
Nancy Couter
Grace Curry
Betty Curtis
Julienne Davis
Mary Beth Davis
Wanza Davis
Aimee Davison
Cynthia Denby
Eileen Denham
Sandra DeNotto
Diana DeWeese
Sarah Dietel
Julie Dill
Kim Dixon
Sara Dobron
Anne Dondanville
Kathleen Dowling
Patricia Downen
Denise Druhot
Carolyn Dungan
Sandy Dunn
Nancy Durbin-White
Nancy Eck
Cathy Edson
Jill Eggebrecht
Trish Egler
Suzette Engerman
Terri Enno
Teresa Ess
Lisa Esslinger
Julie Evans
Susan Fairfield
Nancy Ferguson
Julia Ferner
Lorraine Ferry
Kathleen Fetter
Ellen Fiersten
Dee Funk
Christine Gaffigan
Jacqueline Gerber
Linda Gerber
Katherine Germeraad
Kathryn Gietl
Sandy Giganti
Elizabeth Gildner
Rosalynne Gillespy
Riv Goldman
Gayle Gonzalez
Elizabeth Grady
Vesta Gray
Violet Greenwood
Karen Gronewold
Pat Gross
Janice Gvazdinskas
Anne Haaker
Amy Haas
Ceceilia Haasis
Sharon Hadsell
Denise Hall
Diane Harvell
Jane Hasselbring
Linda Hayes
Mary Hedges
Mary Heid
Susan Helm
Rebecca Hendricks
Barbara Hennessy
Catherine Higgins
Brenda Hill
Elizabeth Hodgson
Valorie Hofferkamp
Kathi Holley
Donna Holmes
Louise Hughes
Cathy Humphrey
Patrician Humphrey
Pat Hymans
Patricia Jacobs
Ann Jakowsky
Julie Janssen
Mary Ann Janssen
Barbara Jason
Patricia Johnson
Laurie Karman
Betty Kay
Patricia Kearney
Julie Kellner
Genevieve Kelly
Rita Klemm
Stephanie Knight
Georgina Knox
Camille Koertner
Carla Kopec
Lori Kornish
Karen Korsgard
Danute Kuprenas-Durbin
Bobbie Kurmann
Julie Kyes
Mary Kay Lackman
Elizabeth LaFata
Shirley Lampros
Nancy Lane
Shirley Lanphier
Pamela Larson
Susan Laue
Joyce Lawton
Julie Leonard
Marcia Lepinski
Debra Locher
Nancy Loeb
Sara Lopinski
Susan Lowery
Jennifer Ludwig
Jane Luers
Peggy Lynch
Donna Lynn
Michelle McCarthy
Pam McDonald
Chris McEvoy
Glenda McNichols
Tara McVary
Vivion Maisenbacher
Cheri Manson
Patricia Marriott
Rebecca Martin
Colleen Maskel
Cheryl Mataejka

Ellen Matlins
Martha Mauterer
Elaine Mayer
Lucinda Meyer
Victoria Mlacnik
Anne Morgan
Linda Morrison
Deborah Murphy
Laura Myers
Karen Nachtwey
Catherine Narup
Janet Narup
Teri Neff
Luanne Nelch
Mary Jo Nelch
Elizabeth Noonan
Pat Norris
Jane Novotny
Karen Nuechterlein
Jaylee O'Neill
Mary Ossowski
Brenda Page
Roberta Pape
Jan Parr
Christine Patsche
Kathleen Patton
Suzanne Pettyjohn
Nancy Plochman
Deborah Porter
Debra Prather
Millie Prather

Valerie Presney
Linda Prola
Marjorie Purnell
Elizabeth Rambach
Juleann Randles
Lisa Remack
Mary Renner
Pam Reyhan
Carol Reynolds
Donna Riley
Penny Rinehart
Marion Robinson
Darlene Roe
Cathy Rogowski
Mary Beth Roland
Alice Rolf
Marcia Ross
Diane Rutledge
Mary Ann Salefski
Kathleen Sanders
Ellen Schanzel-Haskins
Jan Schuermann
Kyle Schultz
Barbara Schwartz
Cathy Schwartz
Cathy Schwind
Katie Semanik
Karen Shafer
Patricia Shillcutt
Laura Shott
Deborah Sidener

Cynthia Simmons
Mary Ann Singleton
Catherine Slater
Elizabeth Small
Diane Smith
Elizabeth Smith
Susan Smith
Debra Smitley
Lois Schnepp
Lisa Sondag
Gail Spengler
Sandra Spengler
Patricia Staab
Paula Stadeker
Constance Staley
Katherine Starks-Lawrence
Mary Staudt
Ann Steer
Mary Beth Stephens
Cynthia Stephenson
Doris Stern
Carol Stickney
Kathy Stittsworth
Lisa Stone
Tammy Stone
Janet Stratton
Lois Strom
Margie Stuart
Mona Summers
Carol Taylor

Sally Taylor
Janine Toman
Wanda Tracy
Anna Travelstead
Peggy Traycoff
Laura Treece
Candice Trees
Sandra Tristano
Doris Turner
Anne Unanue
Sharon Vallas
Nancy Vereen
Teena Vincent
Linda Waldron
Salli Ward
Linda Warmoth
Mary Jo Wasser
Debra Weiner
Nancy Wilderson
Beth Wilke
Linda Williams
Barbara Wolfson
Wanda Woodlock
Lynn Woods
Martha Woods
Nancy Woodward
Julie Wright
Cathy Yokley
Janet York
Caren Zentgraf

The Junior League of Springfield, Inc., wishes to thank its members, families, friends, and our community for submitting recipes for Honest to Goodness. We sincerely hope we did not overlook anyone.

Lisa Ahlenius
Jan Andersen
Karen L. Anderson
Patricia Anderson
Linda Anderson
Shelley B. Andrews
Dorothy Anker
Laura Antenan
Helen Appleton
Harriett Arkley
Joanne Ashford
Mary Beth Awerkamp
Marni Baker
Charlotte Balettie
Patricia A. Bally
Irene Barber
Karen Barber
Mary Barber

Charlaine Barker
Colleen Barnes
Carla Barrios
Carolyn Barris
Suzette Barrows
Sherri Barry
Sue Bauersachs
Erin Bauman
Mary Baumker
Mary Beaumont
Molly M. Becker
Nancy J. Becker
Ruth M. Bellatti
Sandy Bellatti
Victoria Benn
Gina Bennett
Paula Bensko
Terri B. Benson

Mina Bentsen
Frances Bernard
Carolynn Bettis
Janice Bierman
Sylvia Bigler
Claire Forsyth Billington
Doris Bishop
Jeanne Blackman
Millie Blair
Eva Mae Blaum
Brenda Bliven
Betty Blythe
Do Boardman
Christina Bock
Mary Lou Booker
Paula Borah
Joan Bortolon
Camille Bourisaw

Bess L. Bowditch
Caren Boyd
Hildegarde Brinkmann
Kathleen Britton
Mary Ellen Brown
Veronica Buckley
Cheryl Bullerman
Cissy Bunn
JoAnn Bunn
Mary Pat Burgess
Barbara J. Burris
Ann Burton
Jane L. Bussing
Janice Butler
Karen "Kay" Buzza
Sally Cadagin
Anne Capestrain
Julie Cardosi

Cindy Carrick
Julie Cellini
Aris Chavez
Stephanie Moore Chipman
Agnes R. Chrans
Lil Clark
Phoebe M. Clarke
Susan M. Clarke
Dee Clump
Nancy Cochran
Joan L. Colangelo
Evelyn Colean
Judith A. Comerio
Sandra F. Conder
Anne Condra
Nancy Couter
Gregory D. Cox
William Richard Creamer
Ramona W. Crook
Anna Grace Curry
Clarissa Cullen
Mary Shea Cummins
Karen Dammann
Shirley B. Davidson
Julie Davis
Marion Davis
Mary Beth Davis
Susan Davis
Wanza Davis
Aimee Davison
Ralph Davison
Judy Dees
Kathryn DeMent
Sandy DeNotto
Sandra Derhake
Diana DeWeese
Pam Dick
Jeanne Ann Dietrich
Sara J. Dobron
Betty J. Dodson
Anne M. Dondanville
Patsy Downen
Peter Duer
Susan Dunaway
Sandra Dunn
Nancy Durbin-White
Margaret Dyer
Kris Chapman Ealey
Susan Eby
Nancy S. Eck
Jill Eggebrecht
Dan Egler
Trish Egler
Chris Elzea
Martha Esmond
Teresa E. Ess
Frances Etson
Nancy Etson
Julie Evans
Vivian Eveloff

Phyllis Fairchild
Ellen Feldhausen
Eryl D. Feldman
Christina Fenner
Nancy Ferguson
Julia Ferner
Lorraine D. Ferry
Ellen J. Fiersten
Bonnie Fitzgerald
Mary A. Forsyth
Valla Dana Fotiades
Carol Fraase
Norma W. Francis
Ruth S. Friedland
Marilyn Fruin
Cordelia C. Fues
Willa M. Fuhrken
Tess Fuller-Sakolsky
Deanna Funk
Christine A. Gaffigan
Mary Gail Galle
Esther Gaskill
Elizabeth Gasper
Gail W. Gasper
Kathryn A. Gietl
Libby Gildner
Rosalynne Gillispy
Gayle Gonzalez
Margaret H. Graber
Betty Grady
Sally Graham
Vesta S. Gray
Donna Gregory
Patricia Gross
Janice T. Gvazdinskas
Catherine Gwaltney
Lillian Haag
Anne E. Haaker
Amy Haas
Nancy M. Becker Hahn
K. Kaisha Halcli
Denise Hall
Susan Hammond
Jim Hampton
Sandra J. Hanner
Julie Harbauer
David N. Harmon
Doreen M. Harris
Gerri Harter
Jeanette Hassebrock
Jane Hasselbring
Shirley Haubach
Linda Hayes
Aggie Hayner
Jim Helm
Roberta M. Helm
Susan Helm
Barbara Hennessy
Catherine A. Higgins
Michael Higgins

Nancy Howard Higgins
Sandy Hill
Carol Hinds
Valorie Hofferkamp
Kathy Hoffmann
Janet Hohl
Donna J. Holms
Margaret L. Holmes
Carolyn Houston
Patricia R. Howard
Patricia Huff
Susan Huffman
Louise Hughes
Cathy L. Humphrey
Mary C. Idleman
Rosemary J. Idleman
Illini Country Club
Theta Jackson
Glenda B. Jacob
Pat Jacobs
Ann Ellen Jakowsky
Bonnie Janecek
Julie Janssen
Mary Ann Janssen
Viola Janssen
Barbara Jason
Kay Johnson
Juanita K. Jones
Lillian Jurgensen
Becky Kagan
Drew Kagan
Carol Kaufmann
Betty Kay
Trish Kearney
Julie Kellner
Kathy Kemp
Katherine R. Kinser
Camille Koertner
Jeannie Koertner
Marguerite Koertner
Karen Korsgard
Suzanne Korsgard
Stefan Kozak, M.D.
Bobbie Kurmann
Julie Kyes
Karen J. Kyes
Kyongok Kim
Fen Hong Lai
Gloria Lamb
Helen Lambert
Bridget Later Lamont
Shirley Lampros
Lou Lane
Nancy Lane
Shirley Lanphier
Phyllis E. Lantis
Pamela A. Larson
Susan K. Laue
Linda Leich
Dorcas Lobdell

Nancy Loeb
Marge Loewenstein
Judy Lofgren
Carol C. Lohman
Irma S. Lowe
David Lumsden
M.K. "Micki" Lynch
Elaine Lyons
Mary McCormick
Mary McCreary
Rebecca S. McDonald
Eileen McVary
Tara McVary
Marge MacPherson
Vivion Maisenbacher
Marge Manson
Alice Markwood
Deanna Marvin
Colleen Maskel
Ellen Matlins
Martha Mauterer
Sandy Megginson
Catherine M. Meyer
Cindy Meyer
Faith H. Mikita
Phyllis Miller
Karen S. Moffat
Carolyn Moore
Anne B. Morgan
Patricia Morgan
Sue A. Morgan
Linda J. Morrison
June R. Murphy
Karen E. Nachtwey
Cindy Nagle
Jean Ann Mitchell Neff
Teri Neff
Kathleen Nenaber
Violet Lance Neuhaus
Mary W. Ninker
Julia S. Noonan
Ellyn J. Norris
Patricia Norris
Rita Nortrup
Jane Trower Novotny
Marge Novotny
Bernice M. O'Beirne
Jaylee O'Neill
Carrie O'Rourke
Mary Ossowski
Kay Owen
Brenda Sue Page
Sandy Paige
Roberta D. Pape
Kathryn parch
JoAnn. M. Passarelli
Shirley S. Patey
Christine M. Patsche
Annabelle Patton
Kate H. Patton

Susie Patton
Diane Pellegrini
Susan Petrilli
Suzanne Pettyjohn
Paula Phipps
Jeanne Pittman
Margaret Pitzer
Marguerite Porter
Millie Prather
Marian Pree
Linda Prola
Rebecca L. Prutt
Juleann Hornyak Randles
Patricia Reece
Roxie W. Reid
Lisa Hendrichs Remack
Mary Renner
Josephine C. Rettke
Pam Reyhan
Jonathan E. Reyman
Claire Richardson
Donna Riley
Penny Rinehart
Carole Roberts
Florence G. Roberts
Sula Mae Roberts
Robert's Seafood Center
Martha Robertson
Patricia Rocha
Darlene Roe
Dale Thomas Rogers
Mary Beth Roland
Alice J. Rolf
Jonas Rose
Mary D. Rose
Marcia J. Ross
Diane Rutledge
Alvora Sandidge
Wendy Sattler
Jan. B. Schuerman
Kyle G. Schultz
Mary C. Schultz
Cathy Schwartz
Gloria Schwartz
Gloria Schwarz
Karen Shoup Shafer
Tricia Shillcut
Deborah J. Sidener
Cynthia Krubel Simmons
Cathy Slater
Patricia H. Slater
Robert Snow
Dolores Hagan Somes
Donna Spencer
Donna Spinhirne
Betsy Sponsler
Margaret Spreckelmeyer
Springfield Area Dental Hygienists
Springfield Symphony Guild
Patricia Staab
Cece Stern
Shirley Stevenson
Jay Stevenson
Kathleen Stewart
Paula R. Stewart
Dottie Stone
Tammy A. Stone
Candy Stout
Doris M. Stoyan
Marjorie Strano
Elizabeth Stuart
Margie Stuart
Mona Summers
Karen Sunderlin
Carol Taylor
Marilyn B. Taylor
Lisa Thompson
Leonard Tiberii
Maureen Timm
Marnie tisckos
Mary Sue Touch
Violet Touch
Wanda Wells Tracy
Wilma A. Tracy
Peggy Traycoff
Robert Tregoning
Sandy Tristano
Mary Jane Trower
Marilyn Tungett
Denise Turnbull
Doris Turner
Mary Helmstetter Turner
Sharon Turner
Eloise Van Fossan
Sally Sedlak Vaughan
Carol L. Velde
Nancy Vereen
Randy Vereen
Sally Vogl
Salli J. Ward
Mary Jo Wasser
Charles F. Wayham
Madeline S. Wayham
Maxine Wolff Weiner
Florence Lee Wellons
Patricia A. Wheat
Sandra L. Wheeler
Cathy Wichterman
Nancy Wilderson
Deborah Moss Wilkins
Dottie J. Willard
Laura Williams
Cynthia Wilson
Barb Wolfson
Esther Wolfson
Sue Wolfson
Gale L.Wolter
Nance Woodward
Audrey Wooldridge
Cathy Yokley
Janet York
Liz Zalar
Caren Zentgraf
Ruby Ziegler

Bibliography

Dyba, Thomas J., and Painter, George L. *Seventeen Years at Eighth and Jackson: The Lincoln Family in Their Springfield Home.* 2nd ed. New York: McGraw Hill Publishing Co., n.d.

Nicolay, Helen. *Personal Traits of Abraham Lincoln.* New York: The Century Company, 1912.

Pratt, Harry. *The Personal Finances of abraham Lincoln.* The Abraham Lincoln Association. Springfield, IL: Lakeside Press, 1943.

Randall, Ruth Painter. *Mary Lincoln: Biography of a Marriage.* Little, MA: 1943.

Sandburg, Carl. *Abraham Lincoln: The Prairie Years and the War Years, Vol. I.* San Diego, CA: Harcourt, Brace, Jonanovich, 1954.

Turner, Justin G., and Turner, Linda Levitt, eds. *Mary Todd Lincoln: Her Life and Letters.* New York: Alfred A. Knopf, 1972.

Editors of American Heritage. *The American Heritage Cookbook and Illustrated H istory of American Eating and Drinking.* New York: American Heritage Publishing Co., Inc., 1964.

Recipes from America's Restored Villages. New York: Valentine, 1987.

A

B

C

Honest to Goodness

Name

Address

City / State / Zip Code

Telephone

Please send me the following as indicated:	Quantity	Price	*Tax	Total
Honest to Goodness		$24.95	$1.93	$

Plus $5.00 shipping and handling each for the first three books ordered and $1.00 for each additional one.

*Illinois residents. Total Enclosed $

Please charge to my VISA or MasterCard Card Number Exp. Date

Cardholder's Signature

Please make checks payable to Junior League of Springfield Publications. Please do not send cash. Sorry, no C.O.D.'s.

Send to:

Junior League of Springfield Publications
P.O. Box 1736
Springfield, Illinois 62705
(217) 787-7802

Profits from the sale of this book are used to support the purpose and programs of the Junior League of Springfield, Inc.

Name

Address

City / State / Zip Code

Telephone

Please send me the following as indicated:	Quantity	Price	*Tax	Total
Honest to Goodness		$24.95	$1.93	$

Plus $5.00 shipping and handling each for the first three books ordered and $1.00 for each additional one.

*Illinois residents. Total Enclosed $

Please charge to my VISA or MasterCard Card Number Exp. Date

Cardholder's Signature

Please make checks payable to Junior League of Springfield Publications. Please do not send cash. Sorry, no C.O.D.'s.

Send to:

Junior League of Springfield Publications
P.O. Box 1736
Springfield, Illinois 62705
(217) 787-7802

Profits from the sale of this book are used to support the purpose and programs of the Junior League of Springfield, Inc.